Current Developments in Economics

STEPHEN C. R. MUNDAY

Foreword by G. C. Harcourt

St. Martin's Press
New York

CURRENT DEVELOPMENTS IN ECONOMICS
Copyright © 1996 by Stephen C. R. Munday
Foreword copyright © by G. C. Harcourt

St. Martin's Press, Scholarly and Reference Division,
175 Fifth Avenue, New York, N.Y. 10010

First published in the United States of America in 1996

Printed in Great Britain

ISBN 0–312–16338–X (cloth)
ISBN 0–312–16339–8 (paperback)

Library of Congress Cataloging-in-Publication Data
Munday, Stephen C. R., 1964–
Current developments in economics / Stephen C. R. Munday.
p.   cm.
Includes bibliographical references and index.
ISBN 0–312–16338–X (cloth : alk. paper). — ISBN 0–312–16339–8
(pbk.)
1. Economics.   2. Economics—Methodology.   3. Economics—History.
4. Economic policy.   I. Title.
HB171.5.M934   1996
330—dc20   96–21861
                                                                  CIP

To all those who have instructed and inspired me in the ways of the 'dismal science', especially **Ray 'The Chief' Jarvis**, **Jeremy Edwards** and **Geoff Harcourt**. With thanks.

Contents

Foreword

Teaching economics well at any level is a great challenge and at an introductory level probably the greatest challenge of all. To achieve effective success, the reading set needs to be authoritative, balanced, lucid, applicable to the world around us, especially as perceived by the students involved, *and* exciting and inspirational. By writing down this list, I have described Stephen Munday's splendid *Current Developments in Economics*.

I had the privilege, first, of lecturing to Stephen when he was a student at Cambridge in the 1980s (I also played cricket against him), and secondly, of seeing a lot of him and of reading his book in embryo when he was school teacher bye fellow at Selwyn in 1994. I learnt a great deal from all these encounters.

Stephen really is the master of his subject. His range is wide; he sees his subject as a means to understand the world, why it works well and badly, and what may be done about it. He is a humane and generous person and these traits inform all that he does and writes. He has a good sense of the nature of political constraints and of the limitations of economic analysis itself. Within these constraints, he has written a book which guides the reader, carefully and with mounting enthusiasm, through current developments in economic analysis and their applications to the pressing economic and social problems of our age. I cannot recommend too highly this excellent introduction to what is still a fine calling, worthy of the attention of all those with cool heads and warm hearts, as Marshall put it long ago, who care about their fellow citizens and their society.

G.C. HARCOURT
Reader in the History of Economic Theory
Fellow, Jesus College, Cambridge
Professor Emeritus, University of Adelaide

Acknowledgements

There are many people who have enabled the writing and publication of this book. I am grateful to all of them.

I was afforded the opportunity to research for the book through a term's leave granted to me by the headmaster and governors of Bishop's Stortford High School. I then spent a wonderful term as schoolteacher bye-fellow at Selwyn College, Cambridge. This must be the friendliest of all the Cambridge colleges, and I am most appreciative of all the fellows who made my term so enjoyable, and especially to the advice and encouragement of both Mica Pani!c and Max Beber. I was fortunate also to renew acquaintance with Geoff Harcourt, who gave much helpful advice and encouragement on the research for this book.

I am very grateful to Tony Thirlwall for commenting extensively on some early proposals that I had about the book and for the several various helpful suggestions that he made about its structure and content.

During my research I found particular books and articles especially helpful for different topics. The *Oxford Review of Economic Policy* is an outstanding economics journal, and I found the review articles on several of the topics that I was handling particularly helpful. I would recommend them to anyone studying economics. Robert Heilbroner's *The Wordly Philosophers* is an excellent summary of the thoughts and ideas of most major economists, and I found the book particularly helpful for the chapter on the history of economic thought. Geoff Harcourt's lecture notes on the topic were also very useful. I found Bronwyn Croxson's lecture notes on the economics of health care particularly helpful for the chapter on the state provision of goods and services.

I am grateful to the Brookings Institution for permission to use the table on the estimated effects of inflation and unemployment upon government popularity in the chapter on economics and politics.

Both Stephen Rutt and Nicola Young at Macmillan have been friendly and helpful and I am grateful to them for their editorial work.

Finally, I owe a great debt of gratitude to my two young daughters and especially my wife, Elizabeth. I sometimes wondered if the opportunity cost of the project was too great and without Elizabeth's tolerance and encouragement the book could never have come into existence. Thank you.

STEPHEN C.R. MUNDAY

Introduction

This book aims to be an economics textbook with a difference. It does not aim at anything approaching universal coverage of the subject matter of economics. Topics such as the basis of supply and demand theory and the different competitive models in the theory of the firm are hardly mentioned. As such, it is in no way intended to be a substitute for a sound, basic economics textbook. Rather, it is designed to complement such texts. The purpose is to pick on issues within economics that either are often insufficiently covered or entirely neglected in many of the standard textbooks, or where there have been important new developments in the relevant economic theory which have generally not found their way into the textbooks. Often, such developments occupy much space in the standard economic journals and form an important part of many economics and related subjects degree courses. However, they are rarely found in a general textbook. The aim of the book is thus to bridge that gap.

Within that overall aim, this book has certain other principles. The general approach of each chapter is to take a topic of interest and importance in the study of any economics course. The relevant theory concerning that issue is then explained, often with two sections, one summarising what might today be called the 'traditional' economic theory and the other then considering relevant new theory in that area. Once this is done, topical case studies are chosen to which it is possible to apply the relevant theory. Where possible, the implications for government economic policy are also considered. The suggestion is thus that the economist can arm himself or herself with certain important principles and theories which can be used as a lens with which to view a whole host of important issues in order to aid understanding and analysis. The book also aims not to use any mathematical language. The logic and significance of the theories in economics can be appreciated without having to be expressed in a language that remains foreign to many who endeavour to study the subject of economics. Thus those who are uncomfortable with mathematics should be entirely comfortable with the approach of this book (as indeed should those who do feel comfortable with mathematics!).

The book is divided into three separate sections. Part I, an overview of economics, is in some ways an introduction, but more a look at three overarching fundamental issues in the study of economics which are generally virtually entirely ignored in most standard economics textbooks. The first concerns economic methodology (Chapter 1). The general tendency is to dive into the subject content of economics without considering how the subject should be studied and used. This chapter looks at the issues involved. Chapter 2 attempts the ambitious task of giving a brief overview of the history of economic thought. So often economic theory and practice is better and more fully appreciated within its historical perspective, yet this is equally often simply ignored. Chapter 3 addresses the standard divide in the subject of economics between microeconomics and macroeconomics. Usually, the difference between these is defined in economics textbooks, and then they are treated as almost entirely separate subjects. The problems with this are discussed, as are the reasons why the two must be seen as a coherent whole.

Part II of the book picks on various topical issues within the subject of economics which are usually seen as part of microeconomics. Game theory has received great attention in the study of economics in recent years, but little of this has found its way into the standard economics textbooks. Chapter 4 attempts to overcome that problem. Privatisation is an issue that does appear in many textbooks, but Chapter 5 here looks at relevant theory that is less frequently considered and discusses how its application is relevant to the topic. The environment is an issue of particular current concern. There is much important and relevant economic theory that can be applied here, and that is what Chapter 6 attempts to do. Consideration of the rationale of the government provision of goods and services goes to the heart of important theory and theoretical differences within economics. The whole range of relevant economic theory, both old and new, is considered and applied to the topics of health care and education in Chapter 7. Taxation is a political hot potato, but Chapter 8 on this topic looks at how a proper understanding of the relevant economic theories can help to clarify and to understand what are the important issues at stake. finally, Chapter 9 on the economics of trade looks at new trade theories that challenge the standard theories of trade which form the usual presentation of economics textbooks.

The final section of the book, Part III, examines some of the fundamental and topical issues within the area of macroeconomics. All standard textbooks look at some or all of the macroeconomic models that are available for studying the subject. However, the purpose of Chapter 10 is to put the different models side by side and to consider which issues are best understood through which models, and what are the shortcomings of each of the models. Chapter 11 on inflation, unemployment and the Phillips curve attempts an overview of these related fundamental topics within macroeconomics. As such, it is more of a general chapter than many of the others which pick on particular, tighter themes. However, understanding the issues here is fundamental to understanding the study of macroeconomics. New developments and their implications are considered wherever they are relevant. Chapter 12 on economic and monetary union looks at general theory in this area to try to clarify the issues. In particular, an understanding of optimal currency areas is important. Public choice theory is hardly dealt with in the standard textbooks, but it is an important area of economic theory and helps to understand the issues behind political business cycles and independent central banks. Chapter 13 investigates this. finally, Chapter 14 on economic growth suggests that a greater prominence should be given to this area of economic theory in textbooks and explains important recent theoretical developments in this area.

Part I

An Overview of Economics

1 Economic Methodology or How To Do Economics

Most students of economics are happy to be asked the question 'What is economics?' The answer to that question is confidently answered in any first chapter in any introductory textbook. A world of scarce resources and infinite human wants provides economics with its subject matter. However, ask any student of economics the question 'How do you do economics?' and the reply may be far less confident, if indeed the question is understood at all. It is to that second question that this chapter addresses itself by considering what is meant by economic methodology.

Economic methodology is something from which economists have often steered well away. Yet it is important to ask what is the appropriate way in which to study a subject. In attempting to consider this issue with regard to the subject of economics, this chapter will concentrate on three particular areas:

1. The different possible methodological approaches in economics. Several different possible methodologies can be identified, and the purpose of this section is to identify and explain each one. Some of the merits and demerits of each approach will also be considered.
2. The question of whether economics can be deemed to be a science. It is usually asserted that economics is indeed a science. In many ways this can be considered as a methodological question and thus is considered in this chapter.
3. A consideration of the common practice of economists in studying their subject and what this may suggest about the methodology that is actually used in economics.

DIFFERENT POSSIBLE ECONOMIC METHODOLOGIES

In general, methodology means the study of method. This is an activity concerned with the procedures and aims of a subject and a study of the organisation of a subject. With regard to economics, Blaug (1986) suggests that methodology can be defined as 'the study of the principles which we regularly employ to establish and validate economic theories'. In practice, a number of different possible economic methodologies can be identified.

3

1 'Deductivism' or '*a Priorism*'

This is an approach to study that can reasonably be traced back to J.S. Mill (see Chapter 2 on the history of economic thought). The approach suggested is that of inductively establishing basic laws or axioms and then deducing economic implications from those fundamental laws. In other words, the study of economics involves, by some means or other, establishing certain key ideas or tendencies in life (as relevant to the study of economics) and then considering what the implications of these are in different economic situations.

Economics can be seen to operate in this fashion in various situations. For example, when studying the behaviour of firms, traditional economic theory established the suggestion that firms aimed to maximise their profits and then considered the implications of that in different theoretical models of competition. On a more general level, economics nearly always holds on to the axiom of rationality and derives theories and expected behaviour from that starting point. This way of studying economics can clearly be identified as deductivism. The approach was well summarised by Robbins (1935): 'The propositions of economic theory, like all scientific theory, are obviously deductions from a series of postulates ...'. These words from Robbins's famous essay imply both a certain view of what constitutes a science and a belief that the study of economics can be seen in the same light as the study of all science subjects. Both of these views could be open to question, as will be seen later.

It is important to note that the established axioms or laws are best referred to as 'tendencies'. This suggests that they may not hold true in every circumstance at every time in some rigid fashion. Rather, the assertion is that, on average and often, the identified 'laws' probably hold true (unlike in the physical sciences where the laws tend to be seen as holding in all circumstances). Thus, there has to be an element of uncertainty in all economic theories that are derived in this fashion. The laws, and hence the theories, are unlikely to be universal. If economics is to be considered a science, then it must be considered as a inexact science.

A further question that might reasonably be asked about this approach is from where exactly the tendencies come from which deductions are made. The 'inductive' method might suggest that tendencies are derived from observations of the world which can then be tested. The testing of observations or hypotheses is really the hallmark of a 'positive' approach, the next methodology to be considered.

2 'Positive' or 'Popperian' Approaches

Following the work of Popper (1959), the 'correct' form of scientific methodology can best be described as 'falsificationism'. The correct way to 'do' science (and hence the correct way to 'do' economics) is to attempt to falsify hypotheses. It is not possible to prove anything, but it is possible to disprove things.

This approach is best understood through a well-known example. Take the hypothesis that 'All swans are white'. It would never be possible to 'prove' this statement. Even if all swans ever sighted were white, that could not preclude the possibility that there was a black swan hiding somewhere on the earth that had not yet been seen but might one day be discovered. The theory is not proven. However, it would be possible to falsify the hypothesis simply by reporting the sighting of a black swan. Until this was done, it would be reasonable to continue to hold on to the theory that 'All swans are white'. Once a black swan was discovered (and appropriate tests had been done to ensure that it was indeed a black swan!), then the theory would have to be discarded in favour of an alternative that had not yet been falsified. The alternative might be the 'null hypothesis' used for the purposes of testing, in this case perhaps that 'Some swans are black'.

This methodological approach suggests a tentative and uncertain approach to knowledge. Nothing can be viewed as categorically true and accurate. Rather, theories about behaviour can be held for as long as they are not clearly seen to be false. As soon as they are seen to be false, then they must be dropped.

A Popperian approach to the study of economics suggests that the principal activities involved in 'doing' economics should involve the creation of theories which are capable of being tested, and then appropriate research which attempts to falsify the stated theories. The hypotheses generated can be held to be useful and usable until they are falsified. This approach suggests an interrelated point, namely that economics must be 'positive' in nature. It must deal in propositions that can be tested by an appeal to evidence. Therefore economic theories should not contain value judgements which, by their very nature, cannot be tested by appealing to relevant evidence. Thus, the approach may reasonably be referred to as 'positive' as well as 'Popperian'.

An implication of this methodology is that the deductive approach mentioned above cannot be described as scientific and is not an appropriate methodology for economics. The postulates that are generated through the deductive approach are not truly testable insofar as they stem from beliefs about the basic tendencies regarding human nature which it may not be possible to falsify by an appeal to evidence. However, it is sometimes asserted that this represents a potential weakness of the falsificationist approach as applied to economics. Given the complex nature of human behaviour, which is the basis of economic activity, it may be difficult and perhaps inappropriate to try to reduce all economics to statements and hypotheses which can clearly be falsified by an appeal to the appropriate 'facts'. The inner motivations of humans that create economic behaviour may not fit well into such a framework, yet they are clearly important to the study of economics.

A further difficulty which may suggest itself in the application of this methodological approach to the study of economics is the apparent difficulty in falsifying economic theories. Statistically, it is not possible to be entirely certain that the evidence collected has fully falsified a theory. There is always the possibility of an atypical sample and other inaccuracies. Thus, a decision must be made about what level of certainty is required in order for a theory to be falsified. Must we be 99 per cent certain, or 95 per cent, or perhaps 90 per cent certain? There is no clear answer. Further, the nature of economic theory seems to be such that is possible to continue to hold to the validity of a particular theory, even in the face of what appears to be contradictory evidence. This must be so if it is possible for conflicting theories to be held concurrently, as frequently appears to be the case within economics (such as in the various controversies that persist within macroeconomics, for example over the potential effects on the economy of an attempted fiscal expansion by the government). The problem is that it appears highly possible to claim mitigating circumstances in the face of unfortunate evidence for any particular theory. The evidence is seen not as contradicting the theory, but rather to be consistent with the theory given the particular conditions of the time. Thus an increase in price appearing to lead to an increase in demand for a product would not be seen as contradicting the 'law' of demand, but rather would be due to something else causing demand to rise. This may well be an entirely reasonable explanation. However, it may be indicative of a reluctance to allow economic theories to be falsified, the essence of the approach suggested by Popper.

3   'Predictionism' or 'Instrumentalism'

An alternative methodology for economics is derived from Friedman's famous essay on the topic (1953): 'The Methodology of Positive Economics'. The starting point of this approach is the observation that the basic goal of economics is prediction. Blaug (1992) would not disagree with this view, asserting: 'the central aim of economics is to predict and not merely to understand'.

From this position, Friedman moves on to suggest that the way to judge economic theories should therefore be by their predictive success. That is the ultimate way to test a theory. In particular, the suggestion is made that the realism of the assumptions used in any theory is not of any consequence or interest. All that matters is how successful any theory is in predicting economic behaviour and events.

It is certainly the case that economic theories have simplifying assumptions. Without these, economics might be little more than a description of the world as we see it. Assumptions generally form the twin purposes of simplification in order to aid understanding (such as the two-sector model in macroeconomics) and a statement of the conditions necessary for a theory to hold (such as the different models of competition in the theory of the firm). Thus 'models' are frequently encountered in the study of economics and are seen as an important tool in aiding economic analysis and understanding. The question here is whether the realism of the assumptions used in such models is of any interest or consequence. According to Friedman, this is not the case.

Several criticisms of Friedman's methodology have been made. One point is that unrealistic (or false) assumptions are likely to lead to false predictions. It seems reasonable to suggest that a theory with realistic assumptions is more likely to yield accurate predictions than one with unrealistic assumptions. To take the point a stage further, what should be done with a theory when a prediction fails? How does one investigate the possible reasons for the cause of the failure? One of the likely starting points is to consider the validity of the assumptions of the theory in question and to use that as a possible means of developing the theory so that it might yield more accurate predictions. Taking possible criticisms further, it has been asked whether it is right to see accurate predictions as the sole judge of the validity of a theory. Might other possible criteria, such as the internal logic and consistency of a particular theory, be seen as other possible means of judging what is a 'good' theory? It might then be said that this is only so if the predictions prove to be accurate, but it could provide another profitable means of investigating the possible causes of a theory that yields inaccurate predictions.

A further difficulty with Friedman's approach is that it is entirely possible to have any one piece of evidence consistent with more than one set of assumptions. The problem would then appear to be to discriminate between the different hypotheses to judge which might be the 'best' to continue to use. One method of attempting to discriminate between such theories could be to examine the perceived realism of the assumptions. A classic example of this can be seen in Friedman's own domain of the relationship between changes in the supply of money and the price level. An observed association between the two is entirely consistent either with the assumption that changes in the money supply cause changes in the price level or with the assumption that changes in the price level cause changes in the money supply.

4 Eclecticism

A relatively recently identified approach to economic methodology might best be described as 'eclecticism'. This approach is identified by McCloskey (1983). The suggestion here is that it is not possible, nor even desirable, to identify any one particular economic methodology as 'best' or 'right'. Rather, different methodologies are used, and appropriately so, in different circumstances. Much of the practice of economic methodology, regardless of what may be preached, is seen by McCloskey as 'rhetoric': it is seen as the use of whatever literary and methodological device is appropriate in order to justify, explain and defend a particular theory that is being espoused. Economists are happy to make use of analogy and appeals to both logic and emotion in explaining the validity of their theories. This is seen as both healthy and positive. McCloskey cites the example of the theory of rational expectations which uses many literary devices, including analogy. This is not a criticism, but an observation of the methodology actually used.

McCloskey looks at two pages of Samuelson's work (1947) and suggests that he frequently makes use of some of the following methodological devices:

1. The use of complex mathematics, frequently in a nonchalant fashion. This is seen as a device to add authority to the author's work. In practice, the mathematics is often of peripheral importance.
2. Appeals to authority. On several occasions, Samuelson appeals to 'higher' authorities, such as Aristotle and the obligatory reference to Keynes, in order to strengthen his argument.
3. Appeals to relax assumptions. For example, Samuelson speculates about the admission of uncertainty with regard to the demand for money.
4. The use of hypothetical, 'toy' (McCloskey's term) economies (such as the two sector model) in order to draw practical results.
5. The use of analogy. Metaphor and analogy are seen by McCloskey as common devices in economics.

The obvious point that McCloskey makes is that the practical methodology of economics is far removed from the supposed 'official' methodologies suggested above, particularly from the scientific method suggested by Popper. He does not condemn this, pointing out that most academic disciplines use these, and other devices, and that it is perfectly legitimate to use them, as economists do, in the study of economics. However, McCloskey is keen to stress their existence and importance, stating: 'The range of persuasive discourse in economics is wide, ignored in precept while potent in practice' (1983).

Such a view of economic methodology can be criticised as offering no guidelines as to the 'correct' way to do economics. Are all methodologies to be seen as equally valid? Are conclusions reached in one way any more or less legitimate than conclusions reached in another way? These are questions that an eclectic approach to methodology cannot answer. However, perhaps the most important point is that this approach attempts to indicate that various methodologies are in practice used by economists, regardless of what they might preach.

5 Subjectivism

The work of Hayek (1942) can be described as subjectivist in its methodology. This approach attempts to draw a clear distinction between the natural sciences and the social sciences (economics clearly being seen as belonging to the latter). This approach, then, is different from the Popperian methodology which claims to be a scientific methodology wherever it is applied, be that physics or economics. The essential difference between the natural and the social sciences is that social science should be concerned with 'bigger' issues such as the explanation of meaning and the tracing of conceptual connections within society. The domain of social science is not to be concerned with universal empirical regularities: that is the area of the natural sciences. In practice, this suggested methodology has tended to imply an impoverished role for social sciences compared to that of the natural sciences given the far more tentative nature of the knowledge and statements that must be implied by attempting to suggest answers to the 'bigger' questions.

6 Realism

A final possible methodological approach that can be identified for economics is 'realism' or 'critical realism'. Such an approach is suggested by Lawson (for example, 1992). Here, science is seen as unified with no distinction between the natural and the social sciences. The basis of the view is that science is (or should be) primarily concerned not with the flux of events, the observation of empirical regularities, but rather with identifying the relations and mechanisms that govern the perceived flux of events. It is about underlying causes of events rather than events themselves.

This scientific methodology can be applied to economics. For example when looking at the labour market, the appropriate approach and focus of activity would be to try to identify and analyse the underlying structures that cause the observed behaviour within labour markets. Key relationships, such as those between employer and employee, unskilled and skilled workers, and males and females, would be important areas upon which to concentrate as they could be seen as dictating many events within the labour market.

This approach is seen to be in conflict with the methodologies suggested earlier. It sees the role of economics as trying to explain rather than to predict (thus being in opposition to Friedman's view of economic methodology). The positivist approach is seen as being far too narrow: it does little or nothing to explain events.

IS ECONOMICS A SCIENCE?

The classic methodological question to ask of economics is whether it can or should be deemed to be a science. Much of the above consideration of the various suggested methodologies for economics have implicit, or explicit, views concerning the nature of science and how economics may, or may not, fit within that framework. Indeed, it is clear that part of the reason for the lack of a single, agreed methodology for economics is that there may not be a single agreed methodology for science in general.

In some ways, investigating the validity of economics' claim to be a science can prove to be a false trail. The real problem is that science must be defined before the question can be answered. As different definitions of science are offered, then clearly it is likely that economics will fit some of those definitions better than others. This is indeed the case.

Some traditional points about the nature of science suggest that economics cannot fully fit into the framework. Science is often associated with the identification of universal laws which can explain and predict behaviour. Given the ever-changing economic environment, it is not possible to have universal and unchanging laws in economics. It could, perhaps, be argued that attempts to maintain universal laws within economics are a reason why economic predictions have been seen not to work in practice on many occasions. However, this point can be partially countered by suggesting that although universal laws might not be possible, specific laws for specific situations can be identified. This may not be so different from some of the other sciences. For example, environmental changes could change certain 'laws' of biology.

A standard objection to labelling economics as a science is that it is not possible to conduct experiments, experimentation being seen as one of the key characteristics of a 'true' science. Even if it were ever considered an ethical possibility, experimentation would be of little or no value. The problem is the impossibility of having a control experiment which holds all other factors constant (the economist's assumption of 'ceteris paribus'). Imagine trying to experiment with the effects of an increase in government expenditure upon an economy. An experiment might try to increase government expenditure in one country and leave it constant in another. The effects might then be compared. Of course, the comparison would have little meaning. The two economies would have had different people with different motivations and would have been affected by different economic events in different ways. The experiment could have no validity in suggesting the impact of government expenditure in general. Again, it could be noted that other subjects that make pretensions to being sciences, such as zoology and astronomy, have similar problems with regard to experiments.

A further objection to the status of economics as a science is that it is inexact. The sharp and precise formulae of physics could never be used in the same way in economics. The complex and changing nature of economies and economic individuals suggests that overall tendencies and directions might be identified in economics, but that it is difficult and dangerous to try to be more specific than that. A further point here is the difficulty in ever refuting a theory in economics. As noted before, there will always be sufficient mitigating circumstances and other factors at work to be able to claim that a theory has not been refuted. If an increase in the money supply did not lead to inflation it might be because households' behaviour had altered, implying that the definition of money used was inappropriate. The theory is not refuted. Again other sciences cannot claim to be free of such problems. Any observation that appeared to contradict the law of gravity would be explained by particular conditions. It would not refute the theory.

In what ways, then, might economics be deemed to be a science? The answer lies in its methodology. If the positive approach to economic methodology is seen to be the correct one, then the methodology used is the same as that used in science and is indeed part of the definition of science. Insofar as economics attempts to generate testable hypotheses and then gathers data in an effort to refute those hypotheses, then its approach could be described as 'scientific'. This is the way that sciences attempt to proceed. If economics produces testable statements which it attempts to refute, then, according to some definitions, it can be described as a science. As mentioned above, however, there are problems applying the methodology to economics. Taking the above example of increases in the money supply leading to inflation, the following problems could be encountered:

1. The problems of defining money.
2. The difficulty of identifying the line of causation. Do changes in the supply of money cause changes in the price level, or does the causation run from changes in the price level to changes in the money supply?
3. The tools that are used to test the relationship could change the nature of the relationship. Gathering information about the money supply could change the behaviour of financial intermediaries, for example.
4. The knowledge of the relationship could cause the relationship to change or even disintegrate. This is the nature of the so-called 'Goodhart's Law' (named after Charles Goodhart, formerly of the Bank of England). An example might be that if a relationship between one definition of the money supply and the price level were perceived, then an attempt to control that definition of the money supply might cause the relationship to disappear as people changed their behaviour and, for example, found alternative ways of borrowing that were not included under the particular definition of the money supply being employed.
5. The overall problem, partly seen from some of the above points, is that no theory can be conclusively rejected. A decision will have to be made about the level of probability required to accept that the theory has indeed been refuted.

The philosophy of science has developed further suggestions of what may constitute science. These differ from the approach of Popper, and it is interesting to see how well economics fits within the descriptions. Kuhn (1970) points out that scientific knowledge tends to develop fitfully. He explains this by identifying 'colleges' which tend to dominate a subject at any one time. The dominant 'college' of people holds to a particular paradigm within the subject. This paradigm is not open to questioning or refutation: it is accepted as true by the dominant college and cannot effectively be challenged, despite possible evidence which may appear contradictory to the paradigm. During this time, there is little or no scientific progress. However, there are certain time periods when the pressure upon the dominant paradigm has become so great in terms of anomalies and contradictory evidence that the paradigm is rejected and replaced by a new paradigm dominated by a new college of people. This period of transition represents revolutionary change within the subject and is followed by another passive period.

It is interesting to see if economics fits within Kuhn's description of a science. Certainly there is an important point for economics that fundamental theories may not truly be open to refutation in the manner suggested by Popperian methodology. It simply is not felt to be possible that certain underlying theories could be found to be wrong. Whether economics has witnessed a paradigm shift is another important question. It could be argued that the Keynesian 'revolution' was such a shift, and its following rejection a further shift. However, it could also be argued that economics has never moved from an overarching domination by the neoclassical paradigm based on the axiom of rationality and, perhaps, human greed. This might suggest a lack of 'progress' in the subject.

Lakatos (1970) suggested that science was characterised by 'Scientific Research Programmes'. In some ways, this can be seen as something of a mixture of the approaches suggested by Popper and Kuhn. Scientists hold on to a hard core of theory within a subject that is not open to refutation. This is surrounded by a protective belt of theory where testing does occur and refutation is possible. A refutation within the protective belt need not challenge the hard core. However, persistent refutation within the protective belt could lead to a questioning of the hard core itself. This could be applied to economics. The hard core of neoclassical economics could be seen as the fundamental axioms mentioned earlier. The protective belt could be deemed to consist of such theories as the negative correlation between quantity demanded and price of a product (although that might be close to the hard core).

One further recent development of some importance within science has been the growth and application of chaos theory. This suggests that much of science is in fact characterised by an intrinsic lack of predictability and uncertainty. There are no clear universal laws that can be held as true over a period of time. Within biology, for example, population growth of species is best explained by a random variable. If this approach to science is held as having any validity, and that is open to future question, then perhaps economics can sit more easily with other sciences. Its lack of universal laws and imprecise nature is something that may be true of all sciences.

So is economics a science? A review of some of the different descriptions and interpretations of science suggests that the question cannot clearly be answered. It really depends upon how science is defined.

APPLYING METHODOLOGY: ECONOMICS IN PRACTICE

It appears that there are many possible ways of 'doing' economics, at least in principle. However, much of the above discussion may be of little help without looking at what economists do in practice: what methodology is actually used in economics? McCloskey makes the point that the methodology employed may be very different from that preached.

If a positive methodology is the dominant methodology of economics, then the study of the subject should be charactised by the devising of testable hypotheses, and the basis of economic research should be the gathering of information that endeavours to refute those hypotheses. Regardless of whether this is felt to be the 'correct' methodology of economics, it is hard to argue that this is how the study of economics is in fact conducted. A careful examination of the articles written in leading economics journals would find that very few are devoted to attempting to falsify testable theories. That does not appear to be the way that economists behave. It is not at all clearly stressed to students of economics that to do economics must mean the generation of theories which should be tested.

A more obvious methodology of economics is deductivism. When looking at what economists appear to try to do (which, as McCloskey points out, may not be the same as they actually do), it is hard to disagree with Robbins's words mentioned earlier. Much of the practice of economics appears to be deductions from a series of postulates. This seems to be the essence of economics as studied by most students of economics. Given that consumers are held to be rational and aim to maximise their utility, how will they behave in different situations? What theories of consumer behaviour can we derive from this starting point? If firms are held to be run by rational individuals who aim to maximise profit, what theories can we generate regarding the behaviour of firms under different levels of competition? This is the way that economics proceeds in practice. It might well be argued that it would do well to proceed in a more clearly Popperian fashion and devote more energy to refuting important theories. However, it does not, in general, do so. Rather, it devotes its energy to thinking through and developing the implications of certain important starting points or postulates. Referring to the previous discussion of economics' claim to be a science, if deductivism is seen as being an appropriate methodology of science, then economics can properly claim to fit within that description.

CONCLUSION

Not much time is spent by most economists and students of economics on considering how to do economics. Perhaps that is because it is felt to be an avenue that does not much help the subject in terms of any practical use. Perhaps it is because there is no agreement regarding how economics is or should be done. However, reflecting on the practice of economics may be an important part of improving its study. Considering Popper's methodology might lead to such helpful questions as what exactly would be required in order for an economic theory to be deemed as invalid. Looking at a deductivist approach might suggest the key importance and role of underlying laws and postulates. What would happen if any of these were seen, in general, not to be true? Any study of economics is likely to be richer and more effective for a consideration not just of the subject matter of economics, but also of how economics is done. Further, it is notable that different methodologies can often be associated with different economists. Thus, not only can understanding methodology aid economic understanding, but understanding something of the economists responsible for different areas of economic theory may also be important. Such is the purpose of the next chapter.

References

Blaug, M. (1986) *Economic History and the History of Economics* (Cheltenham: Edward Elgar).

Blaug, M. (1992) *The Methodology of Economics*, 2nd edn (Cambridge University Press).

Friedman, M. (1953) *Essays in Positive Economics* (University of Chicago Press).

Hayek, F. (1942) 'Scientism and the Study of Society', *Economica*, August.

Kuhn, T. (1970) *The Structure of Scientific Revolutions*, 2nd edn (University of Chicago Press).

Lakatos, I. (1970) *Criticism and the Growth of Knowledge* (Cambridge University Press).

Lawson, T. (1992) 'Realism, Closed Systems, and Friedman', *Research in the History of Economic Thought and Methodology*, vol. 10.

McCloskey, D. (1983) 'The Rhetoric of Economics', *Journal of Economic Literature*, June.

Popper, K. (1959) *The Logic of Scientific Discovery* (New York: Harper Torchbooks).

Robbins, L. (1935) *An Essay on the Nature and Significance of Economic Science*, 2nd edn (London: Macmillan).

Samuelson, P. (1947) *The Foundations of Economic Analysis* (Cambridge, Mass.: Harvard University Press).

2 A Brief History of Economic Thought

In economics, we appear to assume that it is entirely possible to study our subject to a high standard with scant appreciation of its intellectual heritage. Most economics courses give little or no role to the history of economic thought. Standard textbooks do not give chapters to the topic. The message appears to be that it is unimportant. This is intriguing if not indeed disconcerting. It is hard to see how having an appreciation of the historical development of economic ideas could not be of benefit to a contemporary study of economics. The purpose of this chapter is to give a brief overview of the history of economic thought. The belief is that through this, all the other topics considered later on will be better understood and appreciated.

There are several justifications that can be offered as to why some study of the history of economic thought can be a valuable use of an economist's scarce resource of time. One obvious point to make is that if economics has any pretensions whatsoever to being a science (see Chapter 1 on economic methodology) then at the very least studying the history of economic thought will increase the size of the laboratory for the economist. Previous tests and developments of theories can be taken as data together with contemporary research. Such an increase in the amount of information available can only aid the good study of economics. Keynes, in his famous adage, suggested that many politicians and others proffering views of significance to society were often simply the slaves of some defunct economist. If this is so, then we may as well know the person to whom we are a slave. We might understand why we think what we do if we knew who first articulated the thought. The historian would go further still and suggest that it is only with an awareness of history that we can understand and appreciate the present. Without an awareness of the history of economic thought, we cannot appreciate and understand contemporary economic thought. One obvious and related point is the uncanny tendency of history to repeat itself. This applies to economic thought as much as to any other area of life. At the very least, a study of the history of economic thought may help to stop us endeavouring to reinvent the wheel. Thus, there is good reason for this chapter to exist.

This chapter will divide into several different sections, each one representing an important stage in the perceived development of economic thought. Each development is associated with a particular person or group of people.

ECONOMICS BEFORE ADAM SMITH

It is often suggested that the publication of Adam Smith's *Wealth of Nations* in 1776 marks the birth of economics as a subject. While this might in some senses be true in terms of a subject that becomes defined as an area of academic study, in other senses it is not really accurate. In one way, of course, economics has always existed insofar as mankind has always been confronted with the basic economic problem of how best to use the limited resources available to meet the unlimited wants of members of society. This problem has been thought about and decisions made on its best resolution in any number of different situations. However, in another sense it can be asserted that economics, as we know it today, only came into existence with the advent of what can be called the 'market system'.

The profit motive and the idea of gain, so central to any contemporary study of economics, have to be seen in many ways as only as old as modern man. The Church, the most important social institution of western societies until relatively recent times, saw the concept of endeavouring to make a personal gain as in some sense sinful. It was wrong to aim to behave in such a fashion. There was little concept of aiming to 'make a living'. Work was part and parcel of the essence of life and an end in itself. There were markets for goods, but no real market system. As such, there was no real economics, as we see the subject today, to study. According to this view, it is only really with the arrival of the Industrial Revolution that the time for economics and economists can be deemed to have arrived. It is with the arrival of the Industrial Revolution that we see the development of the market system. With the emergence of clearer national polit-ical units in Europe, the lessening of the perceived importance of traditional Christian thought, and the increases in material standards of living, market systems as we now define them came into existence. The concepts of making profit and making a living were now real. The stage was set for Adam Smith's entrance.

ADAM SMITH

Adam Smith was born in 1723. He attended the University of Oxford at the age of seventeen, but it was at Glasgow University that he embarked on much of the academic enquiry that led to his now famous publications. In 1751, he was given the Chair of Moral Philosophy and in 1759 his *Theory of Moral Sentiments* was published. It is worthy of note that economics, in its early years, was not seen as a distinct discipline in the manner in which it is often studied today. It was rather part of a broader moral and social science.

Although it was to be Smith's *Wealth of Nations* published later that was to be the work that posterity was to view as his great contribution to the development of economic thought, it can be argued that it should always be considered in conjunction with his *Theory of Moral Sentiments*. In this, Smith asked himself the question of how there could be any moral judgements formed in a world of selfish individuals. A related question was how there might be social cohesion in such a world. The answer to his first question was that we must and are able to put ourselves in the position of a third party, and thus can make detached judgements upon issues. Thus, moral judgements are possible. The answer to the second question was that it was necessary to foster a sense of responsibility for others. This was done through society constructing institutions which helped to do this. In light of Smith's later apparent eulogising of self-interest, the answer to his second question is sometimes seen as significant. The self-interest of the *Wealth of Nations* needs to be seen in conjunction with the sense of responsibility of the *Theory of Moral Sentiments*.

In 1764, Adam Smith gave up his Chair at Glasgow in order to embark upon a Grand Tour of Europe as the personal tutor of the son of a Duke. This tour was to last eighteen months and was significant both because he came into contact with the so-called 'Physiocrats' who had developed certain economic theories, and because it was where he began his work on the *Wealth of Nations*. It was not until 1776, the year of American Independence, that the great book was to be published.

The ultimate purpose of Smith's book is explained in its full title: *An Inquiry into the Nature and Causes of the Wealth of Nations*. Smith wished to discover and to explain how societies grew and developed wealth. However, within this overall object, many other issues are considered in a remarkably wide-ranging and scholarly work. Perhaps one of the most enduring ideas to emerge from the book regards the working of the so-called 'invisible hand'. This was the wonderful mechanism by which 'the private interests and passions of men' manage to achieve an outcome 'which is most agreeable to the interests of the whole of society'. For many, this was the greatest insight of the book, and one whose significance and importance drives much economic theory and policy today.

The essence of the workings of the invisible hand is perhaps best summed up in one famous passage: 'It is not from the benevolence of the butcher, the brewer, or the baker that we expect our dinner, but from their regard to their self-interest. We address ourselves, not to their humanity, but to their self-love, and never talk to them of our necessities, but of their advantages.' It is through the self-interest of producers that they are led to produce those things that individuals and society most want, for only thus can they fulfil their selfish desire for profit and gain. The selfish motivation of the producers led to something that is socially desirable. However, this is not the whole picture. The selfish ambition of an individual producer needed to be regulated by the selfish ambitions of other producers. There needed to be competition. This would prevent any one producer charging anything but the lowest of prices, for if he did not, then one of his competitors would do so. Equally, it would force each producer to produce at the lowest possible costs so that he could not be driven out of business. Thus, competition was integral to the successful functioning of the invisible hand. An important corollary of this was that any movement away from competition could only be a bad thing for society: 'People of the same trade seldom meet together but the conversation ends in a conspiracy against the public, or in some diversion to raise prices.'

For the invisible hand to achieve its desirable ends, it also required the free movement of prices. This would ensure that society's scarce resources always moved in the direction where they were most wanted. If consumers decide that they now have a preference of one product over another, then the increase in the demand for one product will cause its price to rise and the fall in demand for the other product will cause its price to fall. This will encourage profit-seeking producers to aim to move production to the more popular product in response to the better price that is available. This is exactly as society desires. The process is reinforced by what will be happening to wages. Where prices are rising, producers wish to employ more workers to raise output. Thus there is an increase in demand for workers which increases wages. This will encourage a movement of labour from the other industry where the fall in demand for the product will have lowered the demand and the wage for workers in that industry. The overall result is that the selfish motivation of the producer, regulated by the forces of competition and facilitated through the free working of the price system, produces a system where the consumer is the main beneficiary. This accorded with Smith's view that 'Consumption is the sole end and purpose of all production.'

If it was Smith's ideas concerning the functioning of the invisible hand that can be seen as the most important of his ideas, there were other significant points that he made in the *Wealth of Nations*. In a famous passage, he describes the specialisation that he witnessed at a pin factory employing ten workers. Such specialisation was seen as a most important cause of the increasing wealth of nations.

> I have seen a small manufactory of this kind where ten men only were employed and where some of them consequently performed two or three distinct operations. But though they were very poor, and therefore but indifferently accommodated with the necessary machinery, they could, when they exerted themselves, make among them about twelve pounds of pins in a day. There are in a pound upward of four thousand pins of a middling size. Those ten persons, therefore, could make among them upwards of forty-eight thousand pins a day … But if they had all wrought separately and independently … they certainly could not each of them have made twenty, perhaps not one pin a day.

This division of labour was in turn recognised by Smith as being limited by the size of the market. Specialisation was only worthwhile where the market was sufficiently great to warrant the large production that would occur through specialisation.

Adam Smith died in 1790. It is not difficult to see why he may be considered so important in the development of economic thought. Some of his central ideas appear as powerful (or perhaps more powerful) today as when they were first presented. A belief in the efficacy of the invisible hand has been the driving force behind many of the significant economic policy developments of the past decade, such as the privatisation programmes and the reform of health care and education provision discussed later in this book. It also lies behind the resurgence of free-market macroeconomic views. The increased size of the European market which allows firms to gain the fullest possible benefits from economies of scale is recognised as one of the most important points in the movement towards a single European market. This emphasis on the increasing returns available through higher levels of output in the long run is also central to the new growth theory developed in recent years (see Chapter 14 on economic growth). Smith's influence is as great as ever.

THOMAS MALTHUS AND DAVID RICARDO

Malthus and Ricardo were contemporaries. Malthus was born in 1766 and died in 1834, while Ricardo's life spanned the years 1772 to 1823. They were in fact more than simply contemporaries: they spent much of their lives in fierce opposition to each other's theories regarding the economy. For example, Malthus was to suggest that economies could suffer from the problem of surpluses due to the fact that savings could imply the possibility of insufficient spending in the economy (a suggestion remarkably similar to one of Keynes's fundamental points, a point which Keynes himself acknowledged). However, Ricardo refuted this possibility, suggesting that saving only ever occurred for the purpose of spending, and thus there would be no shortfall of demand and consequent surplus in the economy (a view similar to the classical view of savings which Keynes was keen to refute). On similar lines, Malthus was to suggest that the landed gentry in the country were in fact a useful part of society due to the injection of spending from their wealth that they provided. Ricardo believed that they were undesirable for the economy as the surplus that they gained from their land was not beneficial and would effectively lead to the demise of industrialists in the nation. Despite these and other disagreements, Malthus was to write about Ricardo that 'I never loved anyone out of my family so much'.

Malthus had Hume and Rousseau for godparents and read mathematics at Jesus College, Cambridge. He then taught at Haileybury school. It was his *Essay on Population* in 1798 that was to lead to his lasting fame. Godwin, a minister of the church, had suggested prior to Malthus that the natural development of society was to lead to the future improvement and possible perfection of humanity. Malthus refuted this utopian view and suggested that mankind was rather destined for future misery. His basic model was deduced from two axioms: food was necessary for man's existence, and passion between the two sexes was a natural and necessary part of life that would remain. Godwin had suggested that the latter of these axioms would tend to fade. These two axioms presented a fundamental problem. The population will tend to grow at a geometric rate while the amount of food available to humanity will only grow at an arithmetic rate. Malthus put it thus: 'the human species would increase in the ratio of 1, 2, 4, 8, 16, 32, 64, 128, 256, 512, etc. and subsistence as 1, 2, 3, 4, 5, 6, 7, 8, 9, 10, etc. In two centuries and a quarter, the population would be to the means of subsistence as 512 to 10.' The corollary was that as the population pressed on the means of subsistence, then so there were bound to be wars, famines and other disasters which would return the population to a sustainable level. This process could also work through the mechanism of the wage rate. If the market wage were to move above the 'natural' or subsistence wage, then there would be a growth in the level of population permitted by wages above those just necessary to survive. This would put pressure on the market wage (the supply of labour would rise) and force it back to its subsistence level. Thus, the only wage level that was sustainable in the long run was the subsistence wage. It is perhaps not surprising that, upon reading Malthus's analysis, the historian, Thomas Carlyle was to dub economics as 'the dismal science'.

Ricardo was a highly talented man. No more was this in evidence than in his highly successful stockbroking career where he made much money. However, it was his writing, encouraged by James Mill, that led to his enduring importance. In particular, his *Principles of Political Economy*, published in 1817, is one of the classic works in the development of economic thought. Two particular aspects of his work can be seen as especially significant: his arguments in favour of free trade and his theory of economic growth and its implication for society. The theory of comparative advantage developed by Ricardo is still seen as a principal explanation of the economic desirability of trade between nations in contemporary textbooks. Although modern versions of the theory do not hold to the labour theory of value that underpinned Ricardo's analysis (the suggestion that it was the amount of labour that was embodied in a product that determined its value and price), the logic is the same. If individuals, regions and countries produce those things in which they have a comparative advantage compared to others and then trade with each other, everyone can be better off. It does not matter if one country or individual is better at producing everything (has an absolute advantage in everything) as long as the advantage held is not the same for all products. It can be simply shown that by specialising in those things where the advantage is greatest and allowing others to specialise in producing where their disadvantage is least, total production can rise and thus all can gain through appropriate trade.

Ricardo's model of economic growth, which was inextricably bound with a model of distribution, accepted Malthus's analysis that the market wage would tend to be equal to the subsistence wage. Coupled with the existence of diminishing marginal returns (the suggestion that the more output that is squeezed out of certain resources by adding more labour to them, the less the increase in output will be with each addition of labour) and the increase in population suggested by Malthus, Ricardo's prognosis for the long-run growth of the economy was very gloomy. National income was seen as divided between wages received by workers, rent received by landlords for their land and profits received by industrialists upon the production and sale of manufactured goods. It was profits that were the key to economic growth as they provided the finance for accumulation by industrialists which could lead to higher production in the future. The problem was that there would be an inexorable squeeze on profits to the point where there would be no more accumulation and the economy would reach a stationary state. As the population grew, so more land would be pressed into agricultural usage in order to feed the population. The problem was that the land would suffer from diminishing returns and thus the extra food would be more expensive to produce. This would force up food prices which in turn would force up the subsistence wage. Thus the wage rate would have to take up an increasing proportion of the national income. Given the demand for agricultural produce, the rent received from landlords on the use of their land would certainly not decrease: if anything it would increase. This left one part of national income that would decline: profits. These would decline to the point where they were insufficient to motivate industrialists in their work (below normal profit) and the economy would grind to a halt. This provided another important argument for free trade since the international division of labour permitted through free trade would delay the evil day of the stationary state as it would lessen the immediate problem of diminishing returns.

It is not surprising that Ricardo was a strong opponent of the Corn Laws in force at the time (a restriction upon the import of corn from other countries). According to his analysis, such laws could only possibly be bad for the economy. This view accorded well with the hardship caused by the then rising price of corn resulting from the Corn Laws. As such, this can be seen as one of several examples in the development of economic thought of an economic theory emerging that was in tune with the mood of the times. Necessity can sometimes be seen as the mother of economic theory.

Malthus and Ricardo are significant not just because of their specific contributions to individual parts of economic thought but also because of their approach. Both of them developed economic models, simplifications of reality which allowed analysis to be conducted and general implications to be deduced from particular circumstances. This is the approach of economics, in large part, today. Indeed, excessive simplification and ignoring of certain facts is referred to as the 'Ricardian vice'. In addition, Malthus and Ricardo had effectively given a very different message from that of Adam Smith. They had both suggested that if the economy was left to its own devices, disasters were quite likely to be in store. For Smith, all would be well. It is not much of a step from suggesting that the economy will naturally tend towards disasters to suggesting that governments should intervene in the economy to improve the situation. This debate, of course, can be seen as one of the fundamental themes of disagreement in economic thought and prescription for policy.

JOHN STUART MILL

John Stuart Mill was born in 1806. At the age of three he began to learn Greek, by the age of seven he had read much of Plato and by the age of eight was studying Latin. It may have been inevitable that he became a seminal thinker of his age. Mill is perhaps best known to us as a philosopher with works such as *System of Logic*

(1843) and *Utilitarianism* (1867). However, he was an economist, and in 1848 published his masterpiece on economics, *Principles of Political Economy*. This was a great survey of the field of economics as it existed at the time, incorporating Smith, Malthus, Ricardo and much else. Of most interest to us is the specific development in economic thought that this work suggested: that the province of economics and economic laws lay within production and the productive process and that alone. Specifically, it did not lie within the realm of distribution. This was clearly different from Ricardo. Ricardo had suggested that the productive and distributive aspects of society were inextricably linked. Indeed, they would work together to produce a stationary state. Mill's observation was simple: the state of distribution did not have to be taken as given. If, for whatever reason, it was seen as undesirable, then it could be changed through redistributory taxes and other forms of government intervention. Thus, the squeeze on profits implied in Ricardo's model could be overcome by a more favourable tax treatment of profits than of rents and wages.

Mill's insight is significant for it is accepted by much of mainstream economics today. The province of economics is seen as lying within the various aspects of the productive process and associated consumption. Distribution is outside of this and is generally seen as outside of the province of the economist. Society and politicians, not economists, should make judgements upon distribution.

KARL MARX

Karl Marx was born into a Christian family (which had Jewish origins) in 1818. He attended university at both Bonn and Berlin, at the latter encountering Hegel's views which were to prove an important influence on his later work. He worked as a journalist and married his wife, Jenny, who bore him five children. By the time of his death in 1883, he had produced written work – much of which was done during his daily stint from 10.00 a.m. until 7.00 p.m. in the British Museum – whose impact was arguably as great as any other upon the twentieth century.

Attempting to sum up Marx's ideas and contribution to economic thought is not straightforward. *Das Kapital*, published from 1867, contains more than 2500 pages. *The Communist Manifesto*, published in 1848, is also a significant and important piece of work. All that can be done is to try to distil certain of the key themes and ideas and to consider their place within economic thought. One such theme is the influence of Hegel's ideas upon Marx. Hegel's philosophy suggested that history progressed in a dialectical fashion: two opposite forces proved to be the driving force behind the movement of events. This concept was central to Marx with regard to his views upon the opposed interests of different classes in society. The ending of the processes of history would come when there were no more opposing forces. For Marx, this would mean that the state of communism, where there were no longer classes with opposed interests, represented the logical finishing point of historical development. This dialectical view of history was taken further to include what is termed a 'materialist' view of society. Marx's philosophy is thus often described as 'dialectical materialism'. Engels, who worked closely with Marx, summed up this philosophy in his tract called *Anti-Duhring* (1878) when he wrote that it suggests that 'the ultimate causes of all social changes and political revolutions are to be sought, not in the minds of men, in their increasing insight into eternal truth and justice, but in changes in the mode of production and exchange; they are to be sought not in the philosophy but in the economics of the epoch concerned'. In other words, man is a product of his economic environment. Human lives are shaped not by ideas but by material circumstances. The state and organisation of the economy dictated the lives of its inhabitants.

In addition to Hegel's influence, Marx received from Ricardo the theories of value, based on the view that labour dictated the value of any product, economic growth and distribution. However, from the 1830s, he was keen to distance his work from other political economists as he saw them as simply helping to support the ruling classes. Mill was the leading classical economist of the time, and his views on distribution were very different from those of Marx. Marx's approach was to be more multi-disciplined.

Marx's work was fundamentally an analysis of the working of the capitalist system. He had a great deal to say about capitalism, but far less to suggest about the post-capitalist states of socialism and communism. That was left to Lenin. Probably the most important theme in Marx's analysis was that the state of capitalism would destroy itself. It contained the seeds of its own destruction and communist revolution ending the era of capitalism was an inevitable part of the history of mankind. Marx described it as follows in the *Communist Manifesto*:

> The development of modern industry ... cuts from under its feet the very foundation on which the bourgeoisie produces and appropriates products. What the bourgeoisie therefore produces, above all, are its own gravediggers. Its fall and the victory of the proleteriat are equally inevitable.

For Marx, the whole of history was the history of class warfare. The organising principle of this analysis of history was the notion of surplus. Under a system of feudalism, the two opposing classes were the landlords and their serfs. The source of the surplus here was plain to see. The serfs worked on their landlord's land, having no choice over the matter. The lords then extracted from the serfs however much production they chose. This represented the surplus of the landlords, acquired at the expense of the serfs. The class exploitation under capitalism is not so transparent. Under capitalism, there is competition between producers and a diffusion of power. Workers are not owned in the same fashion as under feudalism and appear to be free to sell their labour power to whomever they may wish. Where, then, is the exploitation and opposed interest in this system? The answer is that the capitalists, or bourgeoisie, hold the power in this capitalist system. As a class, they own the capital, or means of production. Workers, or the proleteriat, may be free to sell their labour power, but they are only free to sell it to a capitalist, an owner of the means of production. As a whole class, capitalists hold monopoly power. As a class, they only need pay the subsistence, or natural, wage to workers. Indeed, the forces of competition will ensure that all industries have the wage at this level if capitalist producers are to be able to compete with each other. However, the value of the production from each worker may well be greater than the value of the subsistence wage. The difference between this true value of the production of the worker and the actual wage paid represents the capitalist's surplus and the level of exploitation from which the worker suffers.

This system of extracting surplus will, however, begin to run into trouble. Capitalism will suffer from ever-increasing crises as profits show a long-term tendency to decline. The starting point of these crises is where the capitalist system appears to be doing well. Demand for products is high and producers are keen to produce as much as possible in order to make profits. In such times, the market wage is likely to be pushed above the natural, or subsistence, wage as producers compete with each other to attract the labour required for production. However, this increase in the wage also then produces a stimulus for producers to introduce labour-saving machinery in an effort to keep down their costs. The net impact of this is to reduce the amount of labour used by capitalists. But this creates a logical problem. Labour is the sole ultimate source of the capitalists' surplus or profit. Thus, a reduction in the use of labour must equate to a reduction in the rate of profit for capitalists. The response to this that competition then forces upon capitalists is to introduce yet more labour-saving machinery in a further effort to reduce costs. This ultimately further reduces the profit rate. It also creates unemployed workers, or a reserve army of labour. These are the characteristics of a capitalist crisis. When the crisis reaches its climax, various producers are forced out of business entirely. However, others re-emerge with lower costs and are once more viable producers. But there are now fewer firms and less competition and the whole process of crisis again develops, except more severely than before. The reserve army becomes ever larger and the rate of profit declines further. Eventually, profit dwindles to nothing and capitalism collapses.

It might be tempting to suggest that with the apparent lack of collapse of the capitalist system and the decline of communist regimes in Eastern Europe that Marx's work must be judged to be of little enduring worth within the history of economic thought. This would not be right. Marx's ideas are a powerful ingredient behind much of the history of the twentieth century. These ideas may also be judged as having some enduring importance. The suggestion that economics is not a subject on its own, but rather part of a general social, political, philosophical and economic analysis, is a view that still holds much credence today. Perhaps economics can only be properly understood and studied within this wider context. Beyond that, it is hard to fault many of Marx's basic predictions concerning capitalism. The twentieth century has seen economic crises with great pressure on profits and a large reserve army of labour. Indeed, Western Europe almost appears to have accepted today that a significant percentage of its workforce will always be unemployed. The pressure for new techniques of production and the drive to introduce labour-saving machinery have both been clearly distinguishable features of capitalist development in the twentieth century. The tendency for ever greater concentration within industries and the dominance of ever larger firms can be seen throughout the capitalist world. Marx's predictions for the end of capitalism may not appear to hold much credence, but his analysis of its likely development needs to be taken seriously.

LEON WALRAS

Walras was born in 1834. His initial study was in engineering, but he later swapped to literature. Walras may not be seen as one of the great names of economic thought, but his work, and that of some of his contemporaries such as Francis Edgeworth and W. Stanley Jevons, must be deemed as important in the history of economic thought in terms of the nature of what is studied in the subject called 'economics' today.

Walras is particularly associated with the development of general equilibrium theory, a significant part of most contemporary advanced economics courses. Walras saw that a schedule showing the demand for a product at different prices was too partial a view of the economic system, and that a greater whole needed to be analysed. The way to do this was to bring together the equations for all of the markets of an economy and to solve them all simultaneously, thus giving the exact prices in all markets at any one time. Some of Walras's equations are still in use. Perhaps more significant than this, however, is the approach that was now being adopted. Walras believed, following his study of Cournot, that economics could and should be expressed in a mathematical form. Many economics texts today suggest a similar view is held by contemporary economists. Equally, Walras suggested that prices would change continuously in their search for what was termed 'equilibrium'. The importance of this idea can be seen in any of today's microeconomic textbooks.

Perhaps most important of all, Walras developed his own marginal utility theory of value. While Ricardo and Marx had theories which suggested that the amount of labour embodied in the production of anything was what gave it value, Walras suggested that it was rather the level of utility, or satisfaction, that a product yielded that gave it its value insofar as this is what dictated the amount that an individual would be willing to pay for something, and that is ultimately what gave anything value. This was a significant development in economic thought in price theory, and really marked the end of the labour theory of value.

Combining Walras's ideas appeared to lead to a particular approach to economics. The suggestion of the marginal utility theory of value effectively came from a utilitarian philosophy. The basic aim of mankind was to derive utility out of all situations. This fundamental proposition concerning human behaviour could be followed through in a mathematical fashion to lead to a whole set of suggestions regarding different economic situations. Edgeworth attempted to combine the approach with a world of perfect competition to suggest that the market would lead to a situation of maximum possible utility for all individuals.

While it is not easy to pin down an exact definition of neoclassical economics today, the approach seems very similar to that developed by these economists. Perhaps it is also no surprise that Jevons had planned to write a book (which never in fact materialised) called 'Principles of Economics'. It is in the work of these economists that we see the clearest move away from what was before termed 'political economy' to what we today call 'economics'.

ALFRED MARSHALL

Alfred Marshall is not always identified as one of the 'greats' in terms of the history of economic thought. This is perhaps because of the lack of any specific new or radical theory that can be attributed to him and which can be judged to have had a profound influence on society. However, by the time of his death in 1924, he had developed ideas that were the foundation of much of the economics that was studied at the time and much of what is to be found in standard (microeconomic) textbooks today.

Marshall's greatest work was his *Principles of Economics* first published in 1890. Various fundamental points were embodied in this work. Perhaps most famous of all was the work on supply and demand. Economists had long studied and written about what exactly determined prices within society. The classical approach, as embodied in Ricardo and Marx, was to suggest that the amount of labour involved in production dictated the value (or price) of anything. Walras and others had moved away from this. Marshall himself stressed that utility was what determined demand schedules: the amount that a product was worth to a person dictated the amount that that person was willing to pay for it (this idea is now referred to as cardinal utility). However, the ultimate determination of prices rested upon the workings of both the productive side of economies, the supply side, and the utilities of consumers, the demand side. It was the interaction of supply and demand that determined price. Thus supply and demand were, in Marshall's words, 'the blades of a pair of scissors'. Where the blades crossed, then there was the equilibrium price. This was thus also the formalisation of equilibrium analysis: everything tended towards some equilibrium point. In the words of Marshall's most famous pupil, Keynes suggested that Marshall had created 'a whole Copernican system, in which all the elements of the economic universe are kept in their places by mutual counterpoise and interaction'.

Marshall was also to identify time as a crucial determinant in the way in which equilibrium prices moved. In the short run, production could not be altered greatly, if at all. Thus, the determinant of price was demand: price fluctuated with demand as supply could not change. However, the longer the time period involved, the more that supply could and would vary, and thus the greater the impact of supply upon market price. Various other important economic ideas can be attributed to Marshall. He is credited with 'discovering' the concept of elasticity of demand, a measurement of how much demand would change in response to a change in another variable, usually the product's own price. This concept is now a central part of any study of microeconomics. Marshall's development of utility theory also led him to derive a labour supply curve based upon the value of marginal disutility that was associated with any particular employment. This remains the standard approach to labour supply curves. He did much work on monetary theory such as applying his supply and demand approach to monetary matters. He developed the use of index numbers in this field and identified the different concepts of money and real rates of interest. Perhaps in particular, he identified a transmission mechanism for the quantity theory of money to help to explain how increases in the money stock actually led to increases in the price level. He also developed the Cambridge version of this quantity theory of money. The importance of all of these ideas will not be lost on anyone studying economics today.

One final thing in which Marshall must be seen as instrumental is the formal development of a subject called 'economics' as opposed to 'political economy'. It has already been noted that his major work was called *Principles of Economics*. More than that, however, Marshall was to establish a separate Economics Tripos at Cambridge University in the first decade of the twentieth century. Economics was thus embodied as a separate subject, for good or ill, in its own right. Marshall hoped that the Tripos would produce young men with 'cool heads and warm hearts'. For him, economics was about the discovery of truth, especially the causes of and possible remedies for the social evil of poverty. The work of his most famous pupil can in many ways be seen as fitting within that outlook.

JOAN ROBINSON

Joan Robinson was born in 1903. Her career was based around Cambridge. She was a graduate of Girton College, Cambridge, married the economist Austin Robinson and spent much of her life teaching economics at the University.

Joan Robinson's work was wide-ranging and frequently challenging of current orthodoxy. Perhaps the piece of work for which she is best known is her development of the theory of imperfect competition during the 1930s. She produced an alternative model of competition to the two traditional models of perfect competition and monopoly which dominated microeconomic theory up until that time. The model bore considerable similarity to the work of Edward Chamberlin in the United States during the same time period. Both models, now commonly referred to as the model of 'monopolistic competition', looked at the importance of differentiated products and the existence of advertising to competition and firms' behaviour. Historically, the development of this model must be seen as significant, as intermediate models of competition between perfect competition and monopoly now dominate much theoretical study of the firm in economics. Equally, such models are also now seen by many as being of considerable importance in developing a proper understanding of macroeconomics, especially the possibility of markets not clearing immediately (see Chapter 3 on microeconomics and macroeconomics).

It was perhaps typical of Joan Robinson that she was later to criticise her own theory of imperfect competition. Traditional, neoclassical theory did not and could not address the matters which to her really mattered, things such as poverty at home or development in the Third World. Different approaches were needed. As significant as anything else in her challenges to current orthodoxy and concern to tackle those issues that might be seen as genuinely important was her work with John Maynard Keynes as he developed his great challenge to the macroeconomic orthodoxy of the 1920s and 1930s.

JOHN MAYNARD KEYNES

John Maynard Keynes was born in 1883, the son of the philosopher and economist, John Neville Keynes. His life was to be one of brilliance on many counts. At the age of fourteen he gained a scholarship to Eton. He read mathematics at Cambridge where he gained a double first. After his degree, he came second in the Civil Service examination and proceeded to work in the India Office for two years. He returned to Cambridge to become a Fellow of King's College. He made large sums of money, both for himself and later as bursar of King's College through speculation on the stock exchange. He established the Arts Theatre in Cambridge and edited the *Economic Journal* for thirty-three years. He was a member of the Bloomsbury group whose members included E.M. Forster, Leonard and Virginia Woolf, Clive Bell and Lytton Strachey (one of his many homosexual lovers). In 1925, he married the famous Russian ballerina, Lydia Lopokova.

From the moment that Keynes became a Fellow of King's College, he aimed always to write at least 1000 words each day. Keynes's serious economics work really started after the First World War. His involvement with the war effort and work with the Treasury led to something of a split with Bloomsbury. However, it appeared to create a more serious outlook within Keynes. He was appalled by the Treaty of Versailles and condemned it in his *Economic Consequences of the Peace* (1919), suggesting that it would inevitably lead to disaster within Europe. From this moment, having witnessed the happenings at Versailles, Keynes developed a strong wish to drive what he saw as stupidity and irrationality from public affairs. During the 1920s, Keynes wrote several notable economics publications. His *Tract on Monetary Reform* (1923) adhered to the quantity theory of money and contained his now famous adage that 'In the long run we are all dead.' In his *Economic Consequences of Mr Churchill* (1925), Keynes argued that Britain had re-entered the Gold Standard at too high a level and that this would prove disastrous for British business. The argument was remarkably similar to concerns over Britain's brief recent entry into the European Exchange Rate Mechanism in 1990. His *Treatise on Money* (1930), written later in the decade, showed Keynes uncertain over some of his views (he changed his mind during the writing of it and disliked the final product) and still staying within the paradigm of the quantity theory of money. In particular, the key theoretical aspect of the quantity theory can be seen as the assumption of full employment in the economy. It was only really during the writing of this *Treatise* that Keynes felt aware that economics lacked a theory of the determination of output as a whole. Perhaps beginning to pave the way for his major work, Keynes also wrote *Can Lloyd George Do It?* (1929), a review of the possible success of public works schemes. His analysis was not all that it might have been as it lacked the mechanism of the multiplier to analyse the possibilities. R.F. Kahn was to remedy this with the development of the theory of the multiplier in 1931. The multiplier was to be an important facet of Keynes's greatest and most influential work, *The General Theory of Employment, Interest and Money* (1936).

A series of lectures entitled 'Theory of Monetary Production' provided the basis of *The General Theory* which was eventually published on 6 February 1936. From the outset, Keynes was in no doubt over the book's likely significance and importance. He wrote to George Bernard Shaw in 1935 that 'I believe myself to be writing a book on economic theory which will largely revolutionise – not, I suppose at once, but in the course of the next ten years – the way the world thinks about economic problems'. Properly to understand Keynes's analysis, three aspects to his approach need to be appreciated. These stem initially from a mathematical work, his *Treatise on Probability* (1921), but underpin his general thinking. The first is that it is appropriate to use a spectrum of languages in any analysis. Sometimes mathematics might be appropriate, at other times poetry. This diversity of language and approach is used in *The General Theory*. The second is that the whole is greater than the sum of the parts. In this, Keynes could effectively offer a justification for the study of macroeconomics as in some way distinct from microeconomics. *The General Theory* is seen by many as the first mainstream macroeconomic textbook. The third point is that we live in a world that is intrinsically uncertain. For some, business uncertainty and its likely impact upon an economy is seen as one of the most important aspects of *The General Theory*.

Probably the most important suggestion made in *The General Theory* was that economies could become stuck in a position of large-scale involuntary unemployment. There could be many people willing and able to work at the going wage (or perhaps even a lower real wage if necessary), but simply unable to secure employment because insufficient employment was available. This was a proposition that ran entirely counter to the standard classical economics (as Keynes called it and as epitomised, certainly in the eyes of Keynes himself, by the work of Professor A.C. Pigou) of the day which suggested that a properly functioning economy, left to its own devices, would deliver a position of full employment. Of course, it was not contrary to Marx's analysis, but Keynes came from a position where he supported capitalism and the established order, and even boasted that he had never read Marx. The fundamental problem for a modern economy was the separation of the decision to save from the decision to invest. In such an economy, Say's law (named after the French economist, Jean-Baptiste Say, a good friend of Ricardo and Malthus) could not be seen as holding true. Supply did not automatically generate its own demand, as the income received from production was not automatically spent: some of it was saved. The problem came when the amount that people wished to save from their incomes was greater than the amount that businesses wished to spend on investment. Malthus had identified the possibility of such a problem in the previous century. If such a position arose, expenditure in an economy would be below the value of production. Firms would thus cut back on their production, making workers redundant in the process. This would further reduce incomes and spending via the multiplier process and thus cause a further cut in output and employment. The process would continue until the point where expenditure was equal to output and savings had been reduced, through the contraction of incomes, to a level equal to investment. The economy would now be in a position of some sort of equilibrium. The problem with this position is that it was associated with large-scale unemployment. This explained the position of the western economies in the 1930s.

The classical view of the above analysis was that as soon as there was any imbalance between the level of savings and investment, the rate of interest would adjust to correct this. However, Keynes suggested that the interest rate was determined not in the market for goods and services, as implied by classical theory, but rather in the money market. It could not fall far enough due to the liquidity trap which implied that there would always be a positive rate of interest, and also because the interest rate was not a sufficiently powerful tool to offset pessimistic business expectations once these had set in. Some perceive the importance of such expectations, as embodied in chapter twelve of *The General Theory*, to be one of the most important aspects of Keynes's analysis. Human beings are complicated and insecure creatures who have vaguely rational fears lurking just below the surface of their lives. If something happens to arouse those fears, then pessimism takes over. In a business context, this represents a lack of desire to invest because of concerns about the future. This cut in investment will lead to a surplus of saving over investment and move the economy towards recession and unemployment.

A further aspect to Keynes's work was his explanation of how the wage rate will not adjust appropriately to cure the problem of unemployment. This was the other mechanism through which the classical economists preceding Keynes believed any emerging unemployment would be cured. Keynes suggested that individual groups of workers would be unwilling to see their wage decline, given their concern over relative wages. However, even if it were to decline, only the money wage would fall. This would cause firms' costs to fall and thus cause a fall in prices. The real wage would remain unaffected. The wage rate could provide no answer to the problem.

Given this analysis, there was only one logical conclusion: the government must do something. In some way or other, and really it did not matter how, the government must raise the level of spending in the economy so that firms would be induced to produce more and thus increase their employment. The government might borrow in order to increase its expenditure and/or reduce taxes.

Insofar as it was posssible, it might also lower interest rates. It would only be through such government action that the economy could be guaranteed to move from its position of unemployment. Without such action, the economy might simply stay there.

By the time of his death in 1946, Keynes had illustrated, in his publication *How to Pay for the War* (1940), how this analysis could also be applied to inflationary situations. Such positions for the economy were simply a reverse of the previous problem: there was now too much rather than too little expenditure in the economy. It was an analysis that was to dominate the formulation of macroeconomic policies of virtually all western governments after the Second World War right through until the middle of the 1970s. Despite apparent problems today, some still suggest that there is no more coherent analysis of the basic framework of how to manage an economy.

CONCLUSION

By the nature of this chapter, its treatment of such a wide topic is but cursory. It has done little more than give a flavour of some of the important developments in economic thought and their impact upon the economics that we study today. Many other economists would be good contenders for inclusion in the survey. It is possible to think of people such as Schumpeter whose view of monopolies as being involved in the 'perennial gale of creative destruction' within capitalist development might be seen as an important insight into the workings of many modern economies. However, the reason for the choice of the individuals in this chapter is that their ideas seem to have had the greatest influence upon the development of what we call today 'economics'.

It might well be asked why the survey finishes about fifty years ago with the death of Keynes. The answer is that it is not easy to discern really significant and radical developments in economic thought since that time. In the area of macroeconomics, Keynes was to be dominant in terms of both academic theory and practical policy until the middle of the 1970s. From then, monetarists and neoclassical economists moved to the fore. However, their ideas cannot be seen as a new development. They were rather a return to the more laissez-faire views that had preceded Keynes's analysis. Today, we live with some sort of uneasy eclecticism, a vague mixture of Keynesian and neoclassical views. Within microeconomics, the approach of Walras and some of his contemporaries appears all-pervasive. The logical mathematical development of models and their implications dominates economics texts. Insofar as new developments in different areas of theory can be discerned in recent years, the purpose of this book is to identify those developments and consider their possible implications.

Can any general themes be perceived from this survey? Three points can perhaps especially be stressed. The first is that significant developments in economic thought are often the product of the situation of the age. Ricardo's strong advocation of free trade came at a time when the Corn Laws were imposing hardship upon Britain. Marx wrote his *Communist Manifesto* in 1848, a year of revolutions throughout Europe. Keynes explained the persistence of mass unemployment during the Great Depression of the inter-war years. Keynes's views went out of fashion in the 1970s when the new economic disaster of stagflation appeared. This begs an important question as to whether economic ideas are the product of an age and thus only relevant to that age, or whether they are in some sense universal. Was Keynes's analysis right for the 1930s but wrong for a later age? This is clearly a crucial question to answer if the best economic policies are to be successfully designed. The second point worthy of note is the clear move from 'political economy' to 'economics'. The subject that we now study is narrower and more specific in its outlook, and aims to see itself as separate from other disciplines that are part of the social sciences. This was not always so, and it may require careful reflection to consider whether we have a better or worse understanding of the workings of economies as a result of this. The third theme appears to be the question of how well capitalist economies work if they are left to their own devices. Smith was highly optimistic; Marx was ultimately highly pessimistic; others sit somewhere in between. It has always been, and it remains today, one of the great questions of economics: how much should the government intervene in the running of an economy and how much should it be left to its own devices? In many ways, to answer that question is to declare one's position as an economist.

References

Engels, Friedrich (1878) *Anti-Duhring* (London: Lawrence & Wishart, 1975)

Keynes, John Maynard (1936) *The General Theory of Employment, Interest and Money* (London: Macmillan, 1973).

Malthus, Thomas (1798) *An Essay on Population* (Harmondsworth: Penguin, 1970).

Marshall, Alfred (1890) *Principles of Economics* (London: Macmillan, 1961).

Marx, Karl (1867) *Das Kapital* (London: Lawrence & Wishart, 1970).

Marx, Karl and Friedrich Engels (1848) *The Communist Manifesto* (London: Martin Lawrence, 1933).

Mill, John Stuart (1848) *Principles of Political Economy* (London: Routledge & Kegan Paul, 1965).

Ricardo, David (1817) *Principles of Political Economy* (Harmondsworth: Penguin, 1971).

Smith, Adam (1759) *The Theory of Moral Sentiments* (Oxford: Clarendon Press, 1976)

Smith, Adam (1776) *An Inquiry Into the Nature and Causes of the Wealth of Nations* (Oxford: Clarendon Press, 1976)

3   Microeconomics and Macroeconomics

It is customary when studying many subjects to divide them into different sections. This makes good sense. It is daunting to feel that the only way to tackle a particular subject is to have to take on the whole of it at once. It makes study far more accessible and easier to organise if there are subdivisions within a subject that allow it to be tackled one part at a time. This helps to explain the logic of the division of economics into microeconomics and macroeconomics. It appears to make the study of the subject a less daunting task if there are two separate aspects of the subject that can be studied.

The purpose of this chapter is to investigate this traditional divide of economics into microeconomics and macroeconomics. The overall message is that the divide is a dangerous one. It is too easy to fall into the trap of seeing economics as two almost separate subjects without considering properly how each relates to the other. In particular, it appears crucial that both parts of the subject should not be contradictory. The structure of the chapter is therefore as follows:

1.   Micro versus macro: the traditional divide. This section sums up the standard presentation of microeconomics and macroeconomics.
2.   Inconsistencies between microeconomics and macroeconomics. The chapter proceeds to consider some of the significant inconsistencies between the two parts of the subject.
3.   Reconciliation between micro and macro. This part of the chapter surveys some of the relatively recent attempts to reconcile the inconsistencies observed in the previous section.
4.   Possible problems of integrating micro and macro. It can be argued that suggesting that macroeconomics is the adding-up of microeconomics is not true and can lead to false conclusions.
5.   Policy implications. The final section of the chapter considers the possible policy implications suggested by efforts to renconcile the two parts of the subject.

MICRO VERSUS MACRO: THE TRADITIONAL DIVIDE

Modern economics courses and textbooks are generally divided into the two sections of microeconomics and macroeconomics. There may be separate examination papers set on the two areas and textbooks are often clearly divided into the two sides. This textbook follows this traditional approach for organisational reasons.

The terms 'microeconomics' and 'macroeconomics' mean exactly as they suggest. Microeconomics is the study of economics on the small scale, while macroeconomics is the study of economics on the big scale. Microeconomics concerns itself with the individual parts of the economy, principally looking at the supply and demand of individual goods and services and the determination of their prices. On the other hand, macroeconomics looks at total supply and total demand within the whole economy. It is thus concerned with changes in the general price level (inflation), the determination of the total level of output and employment in the economy, the rate of growth of the economy's national income and the economy's total trading position with the rest of the world (the balance of payments and related issues). Thus it has been possible to identify what appear to be two quite distinct parts to the subject of economics.

It is important to note that this clear divide of the subject is a fairly recent invention. It is fair to say that before Keynes, mainstream economics concerned itself principally with the study of microeconomics (there are various notable exceptions to this, such as Marx, although they may not be deemed to be main-stream). This is logical given the prevailing view that economies were inherently self-regulating. As long as economies were left alone, they would function well at a level at or near to full employment. Given this belief, there was not a great deal of interest to be studied in what we now call 'macroeconomics' and thus attention was focused upon microeconomic issues. Once Keynes suggested that economies might not be inherently self-regulating and this view came to be accepted by many within the economics profession, then macroeconomics became an area with much of interest and importance to study. Thus we have the current two parts of the subject.

Dividing economics into its two parts seems, then, to be logical and coherent. It helps to make the subject more accessible and allows specialisation. Unfortunately, the divide may have done considerable harm to the subject as a whole as it has caused it to lose an overall coherence. In particular, it appears to have led to contradictions between the two parts of an economics course as studied by many students of economics.

INCONSISTENCIES BETWEEN MICROECONOMICS AND MACROECONOMICS

The problems of dividing economics in the way described above start to become clear when considering various economic issues. A useful starting point might be the contention (widely held by the UK government during the 1980s) that income tax cuts increase the rate of economic growth and reduce the level of unemployment. Stated as such, this appears clearly to be a topic for study within the realm of macroeconomics. However, upon closer inspection, this is less clearly the case. The reason for holding such an optimistic view about the effects of cuts in income tax rests upon observations of individual behaviour. The belief was that work would now be perceived as 'better value' than the alternative of leisure, and thus people would want to have less leisure and more work. Thus the output of the nation would rise and unemployment would fall (such a view ignores the contradictory possibility that people may choose to work less as the same income can now be earned in less hours). Looked at from this perspective, the issue is clearly microeconomic. Thus we have to conclude that this topic, along with many others in economics, is both macroeconomic and microeconomic in nature.

However, the problem may be more fundamental than is suggested above. Many introductory macroeconomics courses make use of the simple so-called 'Keynesian' 45 degree diagram as a starting point for analysing macroeconomic situations. The suggestion of this model is that it is possible for an economy to be in equilibrium at less than full-employment income and thus for involuntary unemployment to persist due to lack of aggregate demand in the economy. This situation is illustrated in Figure 3.1.

Given the level of aggregate demand in the economy, the economy is in equilibrium at national income level *Ye*. The problem is that this level is below the

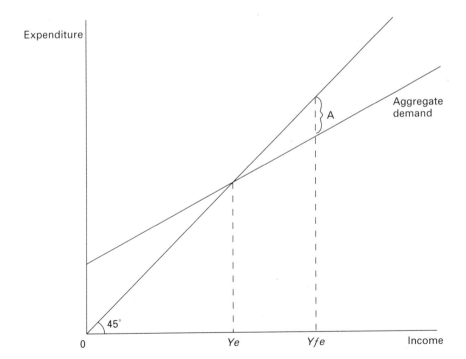

Figure 3.1   *The Keynesian 45 degree diagram*

level that would ensure sufficient output so that resources were fully employed (*Yfe*). Thus, there is a deflationary gap (distance A) and involuntary unemployment. The solution to this situation is straightforward: it is the responsibility of the government to increase the level of aggregate demand in the economy and thus move the economy closer to a full employment level (*Yfe*). This can be done either through the use of monetary policy (lowering interest rates to stimulate consumer and investment spending) or through fiscal policy (lowering taxes and/or raising government expenditure) or both. The effect of the increase in aggregate demand, however generated, is to cause output to rise and thus unemployment to fall as the size of the deflationary gap (A) is reduced. This process can continue until a position of full employment is achieved. After this point, the suggestion is that it will be prices that now adjust due to higher demand and thus that inflation is created. The implicit assumption is that the whole economy faces an aggregate supply schedule as shown in Figure 3.2.

The supply schedule indicates that if demand is increased up until the point of full employment output (Q^*), then output and not price will respond. However, after this point price and not output will respond.

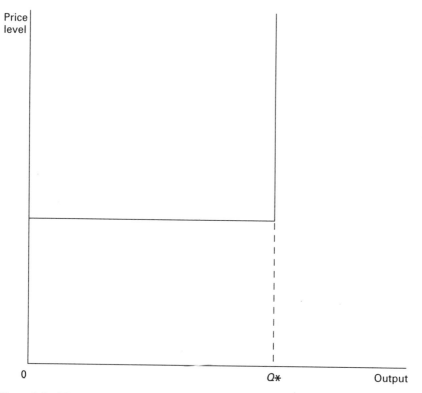

Figure 3.2 *The aggregate supply schedule suggested by the 45-degree diagram*

It is perhaps important to note here that many economists who would describe themselves as in some way 'Keynesian' are most unhappy to see the 45-degree model described above as a proper representation of Keynes's theory. Keynes never dismissed the supply side in the way suggested in the model (see Chapter 10 on macroeconomic models).

We now move over to the standard presentation of microeconomics as encountered in most economics courses. The approach that is taken is to analyse the determination of prices through supply and demand analysis as suggested by Figure 3.3.

The price of any product is given by the equilibrium point where supply is equal to demand (*Pe, Qe*). If demand were to change in this diagram (*D1* moves to *D2*), then output and price will adjust to ensure a new equilibrium (*Pe1, Qe1*). Price is bound to rise given the shape of the supply curve which is derived from the law of diminishing marginal returns.

The beginnings of the problem should already be clear from the above discussion (all of which is probably familiar to any student of economics). We have two models studied simultaneously which suggest that the effects of an increase

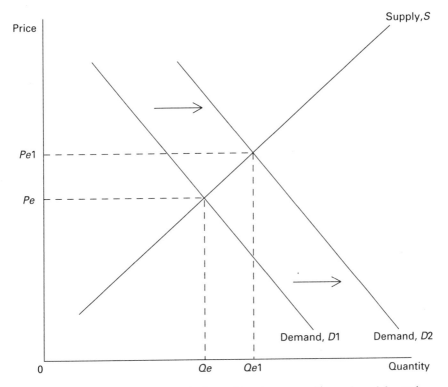

Figure 3.3 *The effects on increase in demand in microeconomic supply and demand analysis*

in demand are different. One suggests that there will be just an output response to an increase in demand if there is less than full employment in the economy; the other suggests that there will be some price adjustment for any increase in demand. The models of macroeconomics and microeconomics appear to contradict each other.

In fact, the problem is even greater than that suggested above. The assumption behind the standard presentation of supply and demand analysis is that there is a high level of competition (perfect competition). In such a world, the idea that the economy could be stuck in a position of involuntary unemployment does not make sense. If markets clear, as will be the case if prices adjust efficiently as suggested in supply and demand analysis, then surpluses of any type of products or resources will not persist. This would include labour. Thus a surplus of labour, people wishing to work at the going wage rate but unable to do so, would not be a position of equilibrium. Prices, particularly the price of labour, would adjust so that supply once more equalled demand. There could be no persistent involuntary unemployment.

Thus careful reflection upon the standard presentations of the two parts of an economics course suggests that they are not compatible. It does not appear to be possible that both approaches can be simultaneously accurate. To put the issue in an historical perspective, it has been suggested that in order to arrive at his macroeconomic conclusions, Keynes should not only have rejected the macroeconomics of his day but should have gone further in rejecting the standard microeconomic approach also. The rejection of the role of the real wage in ensuring an equilibrium between the demand and supply of labour, and thus permitting the possibility of involuntary unemployment, was not matched by a rejection of the competitive functioning of the market for goods and services.

RECONCILIATIONS BETWEEN MICRO AND MACRO

The above discussion appears to leave the study of economics, with its traditional divide between micro and macro, in a highly unsatisfactory state. What is needed is some form of reconciliation between the two sides of the subject. There are several possibilities.

One approach is to take the supply and demand analysis of standard microeconomics as the valid way to conduct all economic analysis and to draw macroeconomic conclusions from that approach. In this approach, the conclusion is that there will be no persisting involuntary unemployment as prices, notably the price of labour, will adjust, in order to ensure that supply equals demand. Prices adjust and equilibrium is quickly established. Thus, there would be no role for governments to expand aggregate demand. The only effect of such a policy would be to create inflation, given that there will be no involuntarily unemployed people to draw back into production at the going wage. These are the conclusions of 'new classical' economists. It is a macroeconomics that appears to be compatible with the standard approach of much microeconomic analysis.

Where, then, does this leave Keynesian macroeconomics? The answer seems to be that it is left in need of appropriate microeconomic analysis that is compatible with Keynesian macroeconomic conclusions. In particular, this appears to suggest the need to have microeconomic models which imply that prices may not vary due to changes in demand, and thus to open the possibility of persisting involuntary unemployment. This has been the approach in recent years of what have been termed the 'New Keynesians'.

There are really two strands to the approach adopted by the New Keynesians. The first is to suggest that there are reasons why wages may not vary, and the second is to consider why the prices of products in general may not vary. The importance of microeconomic models which can give results of a lack of change of wages is that they could help to explain the persistence of labour surpluses which are not remedied by variations in the price of labour. This is an area that is investigated in detail in Chapter 11 on unemployment and inflation. Thus just a very brief outline of some of the suggestions is given here.

One possible reason why wages do not vary (or are 'sticky') is that workers may enter into long-term wage contracts with employers which ensure a stable wage over a certain period of time. This may be desired by risk-averse workers who do not wish to suffer from the possibility that their wage could fluctuate. Employers could be willing to enter into such an agreement if they believe that the stable wage paid would be lower than the average of a fluctuating wage. Thus workers can be seen as paying some form of premium for the guarantee of a stable wage. The implication of this is that wages do not adjust, at least in the short run. Wages may also remain sticky due to the behaviour of trade unions. If trade unions represent those in work, hold some control over entry into work and are only concerned to represent those in employment (as opposed to those not in employment), then wages need not vary, even in the face of considerable unemployment. The unemployed do not exercise downward pressure on the wage rate because they cannot easily enter the active workforce (this could be due to factors other than trade union exclusion, such as lack of appropriate skills). Thus wages do not vary and unemployment persists. This is labelled the 'insider-- outsider' theory. Another possibility is given by 'Efficiency Wages'. The suggestion of this approach is that the wage that is paid affects the productivity of a firm's workforce as it has an impact on workers' morale and incentives. This suggests that it would be unlikely to be in the interest of firms to cut the wages of its workforce since this could have the impact of lowering productivity. This would explain why wages might not fall in the face of unemployment and thus help to explain the persistence of unemployment.

The other approach of New Keynesian economics has been to try to explain why the price of products may be sticky and thus how surpluses can persist and output, rather than price, may adjust to changes in demand. There is one microeconomic model that is studied in most microeconomic courses that yields precisely this result. This is the best known of the oligopoly models, the kinked demand curve. This is illustrated in Figure 3.4.

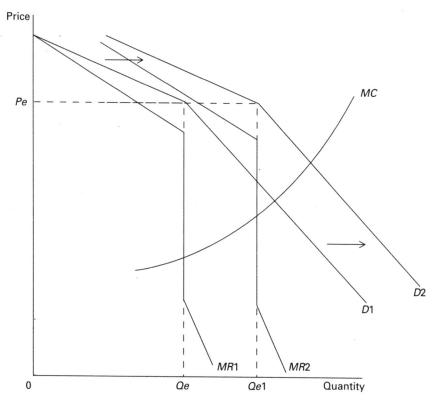

Figure 3.4 *An increase in demand under oligopoly with a kinked demand curve*

There is a kink in the demand curve because it is suggested that if a firm raises its price, others will not do so, and thus much demand is lost, but if a firm lowers its price, others will match this and little extra demand will be gained. Thus the demand schedule is given by $D1$. The shape of this demand schedule yields a peculiar shape of marginal revenue schedule, as illustrated by $MR1$. The kink in the demand schedule gives an area of discontinuity in the marginal revenue schedule. The equilibrium is given by the position where marginal cost, MC, intersects marginal revenue (the position of profit maximisation). This is highly likely to be at a point somewhere in the area of discontinuity in the marginal revenue schedule. Thus the equilibrium position is at output, Qe, and price, Pe. It is interesting now to consider the effects of an increase in demand. The increase in demand is represented by a rightward movement in the demand schedule ($D1$ moves to $D2$). This implies that the marginal revenue schedule will move in a similar direction ($MR1$ moves to $MR2$). Thus there is a new equilibrium where marginal cost intersects the new level of marginal revenue. The key point about this for the current discussion is that the new equilibrium yields a higher output, $Qe1$, but the same price. Thus here is a microeconomic model that has given the same results for a change in demand as that suggested by the so-called 'Keynesian' 45 degree diagram. Output has varied, but price has remained unchanged.

There have been other attempts to explain a lack of price flexibility. One possibility derives from what have been called 'menu costs'. These relate to the fact that there may be various fixed costs associated with changing prices which could imply that the benefits derived for a firm through a change of price do not justify the costs involved, and thus it may be better to allow output to vary (although this must assume that the costs of allowing output to vary are less than those of allowing prices to vary). Some of the costs of adjusting prices are clear, such as the time and resources involved in changing price labels. However, there are further possible costs involved in the need to communicate the price changes to all potential customers and in the possible loss of goodwill from customers deriving from an increase in price. If these costs are considerable, then it may be a rational decision by firms not to change price in the face of a change in demand.

It is suggested that several products now have pricing systems whereby price can only ever be changed at infrequent intervals. A good example of this would be the development of catalogue shopping. The nature of this form of trade suggests that prices have to be decided, then the catalogues have to be produced and distributed. Such catalogues are only likely to be revised once or twice each year, given the time and other costs involved, and thus prices would react very slowly to any change in demand. It would be much simpler under this form of system to adjust the output rather than the price in the short run. Any other institutional factors which cause similarly infrequent price changes would yield the same results.

The 'input–output table' approach may also help to explain price stickiness of complex manufactured goods. In a world in which thousands of firms are buying thousands of components, containing ingredients from many other firms, the informational problem of trying to anticipate the effect of a current increase in demand upon the costs of all the suppliers is probably insurmountable. Thus firms cannot know what their immediate appropriate price response should be to a change in demand. The rational thing, then, to do is not to change price immediately, but to wait to see how different costs have in practice been affected, and then to make a pricing decision in light of that information. This implies a clear element of price stickiness in the short run, and thus the possibility that output may bear the initial brunt of any adjustment due to a change in demand.

Thus the New Keynesian approach has suggested that there could be microeconomic models which yield results of wage and price stickiness which are compatible with Keynesian macroeconomic conclusions. This process has been taken one stage further by certain writers who have attempted to build whole macroeconomic models based on, for example, imperfect competition in the product market and efficiency wages in the labour market. Thus microeconomics has, perhaps, been reconciled with macroeconomics.

Keynes himself never did this as his work can be interpreted as suggesting that involuntary unemployment did not derive from wage and price inflexibility. Rather, it had more to do with the nature of uncertainty associated with a monetary economy: this is a different way of approaching the problem. It suggests the dangers of a label such as 'Keynesian' which clearly covers a multitude of different economic approaches.

PROBLEMS OF RECONCILING MICRO AND MACRO

The apparent reconciliation of microeconomics with macroeconomics may not necessarily be the important achievement that it at first appears to be. Implicit to the approach described in the section above is the view that macroeconomics is simply the adding together of all of microeconomics. Adding together the models of firms' and individuals' behaviour gives an effective macroeconomic model. The truth may not be quite so straightforward.

Perhaps the most famous example of the dangers of carrying the logic of microeconomics over to macroeconomics is Keynes's explanation of why a cut in workers' money wages, even if it could be organised, would not lead to an increase in employment. In most micro models, if workers offer their services at something below the going wage rate, then there will be an expansion of employment: a reduction of the price of labour leads to an extension of demand for labour. However, this logic may not work if applied to macro situations. If all workers receive a cut in their money wages, then the costs of all firms will be reduced. This is likely to lead firms to reduce their prices. The effect of this is that although money wages have fallen, real wages have not fallen in the same way, as the fall in prices has maintained the real value of the wages that are being earned. Thus, if there has not been a cut in real wages, there will not be an expansion of employment. Thus workers are left powerless to reduce their real wage. The logic of microeconomics has not worked in a macroeconomic setting.

There may be other ways in which attempting to add up microeconomics does not give a proper macroeconomic outcome. The two principal ways in which that may be true are to do with macroeconomic externalities and coordination problems. The concept of externalities is explored in Chapter 6 on environmental economics. In a macroeconomic context, it means that adding together many individual markets has an effect greater than the individual parts would appear to suggest: there are spillover effects. For example, if a firm receives less demand for its products, then it may demand less labour. Thus, there has been a spillover effect to the labour market. This in turn may cause a fall in income to labour which implies less demand. Thus, there is a spillover effect into different product markets. This all suggests that adding together lots of micro units, without considering how they have impacts upon each other, would not yield an accurate macro picture.

An example of the problem of coordination can be seen through one version of the explanation of the persistence of involuntary unemployment that is sometimes offered. Workers who are unemployed would be prepared to sell their labour (and thus receive employment) in return for the value of the goods and services that they would produce once employed. The problem is that there is no way of coordinating this. The necessary mechanisms and markets appear not to exist. This is a result that may not have anything to do with the level of price flexibility in the economy.

A further point worthy of mention here is that it may not always just be necessary to try to provide an appropriate microeconomic foundation for any macroeconomic theory. The functioning of any microeconomic theory will be dependent, to some extent, on the current macroeconomic environment. Any prediction yielded by any microeconomic model may be swamped by an important macroeconomic effect, such as a burst of consumer spending throughout the economy due to high levels of confidence and easy borrowing facilities. Such a factor could outweigh any microeconomic reforms which might, for example, be designed to moderate price increases in any particular market. Thus, if macroeconomics should not be studied without a proper understanding of any relevant microeconomics, it could also be argued that microeconomics cannot be properly studied without an appropriate appreciation of macroeconomics.

CONCLUSIONS AND POLICY IMPLICATIONS

The previous section suggests that some caution may need to be taken when attempting to reconcile microeconomics and macroeconomics. However, that cannot be to say that there is no need to consider whether the microeconomics that is studied on an economics course is compatible with the macroeconomics. It still holds that certain microeconomic models of firms' behaviour will yield considerably different macroeconomic implications from others. Thus, even though this book divides itself into the two sections of microeconomics and macroeconomics in terms of the topics that are covered, it is vital to recognise that it is one subject that is being studied and there must be consistency between the two sides of the subject that are so often presented.

The possible policy implications of the suggestions of this chapter are not clear! Perhaps one of the most important questions to ask is whether there is a role for the government in expanding aggregate demand in the economy in a way that will produce beneficial results, namely the expansion of output and employment rather than simply inflation. The answer is that there can be no definite answer to that question. In an economy that is characterised by many different products that are being produced by many different firms operating under many different levels of competition, the overall impact of a general increase in demand cannot be predicted. Some firms may be operating in a situation that is close to the oligopoly model of the kinked demand curve. Other firms may be operating in an oligopoly market that has a price leader who sets prices that all others simply follow. Some commodity markets may not be too far removed from a position of perfect competition. It must be reasonably con-cluded that the response to an increase of demand may be very different between different firms. Sometimes price may adjust, sometimes output may adjust and sometimes both price and output may adjust. Thus it is not clear to what extent an expansion of demand will lead to higher output and employment. The logic of this approach might suggest that it would be a sensible policy to try to target any increases in demand at industries that have sticky prices in order to achieve the greatest output and least price response. However, this would be highly complex to try to engineer, and the spillover effects described in the previous section suggest that it simply could never really work.

Thus the implications of attempting to reconcile microeconomics with macro-economics appear to be to make macroeconomics, and especially the conduct of macroeconomic policy, less than straightforward. However, this may be far better than simply accepting two parts of the subject that are inconsistent.

Part II

Developments in Microeconomics

4   Game Theory and Its Uses

Most of us like games and most of us play games. Our games may be simple (a game of 'snap') or they may be complex (a game of chess). In recent years, economists have come to see this aspect of our human behaviour as increasingly helpful in viewing and understanding a considerable range of economic behaviour. It is the purpose of this chapter to introduce some of the important aspects of this theory of games and to review some of the possible applications of the theory. The theory has usually been applied within the area of firms' behaviour, but the chapter will demonstrate that there may be many other valid applications of the approach.

The chapter is divided into the following four parts:

1. An explanation of the meaning of game theory.
2. A consideration of different possible types of games.
3. A review of some of the major ways that game theory has been applied to the behaviour of firms.
4. A look at various applications of game theory in different areas of economics.

WHAT IS GAME THEORY?

Before we can understand the possible uses of game theory within economics, we need to know what we mean by game theory.

A game can be most simply described as a situation of interdependent decision-making. Schelling (1960) expressed it this way: 'the essence of a game of strategy is the dependence of each person's proper choice of action on what he expects the other to do'. In other words, a game is any situation where a person's decision is affected by the expectation of the reaction of another person. Chess is a good example. All decisions are taken with a view to the likely response of the opponent. All the participants of a game are the players. Each player will pursue an objective. In chess, this would be to checkmate the opponent. In general, players try to maximise their 'payoff': to do as well as possible for themselves in the context of each particular game. Every player will choose a strategy, in other words a plan of action. This strategy will always have to be dependent upon what are believed to be the strategies of the other players as these will have an impact on the likely payoff to be gained by different courses of action.

This, then, is the essence of a game. Sometimes it may also be necessary to go further in specifying the order of moves in a game (straightforward in chess) and how much information is available to the different players of the game. Thus game theory starts from here. However, before proceeding, two fundamental points need to be borne in mind. The first is that, as in economics in general, it must be assumed that players will behave rationally, given the information that is available to them. The second is that we shall only consider this study of games to be a useful theory insofar as it helps to understand or to predict behaviour in concrete economic situations. It is not being studied purely for its own sake.

DIFFERENT TYPES OF GAMES

Games can be divided into different possible types. Some games could be co-ordinated, a situation where all players have exactly the same objective (such as a game of charades). Other games may be conflicting, a game where players have completely opposed interests (such as a game of chess). The most usual situation within economics is a mixed motive game where there is an element of both conflict and coordination of interests.

One of the characteristics of a game stated above was that the best strategy for one player to choose depends upon what the other players choose. In some situations, a player's strategy is best irrespective of what the other players may do. In this situation, the strategy is described as 'dominant'. Such games are easy to predict as it will be rational for players simply to follow their dominant strategies. However, games are usually more complicated, as the best strategy for any one player is often dependent upon the actions of the other players. Any situation where each player is choosing the best strategy available, given the strategies that are being pursued by other players, is called a 'Nash equilibrium'.

Perhaps the most famous of all games in this area is the so-called 'Prisoners' Dilemma'. The situation of the game is as follows. A crime has been committed. Two people have been arrested and it is known that at least one of them has committed the crime, but it is not certain whether both of them are responsible for the act. Therefore, the jury in this case will make their decision depending upon whether the prisoners plead guilty or not guilty. If both of the prisoners decide to plead guilty, then they will both be assumed to have committed the crime and will receive a prison sentence of five years each. If one of the prisoners pleads guilty and the other pleads not guilty, then the person pleading guilty will receive ten years in prison (for committing this dreadful act on his/her own) and the person pleading not guilty will be set free as it will be assumed that that person was not responsible for the crime. However, if both of the prisoners plead not guilty, then it will be assumed that both of them were in fact responsible for the crime, and because they have both compounded their criminal behaviour by lying about their involvement in the crime, then they will both receive a sentence of eight years in prison. Thus, as each prisoner lies in his/her cell contemplating the best way to plea to the jury on the following morning, the permutations can be summarised as follows:

PRISONER A

	Guilty	Not Guilty
	Guilty	Not Guilty

PRISONER B

	Guilty	Not Guilty
Guilty	5 5	0 10
Not Guilty	10 0	8 8

The numbers represent the years in prison that will be received by each prisoner, with prisoner A's sentence shown first, given the different possible combinations of pleas. This, then, is the prisoners' dilemma: to plead guilty or not guilty, knowing the possible outcomes. It should be noted that no attention is paid to who may or may not have actually committed the crime: that is not a relevant part of this game as it is presented. All that is deemed to be relevant is how each prisoner should plead in order to get the best possible payoff, namely the lowest possible number of years in prison.

It is very easy to predict the outcome of this game. In practice, both of the prisoners have a dominant strategy: from their own perspective, there is one course of action that is the best, regardless of what the other person does. For prisoner A, it is best to plead not guilty if prisoner B pleads guilty, but it is also best to plead not guilty if prisoner B pleads not guilty. The same will be true for prisoner B with regard to the behaviour of prisoner A. Thus we can suggest that it is highly likely that both of the prisoners will plead not guilty and receive eight years in prison. The problem, of course, is that both of the prisoners could have received three years less in prison had they both pleaded guilty instead. It is this paradox that makes this game such an interesting one, and, as will be seen later, implies that it has several significant applications in the study of economics.

There are many other examples of games, but just one more will be mentioned. It is a game that represents any decision regarding whether one person may make the decision to challenge or attack another. Imagine a child playing in a paddling-pool on the beach. Another child sees this and decides that he/she would like to play in the pool as well. The complication is that the child already in the pool does not want anyone else in there, and there is the possibility that he/she will resist any possible efforts to enter the pool with force. Thus the child contemplating whether to try to enter the pool is faced with the following decision matrix:

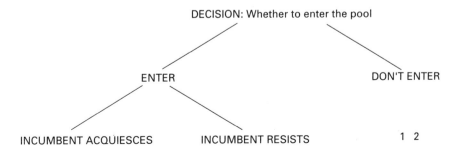

DECISION: Whether to enter the pool

ENTER   DON'T ENTER

INCUMBENT ACQUIESCES   INCUMBENT RESISTS   1   2

There are three possibilities. The numbers after each of the possibilities ranks the desirability of each with the child in the pool (the incumbent) having his/her preference written first. The worst outcome for both children would be if the child in the pool were to resist the efforts of the other child to enter the pool as both children would almost certainly suffer physical pain. This situation might be described as a Nash equilibrium insofar as the decision as to whether the child should enter the pool will depend upon what is perceived to be the likely reaction of the child already in the pool. However, it is worth noting that once the decision to enter the pool has been made, it does not appear a rational decision on the part of the incumbent to resist this. Thus it is possible to see that the outcome of this game may hinge on how credible the threat of the child in the pool to fight really is.

These, then, are the sort of situations suggested by game theory. The rest of the chapter considers how such situations may be of relevance in different areas of economics.

GAME THEORY AND THE BEHAVIOUR OF FIRMS

The most common application of game theory within economics is in the area of the theory of the firm or the theory of firms' behaviour. Remembering the earlier definitions of a game, the theory is not really relevant to a situation of perfect competition (if ever such a situation were to exist) since in that situation each firm is so insignificant that its actions have no impact on the decisions of other firms. Equally, it would appear that game theory might have little to say with regard to monopoly as there is only one firm in such a market (although there could be some relevance insofar as a monopolist may be concerned about potential competition). However, when it comes to a consideration of competition amongst the few, the theory of oligopoly, then it seems clear that the firms involved are in a situation described as a game.

The prisoners' dilemma game can be directly applied to the behaviour of a few firms in a market with some fairly clear implications. It is easiest to assume that there are just two firms in the industry concerned, but there would be little difference in the analysis, except for a greater level of complication, if there were more firms involved. Each firm faces a decision with regard either to the level of output that it will produce or the price that it will charge. In our example, we shall assume that firms set output levels and allow the market to dictate the price of that output. We shall also simplify the output decision so that there is a decision to be made only regarding whether to produce a high or a low level of output. Given this situation, the decision to be made is as it was in the prisoners' dilemma:

FIRM A's OUTPUT

		High		Low	
	High	£2000	£2000	£0	£6000 ·
FIRM B's OUTPUT					
	Low	£6000	£0	£4000	£4000

The figures in the matrix represent the profits gained by each firm in a certain time period with A's profit figure given first. The best situation for either of the firms is to set a high level of output at the same time as the other firm sets a low level of output. That would give the highest possible profits (£6000) as most of the market would be cornered by the firm. The other firm would make no profit due to the limited sales at a moderate price. The next best situation for either of the firms would be if they both set low outputs (implying a profit of £4000 in the time period concerned). This would be better than if both were to set high outputs (a profit of £2000 each) due to the likely price elasticity of demand. Given that we are considering the output of a whole industry, then it is likely that there will be no very close substitutes for the product (this will depend upon the nature of the actual product concerned). In such a situation, demand will be inelastic. Thus, by restricting output, there will be a more than proportionate increase in the market price and it will be possible to make higher profits at a low level of total industry output than at a high level of total industry output.

As with the prisoners' dilemma, it is possible to predict the likely outcome. For both of the firms, the dominant strategy is to set a high output. Whatever the other firm does, it is best for an individual firm to set its output high. Thus the most likely outcome of this situation is that both of the firms will make £2000 profit. The problem with this is clear: if both firms had set low outputs, then they could both have doubled their profits. This appears to go a long way to understanding the nature of collusive agreements in oligopolistic markets. Taking an overall view of the industry, there can be no doubting the logic of a collusive agreement to maximise overall profits. Equally, looking at the situation through the eyes of an individual firm, the motivation to set a high output (which is likely to result in less than maximum profits if all firms pursue that strategy) is clear. Thus we can understand the rationale both of collusion and the tendency to non-collusion.

If the situation described above were simply a one-off decision, then it is hard to escape from the likelihood of high output decisions. However, in practice, continuous decisions have to be made by firms regarding their output decisions over a period of time. The question then becomes whether firms will persist in making the decision that does not maximise total profit. The answer is unclear, depending on such factors as how large the payoff would be for cooperation and how effectively any cheating on an agreement could be dealt with. There are strategies that might be developed by firms to try to ensure that over a long period of time the industry tends towards the low output, high profit option. If there were an agreement, formal or otherwise, that firms should set low outputs, two strategies might help to ensure that this happened. One possibility is the 'trigger' strategy. This strategy implies that the firm adopting this strategy will always adopt a low output so long as the other firm does so. However, as soon as the other firm sets a high output for one time period, then the firm will set a high output decision for the rest of the game. This provides a strong disincentive against raising output. An alternative strategy would be to develop a 'tit-for-tat' system where the firm will always make the same output decision in this time period as the other firm did in the previous time period. Again, this provides a strong incentive to keep output set at a low level.

OPEC: A CASE STUDY

One way to look at this application of game theory further is to consider the most well known of all collusive agreements, the OPEC cartel. While many other cartel agreements have come and gone, the OPEC cartel has managed to remain intact (with varying levels of strength) over a significant period of time. It is instructive to discuss why this may have been so within the framework of the approach suggested by game theory.

The first important point to note is that oil is a resource with very few or no close substitutes for its use in many developed economies. Recent efforts may have increased the substitutability of oil in certain uses, but it remains without close rivals in several important areas (such as powering motor vehicles). The implication of this is that, in the short run at least, the price elasticity of demand is likely to be very low: demand may not change a great deal as price is changed, or price will rise considerably for a relatively small restriction in output. This implies that if the sellers of oil could agree to limit their sales, then there could be a significant increase in total industry profits. Thus the payoff for achieving a low output solution would be large. Therefore, one important ingredient in the successful operation of a collusive agreement would seem to be the size of the reward to be gained through successful collusion.

Even with such high rewards for collusion, there remains the logical temptation for any one member of the agreement to cheat and to produce a higher output which would increase the profits accruing to that nation. OPEC has faced such threats. Of course, if such behaviour were to persist, then the likelihood is that the whole agreement would collapse as other nations also started to cheat upon the agreement. This has been the fate of many other cartels. How then has OPEC survived such difficulties? The early 1980s provide an interesting example. During this time, certain members of OPEC, notably Iran and Iraq, who were at war with one another, began to produce above their quota of oil in an effort to generate more income for their nation. Given the logic of the prisoners' dilemma, this threatened the whole collusive agreement. OPEC was able to survive principally due to the actions of the largest oil producer, Saudi Arabia. As the largest producer, Saudi Arabia clearly had a strong interest in maintaining OPEC and was in the strongest position to be able to do so, especially as its own economy was stronger than most other oil-exporting nations. In effect, what Saudi Arabia did was to threaten a 'tit-for-tat' policy. In other words, if certain members of OPEC did not stop breaking their output quotas, then Saudi Arabia would break its quota in such a way that there would be a considerable fall in the world price of oil. This would harm the Saudi Arabian economy, but it would probably harm the economies of the other nations involved beyond the point of survival. Thus, through this strategy, the OPEC nations were brought back into line and the cartel arrangement persisted. The conclusion from this appears to be that a collusion is most likely to survive when one player in the game can so threaten to harm the others that the agreement is kept.

However, this analysis of OPEC requires further qualification in light of developments in the early 1990s. The world price of oil was forced down to levels that were low compared to the high prices generated when OPEC was at its strongest. There have been two reasons for this. The first is the considerable level of oil output by non-OPEC members (such as the UK). These nations are not bound by any OPEC attempts to restict oil output. Thus a cartel is weakened if it does not contain all members of an industry. The second difficulty arose from a failure to agree what is the appropriate level of oil output, with the two largest producers, Saudi Arabia and Iran, failing to have similar opinions regarding the desired restrictions. Given this failure, countries produce the amount that they desire from their own perspective. The logic of the prisoners' dilemma suggests that this will produce a level of output that is higher than that required to maximise total profit.

BARRIERS TO ENTRY

Another major application of game theory within the theory of the firm applies to barriers to entry into an industry. This might be considered to be relevant to a monopoly market as well as an oligopoly. Bain (1956) defined barriers to entry as: 'the advantages of established sellers in an industry over potential entrant sellers, those advantages being reflected in the extent to which established sellers can persistently raise their prices above a competitive level [and hence earn abnormal profit] without attracting new firms to enter the industry'. The second of the two games described earlier in the chapter, concerning the two children and the use of the paddling-pool, helps to cast light on to this area, perhaps beyond what has been the standard approach to barriers to entry.

There are certain points to be remembered as a background to this analysis. The first point is that it is assumed that firms wish to make maximum (or something close to that) profit. This implies that if they can set prices, they would like to do so in such a way as to make abnormal profits. The problem with this is that, in a free enterprise economy, new firms will be lured into the industry because they can see the possibility of large profits to be made. This would tend to lower the profit of the firm(s) already in the industry as demand was spread around more producers and the higher output pushed down prices. It is therefore in the interest of the incumbent firm to try to prevent the new firm from entering the industry. Thus the situation is very similar to the paddling-pool game:

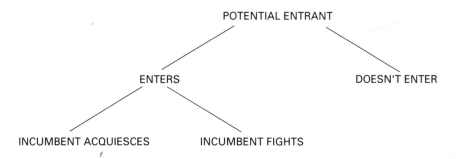

POTENTIAL ENTRANT

ENTERS   DOESN'T ENTER

INCUMBENT ACQUIESCES   INCUMBENT FIGHTS

This situation represents a Nash equilibrium: the decision of the potential entrant into the market will depend upon the perceived likely reaction of the incumbent firm(s). The key thing for the incumbent(s) is to be able to threaten to hurt the new entrant in such a way that the firm decides it would not be a wise decision to enter the market. Thus a study of barriers to entry is directed to investigating how firms may be behaving in such a way. There are several possibilities both on the side of costs and on the side of demand.

One possible tactic on the cost side would be to have an unnecessarily large capital stock given the current level of production. This would imply that the incumbent firm was operating below capacity with the threat that if a new firm were to enter the industry, then the incumbent would raise output and hence lower price, thus making the possible entry unprofitable. Another possibility could be to raise wages if there is a threat of entry, thus again making entry unprofitable.

On the demand side, the prospect of a new entrant may cause the incumbent firm to increase its advertising considerably, making it harder for the potential entrant to gain some of the market. If the entrant is to compete, then there is also a cost effect insofar as it is necessary to indulge in large-scale advertising if it is to be possible to enter the market. Another response available to the incumbent would be to increase brand proliferation given the possibility of a new entrant in order to try to fill any gaps in the market. The most obvious policy to operate, faced with the threat of an entrant, would be predatory pricing: setting market price below cost so that entry into the industry would be unprofitable. The classic example of this can be seen in the airline industry's response to Laker's attempt to enter the transatlantic market in the early 1980s. Prices were lowered and Laker was pushed out of the industry.

Perhaps the key point about all these possible forms of action to deter potential entrants from a market is that no incumbent firm actually wishes to take
them. They are all damaging to the firm concerned insofar as they reduce current
profits. Thus it seems rational that firms should wish the threat of such action to
be sufficient to deter entry without there being the necessity of actually taking
the action. It would then be easy to understand why incumbent firms should be
keen to try to establish a reputation for fighting in the event of new entry. It
could be a good long-term investment for a firm to use resources in building up
that reputation.

FURTHER APPLICATIONS OF GAME THEORY

Whilst the theory of the firm has been the most popular application of game
theory, there are several other areas of economics that may also be deemed as
appropriate to be examined through the lens of game theory. It is the purpose of
this last part of the chapter to examine some of those possibilities.

1 Wage-Push Inflation

One of the most common versions of the theory of cost-push inflation is that
trade unions contribute to the process by demanding wage increases in excess of
productivity. If firms accept these bids (which is more likely to be true in a situation of falling unemployment where the labour market is becoming tighter)
then they are likely to have to raise prices in order not to lose profit margins.
Thus there is the potential for an inflationary process. The logic of trade unions
demanding high wage increases may be seen through game theory.

Considering the wage bids of trade unions in a similar framework to the prisoners' dilemma, we can say that trade unions can either make a low or a high
wage bid. Again, it is easiest to simplify things by looking at the possibility of
just two groups, in this case a single trade union on the one hand and all other
trade unions on the other. From the point of view of the individual trade union,
the best possible outcome is to make a high wage bid while all other trade
unions make low bids. This will have the double advantage of securing a relative
wage increase and also a real wage increase as inflation should be low due to the
low wage bids of all the other unions. The worst possible outcome would be the
exact reverse, since this would imply both a relative and a real wage cut.
Between these two extremes, there are two situations which can be viewed as
leaving relative wages unaffected and real wages changing only by the rate of
productivity. However, it may be viewed as preferable for all trade unions to
make low wage bids than for all trade unions to make high wage bids, as the
former would seem to imply a low inflation economy as opposed to the high
inflation implications of the latter permutation. If it is more beneficial for

workers to live in a low inflation economy than a high inflation economy, as, other things being equal, is usually assumed, then generally lower wage bids will be better than higher wage bids. The problem is the classic problem of the prisoners' dilemma. The dominant strategy for any individual union must be to go for a high wage bid because, regardless of the actions of the other unions, that appears the best option. Thus there is a tendency to generally high wage bids and inflation if the labour market is in a position where workers can realistically make such bids. Whilst for much of the 1980s and the early 1990s this has not been so, it would be difficult to escape the logic of this if the economy were to experience a period of strong growth.

What, then, is the solution to this dilemma? Seen in this way, if cost-push inflation is believed to be a valid theory of inflation, it is necessary to try to move to the position of low wage bids, and the desirability of an effective incomes policy which pushes the solution to the game into this position is apparent. Indeed, the logic of this approach suggests that without such a policy, there are bound to be inflationary tendencies if and when the labour market is strong.

2   European Macroeconomic Policy Coordination

A highly contentious current economic issue is the desirability or otherwise of macroeconomic policy coordination throughout Europe. Game theory may be able to make a contribution to that debate.

The starting point for our analysis is that Europe is in a recession. However, the logic of the approach could possibly be applied to the situation of an inflationary boom. For the analysis to have any credence, it must be believed that an expansion of demand would be capable of helping to move an economy out of recession. It could be argued in this situation that governments have the choice either to take steps to expand demand in their economy, through fiscal and/or monetary policy, or to leave policy unchanged. All national governments face this same decision. It must also be understood how interdependent all European economies have become in terms of the level of their trade with each other.

What, then, are the likely options of national governments within Europe? The best possible solution for any individual nation would be for all other nations to reflate their economies whilst that individual nation did not reflate its own economy. This should ensure some degree of economic recovery given the high level of European interdependence mentioned above, which implies that the nation should find demand is expanded through an increased demand for its exports from all other European nations. This solution has the added benefit that it also implies a strengthening of the current account of the balance of payments and no concerns over some of the possible hazards of an expansionary policy, such as a government budget deficit. On the other hand, the worst possible solution for any individual nation would be for it to reflate its own economy while the rest of Europe did not do so. Not only would this lead to a notable worsening of the current account of the balance of payments as much of the higher demand went on products made elsewhere in Europe, but for the same reason it would prove fairly ineffective in ending recession as most of the higher demand would simply leak abroad. Of the two other possibilities, it would clearly be better if all European nations were to expand their economies, as this would achieve an end to recession, than if all of them were to do nothing which would mean no end to the recession.

When described in the manner above, Europe can be seen to be in a classic prisoners' dilemma game. The problem is that the dominant strategy for any individual nation must be not to reflate its economy, as, regardless of the actions pursued by other nations, that seems to be the best option. Thus there appears to be a tendency for recession to be prolonged as all nations choose not to reflate their economies. The solution would appear to have clear implications for European economic policy. What seems to be needed is a coordinated policy where all nations agree to expand their economies together, or are perhaps even prepared to defer power to a central European institution that will ensure that this happens. The logic of this may be felt to be of relevance to discussions over possible increased macroeconomic coordination throughout Europe.

3 Public Goods

The problem of providing public goods is well illustrated through the perspective of game theory. Public goods possess two important characteristics:

1. Non-excludability. Once a public good is provided for one individual, it is not possible to stop others from benefiting from the provision of the good.
2. Non-reducibility. As more people enjoy the consumption of the good, the benefit to those already consuming the good is not diminished.

There are few examples of pure public goods (although many of quasi public goods). National defence may be an example.

The game theoretic approach is similar to the standard textbook explanation of why public goods will not be provided in a free market. The best solution for any individual is not to purchase the good but to wait for someone else to do so and then to enjoy the consumption from which it is impossible to be excluded. This problem is referred to as 'free riding'. The worst solution would be to provide the good and for others not to pay to do so. The natural logic is that the dominant strategy for all individuals is not to provide or purchase public goods. This is not the ideal solution as these goods yield positive utility which individuals would, in principle, be prepared to pay for. The solution is seen as government provision whereby everybody pays through the tax system and the public good is provided. Thus the outcome is improved by government intervention.

4   Free Trade versus Protection

An interesting and topical example of the application of game theory is the decision of individual nations as to whether to allow free trade with other nations or whether to choose to restrict imports. It might be argued that from the perspective of an individual nation, an ideal solution could be perceived as the rest of the world permitting free trade while that nation restricted certain imports when short-term gains appeared available from doing so. Without needing to describe all the possible permutations, the logic of game theory would immediately suggest that if all nations perceived the situation in the same way, then there would be a tendency for the world trading system to degenerate into ever-increasing protection because to protect would be the dominant strategy for all nations.

What is interesting in this particular example is that, unlike in other examples, the undesirable position has not emerged in the post-war world and the direction has consistently been towards freer trade. It is instructive to consider why this is so. Three factors can be discerned. The first is that the long-run payoff to all nations is perceived as being very high. The incentive for all nations to succeed in producing a system that has free trade rather than protection is thus felt to be great. The second factor is the legitimate fear of retaliation from other nations if a nation were to restrict its imports. It is generally believed that other nations would follow a tit-for-tat policy and thus damage the country restricting imports in the first place. This is a legitimate threat in a world context as it may not be too painful for countries to stop trading with just one country in the world so long as they can continue to do so with all others. The third explanation may be the activities of GATT. While this organisation does not have any formal powers to ensure free trade throughout the world, it does at least manage to bring the major trading nations of the world together in an atmosphere that provides a certain pressure towards increasing world trade liberalisation. These three factors, then, appear to have been sufficient to have prevented the world from degenerating towards protectionism.

5   Keynesian Recessions

A final possible application of game theory that is considered here is that it may help to explain the Keynesian suggestion that economies can become stuck in less than full employment equilibrium.

It is possible to look at the situation from the point of view of either the consumer or the producer. In this example, the producer will be considered. As with all these models, we will give each producer the simple choice between investing or not investing. This game, however, appears to have an important difference from all of the others considered thus far. The best solution for any individual producer in this example would not be to do something different from all other players (a result that has been the case in all of the other examples considered so far). The best solution would be for all producers to do the same thing, namely to invest. If this were to happen, then the effect of the increased demand created would, via the multiplier process, help to lift the economy from recession. This would be better than allowing all other firms to invest but not investing oneself, as this would mean that the firm would not have the capacity to benefit from the higher level of demand that had been created in the economy. As such, this game appears to be a pure coordination game. The problem is that the worse possible situation for the firm would be for it to invest while all other firms did not do so. That could be potentially disastrous for the firm concerned.

The above implies that the psychology of this game is different from that of others. We have a Nash equilibrium as opposed to a dominant strategy. If the firm believes that all other firms will invest, then the best option is to invest. However, if the firm believes that all other firms are not going to invest, then the best strstegy is not to invest. The implication (as with the decision of a potential entrant into a market) is that expectations are crucial. Whatever is forming expectations is dictating the outcome of the game. While all firms would like all firms, including their own, to invest (as everyone's fortunes would be improved from the current recession), if the expectation is that investment will not take place generally, then it is rational not to invest. Hence the economy remains in recession. It is easy to see from this the logic of the standard Keynesian solution to a recession, namely the need for government intervention. Governments might try to alter expectations as a solution ('talk the economy out of recession'). However, if that does not work, the government may have to take direct action to stimulate the economy by expanding demand. The alternative, if business expectations did not change, would be persisting recession.

CONCLUSION

It has been seen that simple game theory has considerable application within economics. This applies particularly in the area of the theory of the firm, but it also has many wider applications, some of which have been discussed in this chapter. The overall message appears to be that there are tendencies for less than ideal equilibria to emerge either for particular groups or for the whole of a society. The implication of this appears to be the necessity of some form of central organisation, in certain circumstances the government, if the solution of the game is to be moved to a more desirable outcome.

References

Bain, J. (1956) *Barriers to New Competition* (Cambridge, Mass.: Harvard University Press).

Schelling, T. (1960) *The Strategy of Conflict* (Cambridge, Mass.: Harvard University Press).

5 Privatisation

Several government economic policies have been the source of considerable disagreement since 1979. One of the most notable has been the government's extensive policy of privatisation. It has aroused considerable passions, both in favour of the policy and against it. As is quite often the case in such debates, the economics of the issue is frequently left trailing in the wake of the political furore that the issue creates. The purpose of this chapter is to examine the relevant economic theories and to consider what they appear to suggest regarding privatisation both in theory and how it has been implemented in the United Kingdom.

In order to address the significant issues within this topic, the chapter will be divided into five areas (although there is bound to be some overlap between these different areas):

1. A discussion of what is meant by the term 'privatisation'.
2. A review of the possible (economic) objectives of privatisation.
3. A careful look at how competition may or may not enhance efficiency (including a discussion of what might be meant by 'efficiency').
4. A consideration of the extent to which actual privatisations have introduced competition into the industries concerned.
5. A review of the relevant theory regarding the regulation of non-competitive industrial situations and how that helps to assess the role of the regulation of the privatised utilities. OFTEL will be taken as a case study.

DEFINING PRIVATISATION

Some discussions regarding privatisation appear to lose their way from the outset by being either unclear or too narrow in their definition of privatisation. At times, the policy appears to be entirely seen as the wholesale selling off of large nationalised industries through the sale of shares to private individuals and institutions. This may be an unsurprising view in light of the media coverage of such events. However, it represents an inadequate picture of the policy of privatisation. A better, and fuller, definition would be: an attempt to increase the role of market forces. This generally implies the transfer from the public to the private sector of the entitlement to any profits to be gained from operating an enterprise. As such, there are three distinct aspects to privatisation policy as it exists:

1. A transfer of ownership from the public to the private sector.
2. Liberalisation: an attempt to permit and to promote competition in areas where previously there was no competition.

3.   Franchising or contracting out: allowing and encouraging private firms to
     make bids to run services that were previously exclusively run by the public
     sector.

The UK privatisation programme can be seen to contain examples of all of
these types of privatisation. The transfer of ownership clearly includes the large
sales of the nationalised utilities mentioned above as well as many smaller sell-
offs. However, it also includes another important branch of Conservative economic policy, namely the sale of council houses to their tenants. A good example
of liberalisation is in the provision of bus services where competition is now permitted in this area having previously been outlawed. There have been examples
also within the private sector, such as allowing spectacles to be sold by outlets
other than registered opticians. The original example of franchising in the UK
was within the area of independent television where companies made bids to be
allowed to run certain areas for a specified length of time. This model has been
used within the privatisation programme in services such as cleaning for schools
and hospitals which are now frequently run by private companies who have been
awarded the contract by the relevant local authority. Thus some privatisations
involve a transfer of ownership, but this is not inherent in all aspects of the term.
      Privatisations could involve more than one of the aspects of privatisation men-
tioned above. For example, the privatisation of British Telecom involved a transfer
of ownership from the public to the private sector and also liberalisation insofar as
Mercury was allowed to set up as a competitor in the provision of telecommunica-
tion services and general competition was permitted in subscriber equipment.
      One final point about clarifying the exact meaning of privatisation is that
certain political debates appear rather groundless. A good example would be the
question of whether the UK health service is being privatised. The answer is
both 'Yes' and 'No' depending on the definition of privatisation that is being
taken. There clearly has not been a transfer of ownership of assets in the health
care industry, but equally clearly, there has been contracting out of a number of
health-related services to private firms. It could also be argued that the attempt
to introduce quasi-markets by encouraging competition between trust hospitals
is similar to the policy of liberalisation.

THE AIMS OF PRIVATISATION

Another difficulty with privatisation is that it has not always been entirely clear
what have been the fundamental economic aims of the policy. Several have been
suggested (and still are in several textbooks), but this section will argue that
there appears to be just one major legitimate economic aim of privatisation, and
that it is that aim that requires investigation. Of course, there have been political
aims that are relevant to any privatisation programme. These are perhaps best
summed up in the phrase, 'rolling back the frontiers of the State'. From a liber-

tarian perspective, all government intervention in a country represents some restriction of individual liberty and is thus intrinsically undesirable. The most desirable state of affairs is the absolute minimum of government intervention. Privatisation fits well well within this philosophy.

One possible aim of the UK's privatisation programme is that it is a means of raising revenue for the government. It is interesting that the government itself has never really claimed this to be the case. Insofar as some sort of economic case for raising revenue from privatisation may have been made, it has been related to an attempt to control the size of the budget deficit, both in order to help to control inflation (as was believed by some policy-makers in the 1980s) and to permit tax cuts which were seen as important in order to provide the necessary incentives for the successful functioning of an enterprise economy. The possibility of raising revenue through privatisation only really applies to the transfer of assets. Little finance would be raised through contracting out services and none through liberalisation. The suggestion has been that the government has been able to reduce the size of its borrowing requirement through selling off state-owned assets, and this may have had beneficial effects for the economy. The main problem with this is that the closest parallel to the sale of assets to the private sector is government borrowing. What is happening is that the government is receiving a one-off payment in return for forfeiting future yearly streams of profit that could have been gained from the assets. This is very similar in nature to borrowing money and then having to pay out annual interest payments to the person giving the loan. Thus it is hard to argue that government borrowing has truly been reduced through the policy.

Another possible goal of privatisation, this time one that is suggested by the government, has been to widen share ownership in the country. The reasons for this are not always clearly articulated. It may be felt to be desirable insofar as it encourages the interest of citizens in the affairs of British industry since share ownership may give them a more direct stake in the performance of British industry. Alternatively, it may be seen as beneficial to have employees of businesses owning shares in those businesses in order to improve their desire to see their company perform well. These arguments may or may not be felt to hold credence. However, the point is that such aims could far more easily be pursued through alternative policies such as encouraging share ownership by offering appropriate tax rebates or other similar inducements. Given this, it is not obvious to see how wider share ownership can be viewed as a vital strand of the economic justification for privatisation.

Another possible objective that is related to the above point is that privatisation may have an impact upon the distribution of income and wealth and that this may be a policy goal of privatisation. Three avenues can be identified through which the distribution of income has been affected by the privatisation programme. The first is that those purchasing shares have generally found that the value of their wealth has increased as the value of the shares have appreciated after the privatisations. The second is that the managers of several of the privatised companies have received considerably larger salaries than was the case before privatisation. The third is that any change in prices due to privatisation of industries may have an impact upon the distribution of real income. This is a contentious area and is not one of the official aims of privatisation. The point to make here, though, is that regardless of what may be seen as certain political objectives it cannot be suggested that this aim is a major economic justification of privatisation. Economists tend to fight shy of discussions about distributional issues because of the value judgements that are involved, and there are, in any case, far more straightforward ways of redistributing wealth and income if this is felt to be an important policy objective.

It has been suggested that another possible benefit of the policy of privatisation has been that it has reduced the problems of public sector pay determination. Trade unions may be in a stronger position to secure unreasonably high wages if working within a nationalised industry than if working for a private company. The reason for this is that public sector managers have weak incentives to minimise costs given the unending potential supply of public money to provide for the industry. However, this argument is not clear. The experience of the miners' strike in the mid-1980s appears to indicate that if the government wishes to resist pay claims made by unions, it is actually in a stronger position to be able to do so than any private company would be, given the financial losses that would have to be sustained.

The last suggestion is often generalised into the point that a major reason for privatisation is simply the poor performance of nationalised industries. There are a whole host of possible reasons given for this, usually to do with the lack of appropriate incentives for those involved in the management of these industries and the undesirable nature of government intervention that always appears to accompany nationalised industries. A problem with this argument is that it is very difficult to make appropriate comparisons between publicly and privately run enterprises. It is very hard to compare like with like, holding all other variables constant. Studies that have been made have to be tentative in their conclusions, and even evidence of a poor performance by a nationalised industry cannot automatically imply the desirability of privatisation.

However, within the previous argument may lie the possible valid economic case for privatisation. A suggested reason for the perceived poor performance of nationalised industries was the lack of appropriate incentives. It could be argued that a major reason for this is the lack of competitive pressures. Thus an advantage of privatisation is that it helps to introduce competition into an industry which in turn helps to improve the economic efficiency of that industry. This must be the legitimate economic argument for privatisation, especially given the initial definition of privatisation as an attempt to extend market forces. Thus, if privatisation is to be properly considered through the lens of economic theory, there are two fundamental issues to be addressed. The first is to consider why, or why not, competition may lead to economic efficiency. The second is to consider whether the policy of privatisation has succeeded in introducing the competition that may lead to efficiency.

COMPETITION AND EFFICIENCY

This section of the chapter discusses why competition is believed to lead to increased economic efficiency. The theoretical justification for this must be clearly established if the policy of attempting to increase competition is to be deemed desirable. However, before this can be done, it must be understood what is meant by the term 'efficiency' in economics.

Efficiency is a word that is frequently to be found on the lips of those involved in public debate, yet it is often unclear what is being implied by the term. Within economics, there are seen to be two aspects to the concept of efficiency. A good starting point here is to remember that the basis of the subject of economics is a study of how mankind attempts to make the best use of the scarce resources available in order to meet as many of its infinite needs as possible. Thus one aspect of efficiency concerns getting the most out of the resources available. Another way of stating this is to say that everything is produced with the minimum cost in terms of scarce economic resources. In economics, this aspect of efficiency is termed 'technical' efficiency. If a firm, an industry or a whole economy is to be technically efficient, it must be producing things at lowest possible cost. It is suggested that competition is capable of leading to this situation. Perhaps the easiest way of understanding this is in terms of what may be described as the 'carrot and stick' of the free market. The carrot of the free market is the incentive of profit that is provided. This causes firms to try to minimise their costs in order to maximise profit. This analysis need not necessarily be fundamentally changed if firms choose to pursue objectives other than the maximisation of profit, such as market share, power and prestige. In order successfully to pursue these objectives it is often still necessary to try to minimise costs. However, if that is not sufficient incentive to ensure technical efficiency, there is also the stick provided in the threat of bankruptcy. In a competitive situation, firms will be forced to produce at the minimum cost, as a failure to do so will mean that rivals will have a cost advantage which enables them to charge a lower price than firms not minimising their costs, thus driving those firms out of business. The corollary of this is that in an uncompetitive situation there will not be the same forces at work forcing firms to be technically efficient.

The second aspect to the notion of economic efficiency is that resources should be used in such a way that those things that yield maximum utility (go furthest in meeting our infinite wants) are produced. It is not sufficient simply to produce things at the lowest possible cost. We must also produce things that are most wanted. This aspect of efficiency is termed 'allocative' efficiency. The condition for allocative efficiency to exist is that price should equal the marginal cost of production. This can be explained at considerable technical length. However, the basic logic of it can be understood by recalling that in a free market economy consumers dictate what is produced by signalling to producers what they wish to purchase at what price, reflecting the utility that they gain from consuming different products. Thus we have 'consumer sovereignty'. This system should lead to resources being used to produce those things that yield maximum consumer utility provided that the price of products presented to the consumer represents the true cost of producing the last unit of each product. This will be so if the price is equal to the marginal cost of production. This should be the result of a competitive market. Under a situation of perfect competition (the highest possible level of competition), price is bound to be set equal to marginal cost as perfectly competitive firms face perfectly elastic demand schedules which means that price is equal to marginal revenue. If marginal cost is equated with marginal revenue in order to maximise profits, then price equals marginal cost. Any deviation from this highly competitive situation will mean that marginal cost no longer equals price and thus that there is not allocative efficiency. For example, monopolies always set price above marginal cost if they wish to maximise their excess profits.

The above may be considered to be the traditional reasoning as to why competition is believed to lead to economic efficiency. As such, it can be considered as the theoretical basis for suggesting that if privatisation leads to a greater level of competition than was the case before privatisation, then there is the possibility that the policy could lead to greater economic efficiency. It should be noted, however, that in order to ensure that all the conditions of efficiency are met it is necessary for there to be perfect competition, something that does not exist even in the most competitive of production situations. That is not to say, however, that greater competition may not be capable of leading to greater efficiency than was previously the case.

Before taking the argument as read that greater competition is desirable on efficiency grounds and proceeding to consider in light of this whether privatisation has the desired effect of increasing competition, a few questions have to be raised. The first is the nature of the costs being discussed earlier in this section. The costs that we wish to be concerned with are the overall costs to society. Unfortunately, the costs that will concern individual firms in their production decisions are only those costs that are private to the firm. These two sets of costs may not be identical, in which case an externality exists. In this situation, there is no guarantee that competition will lead to efficiency. A simple example would be that if in order to minimise its own costs, a firm adopted a technique of production that produced a great deal of pollution. Thus the firm's private costs may have been minimised, but the overall costs to society may not have been. Therefore free competition has not led to efficiency. This could be relevant to certain of the privatisations where safety could be considered in any way to be a factor (coal mines would be a good example). The lowest cost technique of production may carry safety risks that are considered unacceptable in terms of potential social cost. In such circumstances, entirely free competition could be considered undesirable. At the very least, some form of regulation would be required.

Another interesting possibility can be illustrated by considering the nature of the costs faced by many of the nationalised (now privatised) industries. Several of these industries (such as the railways) have cost structures that are dominated by very high fixed costs and where the marginal cost of producing one more unit of output (carrying one more passenger) is negligible. As such, these industries have average total cost curves that are always above the marginal costs of production over all the possible relevant levels of output. In such a situation, the industry concerned can be characterised as in Figure 5.1.

Given this position, the point of allocative efficiency will be at output Q^* and price P^*. This represents the position where marginal cost is equal to price (the instruction that was given to nationalised industries in the 1967 White Paper regarding how they should be setting prices). The obvious problem with this output is that it represents a loss equivalent to the shaded area. Thus we have a situation (which could correspond to several of the relevant industries under consideration) where a loss must be made if there is to be allocative efficiency. The difficulty with this is that a competitive situation could never deliver this position. Under competitive situations, firms will have at least to break even in the long run if they are able to continue production. Thus we are forced to conclude that in the position shown above, competition could not lead to full economic efficiency.

This problem of needing to make profit (or at least break even) can lead to a further difficulty concerning whether competitive situations will lead to economic efficiency. The earlier notions of efficiency have an implicit assumption that the economy is operating at full employment. It must be a prerequisite of

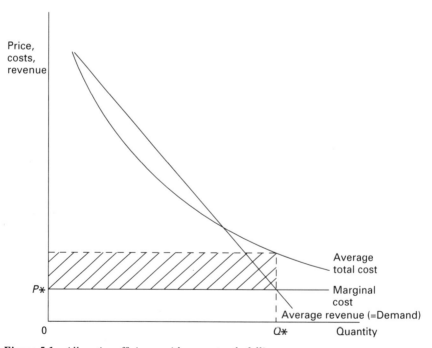

Figure 5.1 *Allocative efficiency with a constantly falling average cost curve*

making the best possible use of all available scarce resources that they are all being put to use. There is little logic in minimising the cost of production and terming that efficient if at the same time scarce resources are lying idle. Thus if there are considerable unemployed resources, then the rules of this game are likely to have to change. A simple example might be the following. A competitive industry that takes over from a previously non-competitive nationalised industry recognises that various of the activities of that industry are making losses and thus makes the reasonable decision to stop those operations. This appears a sensible decision. If consumers do not put a sufficiently high value on the current use of these resources to make a profit possible, then the resources would be better used elsewhere. However, if the economy is in a position of unemployment already, the problem is that there is no guarantee that these resources will be used in an alternative area of production. They may simply lie idle. In that case, it is hard to escape the conclusion that those resources were being better used before competition was introduced. At least then they were being used to produce a certain level of output that would have yielded some positive utility. Now they are doing nothing to meet the infinite wants of mankind. The situation can equally well be described as the social cost of the resources being less than the private cost involved in using them, the exact opposite of pollution (see Chapter 6 on the economics of the environment). Whenever there is a divergence between social and private costs, there is a case for government intervention (see Chapter 7 on the government provision of services). Ultimately, this depends upon what is felt to be the appropriate macroeconomic theory concerning the possibility of long-term involuntary unemployment. However, it again illustrates that there may be more to consider in the link between competition and efficiency than is often thought.

Thus we can conclude this section by saying that there are sound economic reasons for suggesting that competition can lead to efficiency but equally that a certain amount of caution needs to be employed in different situations rather than simply assuming that this statement is always automatically true. We now need to move on to consider whether privatisation does indeed introduce competition.

PRIVATISATION AND COMPETITION

If privatisation is to lead to greater efficiency it is usually held that competition must be increased as a result of the policy. For this we will need an appropriate theory of competition so as to judge the effects of privatisation. We will also need to differentiate between the introduction of competitive forces in the capital market and competitive forces in the product market.

One way in which the transfer of nationalised industries to the private sector through the sale of shares may introduce an element of competition where it was previously absent is through the capital market. The legal owners of an industry sold to the private sector are the shareholders. It is usually assumed that the basic desire of the shareholders will be for their company to maximise profits as this will maximise dividends paid and maximise the share price. This could provide the necessary pressure upon the managers of the firm to minimise costs since this will be an effective way of helping to maximise profit. However, managers may have many of their own objectives, not all of which imply the desire to minimise costs. The problem for the shareholders is one of asymmetric information. The managers know a great deal more regarding the potential profitability than ever the shareholders are likely to do. Thus the pressure to minimise costs may not be great.

The above difficulty may be at least partly overcome by corporate takeovers. Large groups have the incentive and ability to acquire information regarding the potential profitability of a firm. Thus if such a group is aware that the shares of a company are selling for less than their potential value due to inefficient management practices, then they will bid to take over the company and ensure that it maximises profit (presumably through minimising costs). Thus the threat of takeover could be seen as a competitive pressure which will force efficient behaviour. However, certain questions remain, for instance as to whether a government would permit the takeover of any of the privatised utilities (it now appears that, in the U.K., they would do so). Further, if there is the threat of a takeover, it could make sense for individual shareholders not to sell their shares, as they would wish to benefit from the higher share price which would arise from the new management as it increased profits. If all shareholders were to behave in this way, then the bid would fail.

The major area where it might be presumed that competition would be introduced through the policy of privatisation would be in the market for the companies' products. The important things here will be to have an appropriate model of competition upon to which to make judgements and to remember what is meant by privatisation.

According to the traditional theory of the firm approach, the privatisation of the large utilities has probably done little to create competition in the market for the products of these industries. Looking at British Telecom, the introduction of Mercury may have been a move from monopoly to duopoly, although the relative sizes of the two firms might have suggested that this remained a practical monopoly. In any case, privatisation cannot be considered to have moved the telecommunications industry very far along the spectrum of competition towards the most competitive extreme of perfect competition. However, it may be that there is a more helpful model of competition that should be considered.

The theory of contestable markets suggests that the number of firms in any industry is not a significant factor in determining the level of competition in that industry. The key to determining whether an industry is competitive is whether the firm(s) already in the industry (the incumbent(s)) are susceptible to what is termed 'hit and run' entry. This phrase means precisely what it suggests, namely that new firms are able to enter an industry for a period of time and then leave that industry without incurring any costs solely through the act of entering and leaving the industry. If this condition exists, then the market concerned is said to be 'contestable'. If a market is contestable, then all incumbent firms will have to behave in a competitive fashion. Specifically, it will be possible to observe the following characteristics:

1. Firms will minimise their costs.
2. Firms will make only normal profits.
3. Firms will not be able to cross-subsidise one part of their operation from another area of their activities.

In other words, the market has the characteristics of a fully competitive market without requiring the restrictive assumptions necessary for perfect competition. Firms will have to behave in this way due to the threat of hit and run entry. If an incumbent firm were to break any of the above conditions, then there would be scope for a new firm to enter the industry, make temporary abnormal profits and then exit the industry without any cost once the incumbent firm changed its behaviour to become competitive.

An important question then becomes what dictates whether an industry is susceptible to hit and run entry. The key requirement is that there should be no 'sunk' costs involved in an industry. Sunk costs are not the same as fixed costs. A sunk cost is a cost incurred due to entering an industry which cannot be recovered when exiting an industry. A fixed cost need not be a sunk cost. For example, in order to enter the airline industry, it would be necessary to acquire aircraft. These would be classified as a fixed cost, but would not be a sunk cost if they could be sold without loss if the firm wished to leave the industry. If sunk costs exist, then hit and run entry will not be possible as there are irretrievable costs involved in a firm entering an industry. The suggestion must be, then, that the higher the level of sunk costs in an industry, the higher the level of uncompetitive behaviour that will be possible by incumbent firms without fear of new firms entering the industry. In addition, three further factors are required if hit and run entry is to be possible:

1. The new firm must have access to the same technology as the incumbents.
2. The incumbent firms cannot change their prices instantly in response to the threat of possible entry.
3. Consumers must respond instantly to any price difference.

If any of these conditions is broken, then the incumbents have important advantages over any prospective entrants which may deter entry.

The theory of contestable markets can be interpreted as having considerable potential relevance when studying privatisation. The useful thing about the theory is that it gives a clear, simple checklist as to whether an industry can be deemed to be competitive, a list that does not include the number of firms in the industry. In particular, it points to the significance of the level of sunk costs in an industry in determining the level of competitive behaviour that will be required. This is very helpful given that the policy of privatisation tries to increase competition in order to increase efficiency and the fact that several privatised industries operate with a very few firms, sometimes just one.

The way to proceed now is to make some judgement of the privatisations that have occurred and to consider whether they have increased competition in an industry according to the criteria of contestable markets. In particular, it seems appropriate to consider whether the level of sunk costs in an industry has been reduced through privatisation. The most obvious comment to make is that the transfer of assets from the public to the private sector does nothing in itself to affect the sunk costs in an industry. It will leave them unchanged. As such, it will do nothing to encourage competition and competitive behaviour and thus will not achieve the stated aims of privatisation. (It has been argued that there will still be some competitive pressure insofar as firms in the private sector are always faced with the threat of bankruptcy. However, it is very hard to believe that this is a realistic fear with the major utilities or that it is possible for a government to allow this ever to happen.) Thus the major privatisations of the utilities may have contributed little to introducing the desired competition. However, this is not entirely true insofar as some of these privatisations have been accompanied by other measures which may have had an impact on competition. A good example is with the telecommunications industry. When Mercury was created as a competitor to British Telecom at the time of privatisation, Mercury was guaranteed access to certain of Telecom's major telecommunications networks. From the perspective of contestable markets, this represents the elimination of the largest single sunk cost involved in that industry and thus permitted a new entrant into the industry in a way that would not otherwise be possible.

The example of telecommunications appears to suggest that it may be the other aspects of privatisation apart from the transfer of assets that could help to introduce competition. Of particular interest is the policy of contracting out. This policy does not involve the selling off of public sector assets. Rather, it allows private firms to run services within public sector areas. Thus school and hospital meals and cleaning are now frequently provided by private sector companies. In terms of contestable markets, this policy could be interpreted as maintaining the major sunk costs of the industry within the government's hands implying that the firms bidding to enter the industry do not have the obstacle of these sunk costs preventing them from doing so. Thus the level of competition within the industry may be raised and privatisation may have a chance of achieving its objectives.

Given the above analysis, British Rail is an interesting privatisation. In contrast to the other major nationalised industries, there is no selling off of the whole industry to the private sector as an entire, intact monopoly. Rather than this, Railtrack has been created as a separate company which will operate in the private sector and is in charge of the track and the signalling. Private companies can then bid to run services on this track for a certain period of time. There are many logistical difficulties with this system and various concerns about whether the whole policy allows the externalities involved in transport to be accounted for. However, in terms of the theory of contestable markets, this privatisation has the potential to introduce more competition than would have been the case with a simple transfer of all assets to the private sector. Given that the track and the signalling must represent two of the most important sunk costs in this industry, the government has in one sense removed them by allowing companies to bid to run rail services without having to incur the full amount of these costs. Thus, entry into the industry is easier and potential competition greater.

Franchising, then, appears to be a much more promising policy in terms of creating potential competition. Unfortunately, there are reasons why even this policy may fail to introduce the level of competition that is desired. One problem may be that there will be very few competitors for the franchise. This could be due to various reasons such as scarcity of the appropriate skills or knowledge, possible collusion between the bidders and the advantages enjoyed by incumbents (such as greater experience). All of these could apply to the railways. Another problem could be associated with the fear of an incumbent losing the franchise and thus under-investing in the industry. A further problem arises if there is uncertainty regarding the service provided, notably the quality. This would imply the need for complex contracts and considerable monitoring, all of which is using scarce resources in a way that may be deemed to be inefficient.

Thus we are left to conclude that according to contestable markets, the nature of several of the major privatisations suggests that they have done little to introduce competition. The system of contracting out of services appears to offer more hope of achieving the desired goal, but there remain difficulties with this system that indicate that a fully competitive situation will not be achieved here either. Given this, the need for some form of appropriate regulation of privatised industries seems clear.

FURTHER EUROPEAN EXAMPLES OF PRIVATISATION

Privatisation has occurred elsewhere in Europe, other than just in the United Kingdom, since the early 1980s. It is interesting to compare the reasons for and the practice of such privatisations with the UK experience. The examples of Eastern Europe and Portugal are instructive.

Privatisation in Eastern Europe

Perhaps the most significant privatisation programmes are to be found in the former communist nations of Eastern Europe. Privatisations here can be seen as part of a radical general transition from command to market economies. Although the schemes vary between countries, all of these economies are embarking upon significant privatisation programmes. For them, some of the concerns expressed are not of great interest: decades of perceived failure associated with state provision means that privatisation programmes are seen as essential.

A few examples from some of the economies involved give a flavour of the privatisations being undertaken. In Poland, there is small enterprise privatisation taking place where small state enterprises are simply sold off to private buyers. Large companies are being turned into joint stock companies that are initially owned by the state. These may then be privatised by a direct sale to a specific buyer or the sale of shares to a range of individuals, notably employees of the company. State firms are also being liquidated and then either being sold directly to specific buyers or leased out. Finally, state housing has been sold to tenants. In Hungary, agricultural land has been restored from the state to working on the land. Selected small commercial enterprises in the service sector have been sold directly to domestic buyers. Larger individual privatisations have taken place in groups of about twenty enterprises at a time through the sale of shares to foreign or domestic investors. Management and worker buyouts have also taken place. In Bulgaria, there has been the restitution of agricultural land, small shops, some industrial property and residential properties. Small enterprises have been privatised through the auctioning off of such businesses as small shops and petrol stations. Larger enterprises are to be privatised through the sale of shares. Thus, there is wide-ranging privatisation taking place.

Probably the most notable point about these privatisation programmes from the perspective of this chapter is that there appears little recourse to consideration of whether they will beneficially increase the level of competition. The imperative seems simply to be to privatise. The fact that there may well be private monopolies created might be of some concern. In particular, there does not appear to be any suggestion of the need to regulate any of the privatised industries. Such regulation has been seen as intrinsic to the possible success of the main part of the privatisation programme in the United Kingdom. Without it, there must be a fear that the various inefficiencies associated with monopolies may arise.

Portugal

Portugal is another European nation that has witnessed a significant privatisation programme in recent years. The major Portuguese privatisations have been concentrated mainly in the industrial, banking and service sectors in companies that were nationalised in the large nationalisation programme of 1975–6 under the then socialist government. To permit the privatisations to occur, the constitution of the country had to be changed as any such change of ownership would have been deemed illegal under the previous constitution. The objectives of the privatisation process are clearly stated in the 1990 Law which permitted 100 per cent privatisations:

1. The modernisation of enterprises, increasing competitiveness and contributing to needed restructuring.
2. The strengthening of national entrepreneurial capacity.

3. The reduction of the state's stake in the economy.
4. Contributing to the development of the capital markets.
5. The widening of share ownership amongst Portugeuse citizens.
6. The maintenance of the state's interest in the economy.
7. The reduction of the national debt burden on the economy.

These form an interesting list of stated objectives. Some of them are clearly similar to those of the United Kingdom's programme, others are more specific to the Portuguese economy (such as the desired development of the capital markets). One thing that is not so strongly emphasised is the totally central role of increasing competition in order to increase economic efficiency.

A Commission has been established for the privatisation process. This supports and advises the appropriate Secretary of State in the Ministry of Finance. Privatisations are then conducted by the company itself in collaboration with the Ministry of Finance. The shares are valued and a prospectus for the sale is produced. The shares are then sold on Portugal's two Stock Exchanges. The process of privatisation is generally perceived as having proceeded smoothly. There is general political agreement on its desirability. There are, however, two areas of concern. The first involves the level of concentration of ownership. There is a worry that Portugal could witness a return to the domination of industries by strong oligopolies as was witnessed in its pre-nationalisation days. This appears to point to the need for appropriate regulation. The second issue is over the level of foreign ownership of domestic industries that is desirable. There is a concern that too much foreign ownership will make the economy more difficult to manage effectively as the owners of companies will have objectives that may be entirely different from what may be deemed to be in the national interest of Portugal. If this is a real problem, then it is a valid issue for any nation's privatisation programme.

PRIVATISATION AND REGULATION

The regulation of some of the privatised industries is an explicit admission that full (or perhaps even minimal) competition has not been achieved. If it had been achieved, then there would not be the need to regulate if it is believed that competition leads to efficiency. Indeed, in some ways it could be argued that what has happened in practice with privatisation is that one form of the regulation of industry (nationalisation) has been exchanged for an alternative form of regulation (to be discussed below).

A working definition of regulation will be any attempt by the government (or one of its agencies) to influence firms' behaviour via the establishment of rules to guide or constrain those firms' economic decisions. The general economic case for regulation is to try to overcome market failures. There are several market failures that could be the target of regulation, but in the case of the privatised utilities, regulation is aimed at excessive market power. As explained earlier, situations of concentrated market power can lead to economic inefficiency, both in terms of costs not being minimised and prices being set at undesirable levels. Thus the purpose of regulation in this context is to try to move the industry closer to an efficient outcome than would be the case if the industry were left entirely unregulated.

The way that regulation of the privatised utilities has developed has been via the establishment of public agencies which have created rules which the firms in the industries concerned are expected to abide by. Before looking at the specifics of what has been done, it is helpful to consider the general difficulties associated with regulation. The appropriate economic framework for considering regulation is in terms of principals and agents. The nature of this situation is that the principal has objectives which can only be achieved by the agent because the agent has immediate responsibility for the decisions as well as usually possessing better information. This is the essence of the problem confronting a regulator (the principal) who wishes to regulate the behaviour of a firm (the agent). The difficulty is that the objectives of the principal and the agent are different.

The first specific difficulty facing the regulator is lack of information. The firm possesses more information regarding the operation of the industry than the regulator, and it may be possible for the firm strategically to manipulate that information so that its behaviour does not have to become exactly as the regulator would hope. One example of this would be a firm's costs. The regulator will only be able to have clear access to the observed costs of the firm. These may be different from 'true' costs (perhaps due to accounting proceedures) and certainly give little indication of potential costs. It is probably potential costs that are of most interest to the regulator as the aim of the regulator will be to try to get a firm to minimise its costs for a given quality of output. It may be in a firm's interest to try not to reveal these true costs. One possible way to try to overcome this problem is to develop what is termed 'yardstick' competition. The idea here is to try to bring regulated firms in distinct markets indirectly into competition with each other with regard to cost reduction. The technique is to make the price that a firm in one market can charge depend upon the costs of a firm in a different market. This would be true for all firms in the regulated industry. Thus each firm has an incentive to reduce its own costs as this has the potential to raise profit because price is set according to the costs of another firm. Thus the system may work to reduce costs. For this system to work it must assume that firms in different markets face identical cost conditions and that the firms involved do not collude. However, its potential relevance to the privatised utilities where regional, but not necessarily national, monopolies are implied is clear. At the very least, this system gives the regulator more information regarding potential costs than would otherwise be the case.

A further problem of regulation can arise where there is the possibility of regulatory capture. This occurs if a regulatory agency comes to equate the public good with the industry that it regulates. There is always likely to be this danger given the problem of asymmetric information discussed above which makes the regulator highly dependent upon the firm. If the situation is manipulated sufficiently well by the producers, then the regulator could end by simply serving the interests of the firms in the industry. Another point here is that it could be a good use of firms' resources to try to ensure that the regulatory system that best allows them to pursue their chosen objectives is adopted by the government. From society's point of view, that would be an inefficient use of resources. The question that arises from all of this is 'Who regulates the regulators?'. Given that there may always be some tendency towards regulatory capture, there may be a need to create a further layer of regulation in order to guard against that. Such increasing bureaucracy may not be felt to be a desirable use of scarce resources.

There are really two types of regulation that can be used to influence the behaviour of an industry:

1. The structure of the industry may be regulated. This means that the regulation determines which firms are allowed to engage in which activities.
2. The conduct of the industry may be regulated. This is an attempt to introduce measures concerned with how firms behave in their chosen activity or activities.

It could be argued that the practice of privatisation has really meant a move from the regulation of structure (in the form of nationalisation) to a regulation of conduct (in the form of the watchdog bodies setting rules). The key to the success of the regulation of conduct is to set appropriate rules which give proper incentives to firms to behave in an efficient fashion. This is not an easy task given the problem of information discussed above. The main rule that has been created in the UK is the so-called '$RPI-x$' formula. This allows the privatised utilities to raise their prices by the general rate of inflation minus what is deemed to be a reasonable increase in productivity (except in the case of water where prices may rise by more than the rate of inflation in order to finance required investment). Some of these formulae have contingency arrangements, such as permitting British Gas to increase its price if there is an unexpected rise in the price of North Sea gas. The formulae are set for a certain period (often five years) after which they are open to review.

The rationale of these rules is that they should provide the firms concerned with an incentive to improve efficiency in the form of lowering costs. Once the 'x' factor has been set, then firms can increase their profitability if they are able to increase productivity by more than 'x' (or alternatively will find that their profits fall if they do not hit the 'x' target). Thus this rule may be seen as introducing a form of 'pseudo-competition' by providing a framework which appears to give firms a clear incentive to minimise their costs. Unfortunately, the system does have its problems. The difficulty over information implies that it will be very difficult to set the correct 'x' factor. Certainly the system gives firms a very strong incentive to try to mislead the regulators regarding their potential costs in an effort to try to keep 'x' as low as possible. Another difficulty concerns the time period given during which 'x' will remain fixed. If a firm knows that its 'x' is soon to be reassessed, then there is an incentive not to reduce costs as far as possible in the run-up to the reassessment as the more that costs have been successfully reduced in one time period, the larger the likely value of 'x' in the next time period. A final logical difficulty with the '$RPI-x$' formulae is the possibility that product quality does not remain constant. The alternative to reducing costs in order to be able to provide a service at a lower relative price is to reduce the quality of the service so that it is cheaper to produce. There appears to be no way round this difficulty except to introduce further regulation which is designed to ensure product quality. Thus, for example, British Telecom now has performance targets for such things as the speed with which telephone lines are fixed.

OFTEL: A CASE STUDY OF REGULATION

Telecommunications was the first of the major utilities to be privatised and considering certain aspects of its regulation helps to illustrate some of the general points made above. With the privatisation of British Telecom, a structure of regulation was established that provided the model for regulation of the other privatised utilities. Regulatory powers and duties were to be shared between three groups:

1. The relevant government minister who grants a licence to the privatised firm imposing conditions relating to price and service.
2. A regulatory body (in the case of British Telecom, OFTEL) which monitors compliance with licence conditions and has various other duties such as monitoring customer complaints.
3. The Monopolies and Mergers Commission to whom reference may be made concerning contested proposals to change licence conditions (such as possible changes to the '$RPI-x$' formula).

One point to note is that the government had the option to restructure British Telecom at the time of privatisation, for example by divesting Telecom of its local networks which could have become independent local companies. The advantage of doing this is that it could have led to regulation through yardstick competition as described earlier. However, the government rejected this option. This may have been because the government was heavily influenced in its decision by the management of British Telecom which was strongly opposed to restructuring. If this is so, then this could be seen as a possible example of regulatory capture.

The regulation of British Telecom has regulated both structure (in the dictating of the number of competitors permitted) and conduct (in allowing Mercury access to Telecom's network and particularly in the imposition of the '$RPI-x$' rule). The history of the '$RPI-x$' *formula* has been as follows:

1984–9: *RPI*–3 per cent
1989–91: *RPI*–4.5 per cent
1991–93: *RPI*–6.25 per cent
1993–: *RPI*–7.5 per cent

It is interesting to see how the '*x*' number has been increased since privatisation. Given the size of the profits made by British Telecom, it is not surprising that this has been felt necessary. What it implies is that, as long as quality has not suffered and as long as OFTEL has been successful in ensuring that Telecom has stuck to its pricing formulae, there must have been notable cost reduction since privatisation.

CONCLUSION

This chapter has suggested that the policy of privatisation is correctly judged by its effectiveness in creating competition and in turn efficiency. In the lack of

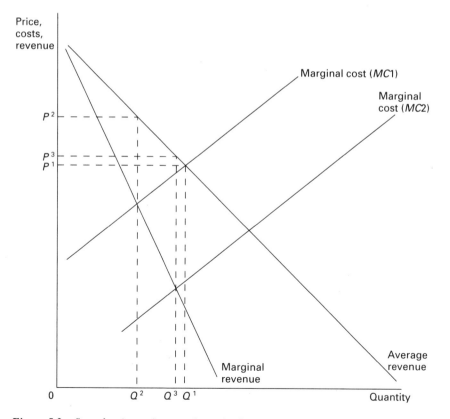

Figure 5.2   *Some key issues in assessing privatisation*

obvious competition, this may include the possible success of regulation acting as a form of 'pseudo-competition'. It is hard to sum up the arguments. However, Figure 5.2 may help to focus on the issues involved.

In the diagram, the position before the privatisation of a public utility is characterised as price $P1$ and output $Q2$. This makes the assumption that the nationalised industry was setting price equal to marginal cost, as suggested in the 1967 White Paper. If the industry is then transferred to the private sector as a noncompeting monopoly, then the immediate effect is that price becomes $P2$ and output $Q2$ as this is the point of profit maximisation. This appears undesirable since there is no longer allocative efficiency. However, if the privatisation succeeds in leading to a long-run reduction in the industry's costs ($MC1$ moves to $MC2$), then price will move to $P3$ and output to $Q3$. The success of the policy then rests on comparing this final outcome with the position before privatisation. This in turn appears to hinge upon how far costs may fall due to privatisation (something that it may be possible to measure in the long run). Of course, all of this ignores the fact that there are various other aspects of privatisation which could have been employed to do more to introduce competition and therefore not to permit the maximum possible abnormal profit.

6 Economic Theory and the Environment

We are all concerned about the environment. Most of us feel that perhaps steps need to be taken to ensure that we do not damage our environment to a dangerous degree. However, we seem highly unsure about what exactly is the problem, and even more unsure about what exactly should be done about it. It is the purpose of this chapter to demonstrate that the essence of the problem is an economic one, and in light of that to consider what might be appropriate policies to deal with environmental problems in general and to consider two particular case studies.

It was from the 1960s that real concern about the earth's environment and the damage that appeared to be being done to it was expressed. Various publications gave voice to this: Boulding's *Spaceship Earth* concept (1966), Galbraith's *The New Industrial State* (1967), the Club of Rome's *Limits to Growth* models (early 1970s), and Schumacher's *Small is Beautiful* (1973). These were but some of the better known examples of a general concern. However, this appeared to lull for a period from the mid-1970s (perhaps coinciding with greater fears over world recession) and it was not until the mid to later 1980s that interest was once more stirred with a growing perception of such environmental worries as global warming.

The government is now committed to certain targets with regard to the environment: to reduce emissions of sulphur dioxide to 60 per cent of their 1980 levels by the year 2003; to reduce carbon-dioxide emissions to their 1990 levels by the year 2000; and, somewhat vaguely, to maintain biodiversity and sustainable development. In addition, there have been various commitments to improve the quality of water and sewage treatment. The environment is on the political agenda.

The suggestion of this chapter is that this whole area of concern over our environment is essentially an economic problem and can properly be set within the framework of economic analysis. When it is remembered that economics is a subject that principally deals with the best use of scarce resources, then the environmental problem can be seen as closely allied to this. Concern over the environment is essentially an observation that we are not making optimal use of our scarce resources: we are using our resources in such a way that we could create significant future difficulties for ourselves. When looked at this way, this is an issue that is at the heart of the study of economics and thus it seems reasonable to suggest that economic analysis must be of relevance.

The chapter will concentrate upon four main areas:

1. The economics of the environment. This section will explain, from an economic perspective, why environmental problems arise. In many ways, they can be seen as another example of market failure.

2. Policies to deal with environmental problems. In light of the perceived causes of environmental problems, various appropriate policies can be suggested.
3. Global warming. The best-known of current environmental concerns will be considered as a case study. The various suggested policies to tackle the problem will be reviewed.
4. Toxic waste. Another contemporary environmental concern gives another context in which to consider the nature of the environmental problem and possible policies to deal with it.

THE ECONOMICS OF THE ENVIRONMENT

There are various aspects to the economics of the environment and the cause of environmental problems. These can all be seen within the context of market failures which are said to exist when the free operation of the market does not provide an optimal use of scarce resources. For a fuller discussion of the general nature of market failures, the reader is referred to Chapter 7 on state provision of health care and education.

The particular market failure that is usually seen as giving rise to environmental problems is that of externalities. Meade (1973) defined the concept of externality as follows:

> An external economy (diseconomy) is an event which confers an appreciable benefit (inflicts an appreciable damage) on some person or persons who were not fully consenting parties in reaching the decision or decisions which led directly or indirectly to the event in question.

In other words, an externality exists when someone (a third party) is affected by the decision(s) of others. The first point to note is that externalities can be either positive or negative. It is possible that the decision(s) of certain people may have beneficial effects on others. Various aspects of health care are often seen in this light. The decision of one person to be innoculated against a particular disease confers the benefit to others that they are now slightly less likely to catch the disease themselves. Equally, the decision(s) of certain people may have harmful effects on others. The decision to drop litter creates a nuisance and an eyesore to other passers-by. It is within the context of negative externalities that environmental problems can be seen to arise.

There are four possible permutations of externalities concerning consumers and producers:

1. Consumer to consumer. For example, loud music being played that is either appreciated or disliked by neighbours.
2. Producer to producer. For example, the use of local road networks to transport products which slows down the transport time of other firms who wish to make use of the same network.

3. Consumer to producer. For example, parking cars in such a way that the delivery of goods becomes more difficult.
4. Producer to consumer. For example, smoke pollution from a local factory that affects people's houses and health in the local area.

It is often this fourth category, externalities from producer to consumer, that is seen as the relevant context for many environmental problems.

In attempting to understand the precise nature of the problem, it is helpful to consider a simple example. Here, the essence of the problem of a negative externality can be seen as a divergence between social cost and private cost. It is important to understand that social cost includes all the relevant costs involved in the production of a particular good. This includes what are called private costs, but may include other possible costs also. That is the essence of the problem. Consider a firm that is producing a particular chemical. There are certain costs that the firm might have to meet in producing each ton of chemicals. These would include raw material costs, labour costs, energy costs and various others. All such costs are termed as 'private' and would be relevant to a firm when considering what would be an acceptable or appropriate market price. These costs are part of social costs. However, in this instance it seems likely that there may be other costs incurred by society due to the production of the ton of chemicals. These would include any dumping of chemical waste, perhaps in a local river, which created clean-up costs, any atmospheric pollution which created clean-up costs and ill-health, and possible road congestion due to the transportation of the chemicals. The problem is that these are not costs that the firm would have to pay when it produced the ton of chemicals and thus would not be relevant to the firm's pricing decision. Thus the market price for the ton of chemicals is likely to be too low when compared to the full cost incurred by society due to its production, and thus there will be over-production and over-consumption. Resources are not being used in the best possible way. This can be illustrated by Figure 6.1.

If the usual assumption of supply and demand analysis is made (perfect competition), then the average revenue (or demand) schedule will be the same as the marginal revenue schedule. In this context, it is helpful to consider these as benefit schedules: they are a measurement of the value of the benefit derived from consumption as expressed by the willingness of individuals to pay certain prices for certain quantities of the good. Thus there is a marginal social benefit schedule (MSB). It is assumed here that there is no divergence between private and social benefit in order to concentrate upon costs. A marginal private cost curve (MPC) can be identified. This constitutes the industry's supply schedule, and thus the usual interaction of the forces of supply and demand yields an equilibrium price, $Pe1$, and quantity, $Qe1$. However, the marginal social costs of production (MSC) are greater than the marginal private costs. This suggests that a more appropriate equilibrium, one in which the full costs of production were taken into account, would be given by price $Pe2$, and output $Qe2$. Thus the externality, the divergence between

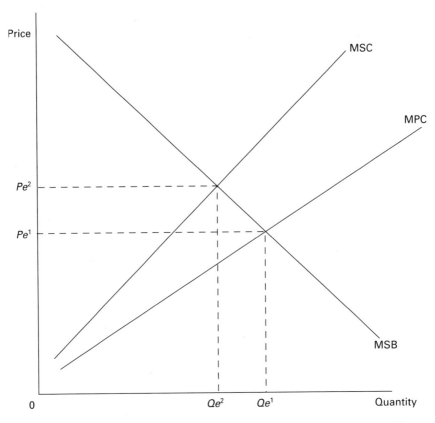

Figure 6.1 *Misallocation of resources due to the divergence of private and social costs*

private and social cost, has led to too many resources being diverted to the production of this good.

The above analysis suggests that the basis of the environmental problem is that environmental damage is not incorporated within the cost curves of private firms. It is not a relevant consideration when a firm is aiming to make profit. However, following the work of Coase (1960), the problem can be conceived of in a slightly different fashion. Coase argued that the basis of the problem was the lack of property rights with regard to such things as the environment. The problem is that no one has any ownership rights of the environment and thus no costs are directly incurred by individual producers through use of or damage to the environment. In a sense, there is a missing market. There is no one who can charge for damage done to or use made of the environment. Thus the environment is different from many other economic resources. Most resources are privately owned, and thus firms have to pay for their use. If firms wish to use labour power in their production, then they will have to buy that from workers. This is not true of the environment. If firms wish to pollute the atmosphere by releasing smoke into it, they do not have to identify an individual or group who must be paid in order to be allowed to do this as no one is perceived as owning the atmosphere. This is highly likely to lead to an over-use of the atmosphere (and thus any accompanying environmental damage), since with a zero marginal cost for its use, firms will continue up until the point where they receive zero marginal benefit. Insofar as society is incurring a positive cost through this use of the environment, then the resource is being over-used. This problem would not occur if the environment were clearly owned and an appropriate price had to be paid for its use.

A further way of understanding the nature of the environmental problem is to consider how the environment has the characteristics of a public good. The problem of the free market with regard to public goods is discussed in Chapter 7 on the government provision of goods and services. The key characteristics of public goods are:

1. Non-excludability. Once the good has been provided, it is not possible to stop people from benefiting from it.
2. Non-reducibility. The benefit to consumers of the product is not reduced by the addition of further consumers.

Clearly, various aspects of the environment appear to come close to these descriptions without matching up to the criteria perfectly. In practice, there are degrees of public goods, with very few examples of 'pure' public goods. Table 6.1 helps to clarify the situation.

The table suggests that there are a whole range of possible goods between the two extremes of pure public goods and pure private goods. The term 'congestible' implies that there is an element of non-rivalry (non-reducibility) in the product concerned, but that after a certain point, the addition of further consumers implies a reduction in the benefit received by current consumers. It can be seen that the major 'goods' associated with the environment (such as the air supply and the atmosphere) can be seen as non-exclusive and congestible. Recent evidence on such effects as the 'greenhouse effect' (discussed later) suggests that such things as the air supply and the atmosphere cannot be seen as

Table 6.1   *Categories of public and private goods*

	Non-exclusive	*Exclusive*
Non-rival	Pure public good Nuclear defence system	Intellectual property
Congestible	Air supply Atmosphere	Private swimming-pool
Rival	Fishery	Pure private good Many consumer goods

truly non-rival. Other environmental goods, such as fisheries, are best described as rival goods (the more one person catches, the less there is available for others) which are non-excludable in nature.

Seen in this light, the essence of the environmental problem is that the goods involved are non-excludable. They are freely available for use by anyone who may wish to use them. In other words, the marginal cost of use to all consumers is zero. Given the usual assumptions of demand theory in economics, this implies that all users of the good will continue until their marginal benefit has fallen to zero. The problem is that this implies over-use. The congestible (or even fully rival) nature of the product implies that there are external costs associated with the use of the good as the benefit to others diminishes as more is consumed. Thus, the true social cost is not zero, and consumption should stop before the marginal benefit has reached zero. In this sense, part of the problem can be seen to be the fact that environmental goods are not pure public goods. If they were, there would be no problem of rivalry, and they could be used as much as desired by all without any diminution in the benefit to others.

An example of the above clarifies the situation. Consider an area of pasture used by goats owned by different goatherders. An individual goatherder may perceive that introducing a new goat to the pasture will allow the goat to put on forty pounds in weight during a grazing season. Given the zero marginal cost of the pasture, this is clearly a sensible decision by the individual goatherder. However, it may well be that the new goat being able to put on forty pounds in weight is entirely at the expense of all other goats currently grazing on the pasture who will now put on forty pounds less in total. Thus the overall (social) benefit is in fact zero and there is no gain being made in a total sense. It is easy to see how this pasture will be over-grazed.

A final economic aspect of the environmental problem is the lack of representation of future generations in current decisions that will have an impact upon the utility of those future generations. The greenhouse effect may lead to undesirable global warming for future generations. A species lost today imposes a cost of lack of benefit from that species upon future generations. The problem can be seen as a missing market. The standard policy decision that is usually suggested for this is that a value must be put upon the future and this must be taken into account in current decisions. The technique used is referred to as discounting. The benefits or costs are not given as high a value in the future as in the present given that consumption now is certain, whereas consumption in the future is uncertain. However, the appropriate value at which to discount the future appears to require a significant value judgement and thus is bound to be problematic.

Economics, then, can do much to aid our understanding of the environmental problem. Having considered this, it is now possible to suggest what may be deemed to be appropriate policies to deal with the problem when viewed from an economic perspective.

ECONOMIC REGULATION OF THE ENVIRONMENTAL PROBLEM

The standard approach of economic theory is to suggest that where market failure exists, then there is a case for government intervention in order to increase efficiency (see Chapter 7 on the government provision of health care and education). Thus, if the essence of the environmental problem is perceived to be some form of market failure, then this can possibly be improved by appropriate government intervention.

While there are several different forms of government intervention that may be deemed to be appropriate in dealing with the environmental problem, there are two distinct traditions that can be perceived:

1. Following Pigou (1932), one approach is to try to tax the value of the negative externality. This approach may be referred to as 'internalising the externality'.
2. Following Coase (1960), an alternative approach is to try to increase the domain of property rights so that the environment has legally identifiable owners.

Both of these approaches need to be considered, together with other possible approaches to different aspects of the environmental problem. One further point that will need to be made is that, as with all forms of government intervention, there is the possibility of government failure. Thus, the possibility of a more efficient use of resources due to government intervention may not be the case in practice.

INTERNALISING EXTERNALITIES

The traditional approach to the problem of externality is to attempt to set a tax (or a subsidy) equal to the relevant externality. The economic logic of doing this is to force individual decision-makers to contemplate the total costs and benefits of any activity before it is initiated. Thus the idea is to set a tax equal to the value of any negative externality, so that private cost equals social cost, and a subsidy equal to any positive externality, so that private benefit equals social benefit. This is best illustrated through a diagram, Figure 6.2.

The basic environmental problem, as discussed in the previous section, can be characterised as the fact that social marginal cost (SMC) is greater than private marginal cost (PMC). The classic example of this is usually cited as pollution: this is clearly a cost to society, but not necessarily one that has to be borne by the decision-makers involved in the activity in question. The appropriate response here is then seen as the imposition of a tax equal to the distance *A*, the value of the negative externality. In this way, the private decision-maker is forced to bear the full social cost of the decision. Thus the production of the

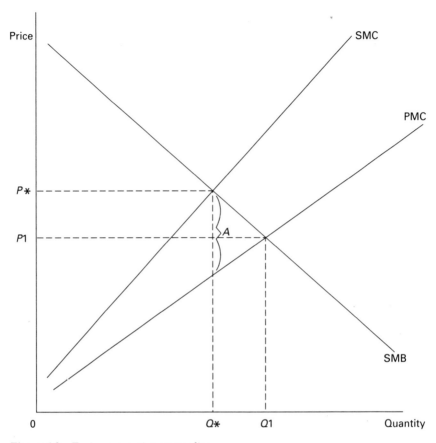

Figure 6.2 *Taxing a negative externality*

good involved is reduced to its optimal level, Q^*, where social marginal cost is equal to social marginal benefit (SMB). In addition, this tax, as with all taxes, will generate revenue for the government. Such a revenue could be used to compensate the sufferers from the pollution, thus further strengthening the case for such a tax.

One important point to note about this analysis is that the production of the good that generates environmental pollution has not been stopped altogether. Rather, it has been reduced to what may be considered as the most desirable level when viewed from the perspective of economic efficiency. Thus pollution is not eradicated. If the cost of the pollution is considered to be an acceptable one in order to gain the benefit of the good produced, then the economic approach would suggest that the optimum use of scarce resources could imply the existence of a certain amount of pollution. Pollution would not be eradicated, but rather reduced to a socially optimal level. This result of economic analysis may not be the same solution as is suggested from alternative approaches which might wish to attempt to ban all pollution. The essence of the economic approach suggested here is simply to force decision-makers to face the cost of the negative externality emanating from their decision.

There are various points that must be noted regarding this suggested 'solution' to the environmental problem. First, it effectively assumes that no other market failures exist. Thus, for example, there should not be any market distortions due to monopoly or oligopoly existing in the markets concerned. The problem in such a situation would be that, even in the event of the successful internalisation of the externality, there will not be an optimal solution if a market is not perfectly competitive as marginal cost will not be equal to price. It might be possible that the final solution could be less desirable than the original position without the tax.

Second, this approach assumes that it is possible to gather all the relevant information. For example, it must be possible to calculate the value of all damage caused by pollution if the appropriate tax per unit of production is to be set. The gathering of this information may prove to be intrinsically difficult (for example, putting a monetary value to noise pollution) and will require considerable scarce resources if a full calculation is to be made.

Finally, it must be assumed that there is no government failure due to the imposition of the corrective tax. The tax needs to be set with the sole aim of maximising economic efficiency rather than any other possible targets, such as the distribution of income. Thus, for example, a tax on domestic fuel could not take regard of distributional issues if it were to achieve the position of maximum economic efficiency.

PROPERTY RIGHTS

Coase (1960) suggested that the introduction of Pigouvian taxes and subsidies was not the best way to deal with the economic problem of externality. A particular objection that he had was that the introduction of any tax or subsidy would have a distributional impact, and the value judgements that were thus implied in the policy were undesirable. A better approach, he suggested, was to try to introduce property rights. The essence of the environmental problem was that no one owned the environment. If ownership rights were given, then the undesirable use of scarce resources could be overcome. Giving property rights would succeed in internalising the externality, but would do so through the operation entirely of the market, within the new legal framework, rather than relying on government economic policy intervention.

Coase's approach can be illustrated in the following manner. Imagine the situation where a company that creates toxic waste through its production activities is currently dumping that waste in the sea. This is creating costs of pollution and other environmental damage. Under the market system as it is, the firm has no private cost due to this activity, and thus continues the activity until the marginal benefit derived from doing so becomes very low or non-existent. Thus, there is excessive environmental damage. According to Coase, the problem would be solved if the sea were owned by someone or by some group of people. If this were the case, then the legal framework of the country could allow the owner of the sea to claim compensation or to sue the polluter. Alternatively, if the legal framework did not permit this, then it would be in the interest of the owner of the sea to bribe the polluter to stop or to reduce the level of toxic waste being dumped. Through this, the level of environmental damage could be reduced to a level closer to its economically efficient level. The same would be true of other environmental problems, such as the over-grazing of common pasture land and pollution. The key issue is to give property rights so that appropriate charges can be made.

Another way of understanding this approach is to refer back to Table 6.1 concerning different types of good and their level of 'excludability'. Most environmental problems occur within the area of congestible goods. Coase's approach can be seen as attempting to move from the left-hand column to the right-hand column for these types of goods. Thus non-excludable common grazing land could become excludable privately owned grazing land and charges made accordingly.

As with the Pigouvian approach, various caveats need to be added to Coase's suggestions. For instance it is often very difficult to define the appropriate market involved in different environmental problems. This is especially true given the global nature of many environmental problems. Thus, for example, the possibility of properly defining the market that is involved in air pollution, identifying the relevant parties and satisfactorily giving property rights is likely to be at best expensive in terms of scarce resources, or at worst impossible.

As with the Pigouvian approach, the giving of property rights will only succeed in producing an optimal use of resources if markets function efficiently. If there is any degree of monopoly or monopsony involved, then the outcome of sueing or bribery may not produce the most desirable outcome.

The Coasean approach may suffer from a particular type of public good problem. It may be that there are significant incentives to try to 'free ride' within the bargaining process implicit in the effort to gain compensation from the party creating the environmental damage. For example, many people may be suffering from the same problem of noise pollution. The temptation for all of these people must be to wait for one individual to establish a compensation claim and then to benefit from that without having to use the resources involved in establishing the claim. As with all such public goods, the difficulty is that the compensation is never established as each party waits for another to act.

Coase's approach does nothing to overcome one important aspect of the environmental problem, namely the lack of representation of future generations in current decision-making. Thus, even if property rights are established, it may be that the principal sufferers of current action will be future generations, but they are clearly in no position to force the full cost upon current decision-makers.

Thus, it must be concluded that neither the Pigouvian nor the Coasean approach can be deemed to be ideal and without cost to implement. It would seem inappropriate to suggest that one approach to combating the environmental problem is intrinsically superior to the other. Therefore it may well be a case of devising what is the most appropriate policy with the lowest cost in each particular situation.

One further economic approach to tackling the environmental problem has gained interest in recent years, namely the possibility of devising marketable permits.

MARKETABLE PERMITS

The approach to the environmental problem suggested through the imposition of taxes on negative externalities is that the price should be controlled and then the market be allowed to dictate the quantity of production at that price. The logical alternative to this is to control quantity and allow the market to dictate the price of that quantity. This is the thinking behind the suggestion that marketable permits might be an alternative economic policy to deal with the environmental problem.

An example of a marketable permit would be in the form of some type of emissions target. This would be set at a certain level and then permits to pollute could be given to all polluters, the total value of the permits equalling the target level of emissions. Once these permits have been allocated, it is at the discretion of the producers as to how they use them. They can simply use them to emit pollution equal to the value of their permit. Alternatively, they may choose to reduce their level of emissions and then to sell the remaining units of their permit to another polluter. Equally, they may make the decision that they wish to expand their production and will thus have to increase their level of emissions. In that case, they would have to buy units of a permit from another producer. Thus this effectively reduces the private costs of those producers who reduce their level of pollution and increases the private costs of those producers who increase their level of pollution. It also allows authorities to control the total level of pollution. Tradable permits could be introduced on an international as well as a national level, with inter-governmental cooperation. Given the global nature of environmental problems, this could be an important possibility.

POSSIBLE POLICIES FOR PARTICULAR PROBLEMS

There are several other aspects of the environmental problem where economic theory may help to suggest appropriate policies.

1 Accounting for Future Generations

One of the aspects of the environmental problem is that the main sufferers from current environmental damage may frequently be future generations. Obvious examples of this are the possible depletion of natural resources and any possible deleterious long-run effects of the use of nuclear power. However, this group, by definition, are not involved in current decision-making, and thus their possible disutility may not be accounted for in current production and consumption patterns.

The usual solution to such situations in economics, as mentioned earlier in this chapter, is to introduce a discount rate: the future is discounted. Current benefits are deemed to have a greater value than those of the future due to the uncertain nature of the future. However, it is clearly not easy to know what number to put on the rate. The number that is decided will have a significant effect upon what is considered to be an appropriate current level of environmental damage.

However, others have further suggested that it is not acceptable to use a discount rate in this fashion as the logic of it is simply to push the problem into the future. It could be argued that it is necessary to hand over the environment to posterity in at least as good a condition as when it was received by the current generation. That would have a considerable impact upon what was deemed to be the appropriate discount rate. One thing that is clear is that no easy solution to this problem can be found. Ultimately, some significant value judgements must be made.

2 Coping with Uncertainty

Another important facet of the environmental problem is the significant level of uncertainty involved in trying to determine precisely what level of environmental damage is being generated by current economic activities. Part of this was considered when noting the difficulty of trying to calculate the appropriate level at which to set a tax in an effort to internalise a negative externality. Once more, there appears to be no easy answer to this problem. Coping with uncertainty is intrinsically difficult. The most positive suggestion that can be put forward is that some form of worst case and best case scenarios can be be put forward. This at least may give parameters within which decisions can be taken. However, even when this is done, there have to be decisions taken as to the appropriate level of risk to take. Is it appropriate always to be risk-averse and to act as if the worse scenario will happen? Again, value judgements appear to be required.

3 The Global Nature of the Environmental Problem

One important aspect of the environmental problem is its global nature. Pollution created in one country has an impact on another. The destruction of part of the ozone layer by one nation has an impact on all nations. The same must thus be true of environmental policy: efforts to reduce environmental damage by one country yield benefits to other countries. A new problem can thus be seen to arise within the area of environmental policy: such policy has a public good nature to it. Once the policy is provided by one party, it is not possible to stop other parties from benefiting from it. Thus there may be the standard problem of attempted free-riding leading to an overall under-provision of such policies.

Perhaps an alternative framework of analysis, that of the prisoners' dilemma (see Chapter 4), may be helpful in suggesting successful policies. The problem is that all countries may end up doing the same as the prisoners pleading 'Not guilty' by not providing appropriate environmental policies, whereas they would be better off by all agreeing to provide appropriate policies. This implies the need to make agreements for cooperative action, and then to have significant legitimate threats that can be carried out against anyone who breaks the agreement. It appears that global coordination and organisation is required if effective environmental policy is to occur.

Much of the thrust of this section of the chapter has been to suggest that economic theory indicates there are no possible universal ideals with regard to environmental policy. Thus the appropriate approach is to look at at each case individually and devise policies that are appropriate to that particular case. Thus, the rest of this chapter will look at two important examples of the environmental problem.

THE GREENHOUSE EFFECT

The best-known of all environmental problems is probably the greenhouse effect (otherwise referred to as global warming). Economic theory may be able to suggest what could be appropriate policies to deal with this. However, first, it is important to have some background understanding of the nature of the problem.

Global warming may occur due to the so-called 'greenhouse effect'. This is caused by the accumulation of certain gases that allow the sun's radiation into the earth's atmosphere but then prevent the escape of some of that radiation. Thus global warming may occur over a period of time. Current human activities are increasing the concentration of these gases, notably carbon dioxide, one of the four major gases involved. The particular reason for the increased concentration of carbon dioxide is perceived to be the burning of fossil fuels. It has been estimated that, if current trends continue, greenhouse gas levels will have doubled by the year 2025. If this is so, it is further estimated (on average) that average global temperatures will rise by 2.5 degrees centigrade by that time.

The effects of such global warming are unclear. However, two main possibilities are foreseen. The first is that there would be an impact on agriculture involving winners and losers. Crudely speaking, those with warm climates at the moment will suffer, while those with currently cool climates will benefit. The second consequence is that global warming may cause rising sea levels. It is suggested that levels may rise by 66 centimetres by the year 2100. This could cause both increased flooding and land loss.

Before proceeding to discuss the possible appropriate policy response to this phenomenon, it is important to note how it fits within the economic framework discussed earlier. Global warming is a clear example of an externality. The activities of certain groups of people are having an impact (be it negative or positive) on third parties. In addition, the principal impact of current activities is likely to be on future generations.

Overall, two possible policy responses to global warming can be identified. The first response is to do nothing and for nations to adapt to the temperature changes. The alternative is to attempt to stabilise or reduce the level of emission of greenhouse gases. The choice between the two may be dictated by what are perceived to be the probabilities of different consequences. Equally, the discount rate that is chosen is important if the major effects are likely to be in fifty years' time. If a risk-averse, worst-case scenario is adopted, then the policy would be to stabilise or to reduce emissions. Indeed, the UK government does have a commitment to stabilise greenhouse gas emissions at their 1990 levels. The rest of this case study will consider what may be appropriate policies to achieve that sort of end.

Suggested policies have often concentrated on the reduction of emissions of carbon dioxide (which accounts for about half of all greenhouse gases). Economic theory suggests that there is likely to be some optimum level of carbon dioxide emissions if account of both the damage costs and the abatement costs are calculated. The situation is best illustrated through Figure 6.3.

When carbon dioxide emissions are zero, then the damage costs must also, logically, be zero. However, the abatement costs that are required to produce zero emissions will be great. The reverse situation is where there are no abatement costs and here the damage costs will be high. Taking into account both of these costs, a total costs schedule can be plotted, as indicated in the diagram. This suggests that there will be an optimum level of carbon dioxide emissions where total costs are minimised, level C^*.

Once more, this pinpoints the need to calculate the relevant costs involved, something that is intrinsically difficult. The position of the damage cost schedule will clearly have a significant impact upon what is deemed to be the appropriate level of emissions. The position of this schedule will also be affected by the chosen discount rate, given that the majority of the damage costs will be in the future.

Once the appropriate level of emissions has been decided, it must be decided what level of emissions are to be permitted by different sectors of the economy. The economic principal here is that emissions should be reduced in each sector so that the marginal abatement cost of each sector is the same. This could mean having a greater reduction in one sector than in another given that it likely to be less costly to reduce emissions in some sectors than in others. The way to achieve this, if a Pigouvian approach is taken, is to set appropriate taxes. This is

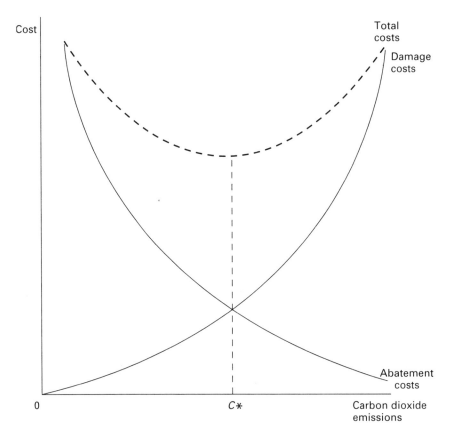

Figure 6.3 *The optimum level of carbon dioxide emissions, given damage costs and abatement costs*

the usual suggestion in economics, given the informational costs involved if the government were to try to calculate the ideal level of emissions for each sector and then to set legal requirements to reach those levels.

One possibility is to introduce a carbon tax. Each of the three fossil fuels, coal, oil and gas, could be taxed according to their carbon content, the carbon content indicating the level of carbon dioxide emissions involved in their use. This appears an attractive option. It would be simple to introduce and should provide the appropriate incentive structure. Further, it would not be distortionary in an undesirable fashion, for example by reducing the incentive to work. However, there are difficulties.

While the tax may be considered to be efficient, there are equity considerations. The introduction of VAT on domestic fuel illustrates this well. There will be redistribution of income away from those who consume a significant level of fuel compared to their income level. This will usually be those on lower incomes. Thus it may be considered necessary to have appropriate offsetting measures to stop this redistribution.

Calculating the appropriate level of taxation will be difficult, depending on such factors as the relevant elasticities of demand. The way round this may be to introduce modest levels of taxation initially and then to adjust them until the desired level of emissions is achieved. This could be a lengthy process.

The tax could suffer from the problem noted earlier in the chapter that there is no way of excluding other nations from benefiting from it. Thus there is the temptation to try to free-ride on other countries' efforts. This implies that it will be necessary to have global agreements and coordination concerning the imposition of appropriate carbon taxes in every country. These agreements could be complicated given that the marginal abatement costs are likely to differ between countries and thus the appropriate tax levels could vary between countries.

A final problem with the tax is the obvious one that it only deals with carbon dioxide emissions. There are other gases also involved, most notably CFCs which account for about 25 per cent of all greenhouse gases. Thus an exclusive reliance on a carbon tax will be inefficient: it will be necessary to impose gas-specific taxes.

As discussed in the overview of economic environmental policy, an alternative to controlling the price of gas emissions would be to control quantity and to allow price to find its own level in the market. It is easy to suggest that this policy has merit in this case because the perceived target is the control of the quantity of total emissions. The policy would be to decide the total level of desired emissions, issue tradable permits to equal that amount and then leave the rest to the market.

One final point concerning global warming needs to be made. It is sometimes argued that it is not reasonable of the developed world to expect the developing world to have to develop technology and to use production techniques that minimise the emission of greenhouse gases when the developed world benefited from such techniques in the past. Apart from other considerations, the developing world may not be able to afford such technology. There are value judgements to be made in this area. However, there could be a strong case for the developed world investing in the energy efficiency of the developing world, both from the point of view of equity and from a position of self-interest insofar as it may be required if there is to be an effective global reduction in the emission of greenhouse gases.

TOXIC WASTE

Another area of particular contemporary environmental concern is the disposal of toxic waste. The UK has a significant role in the world market of toxic waste disposal, the turnover being estimated at £5 billion in 1990. The UK may have a comparative advantage in waste disposal, but it may also be the relative laxity of legal regulations that has led the UK to be so involved in this industry.

Toxic waste can arise in various ways, such as a by-product of extraction and manufacturing industries and redundant substances after usage. The most notorious example probably involves the nuclear power industry. These various forms of waste have potential to create pollution in fresh water, salt water and air. The effects may also not be confined to the country of production. Thus, this can once more be clearly identified as an example of externalities: third parties are having costs (or perhaps occasionally benefits) imposed upon them by other groups of decision-makers. In this situation, it is then possible for government intervention to improve the market outcome, at least in theory.

Three particular approaches to policy can be identified to attempt to deal with toxic waste.

1   Ex Ante Property System

One possible approach is to adopt the standard Coasean idea of attempting to give property rights to all the parties who may be involved. Appropriate legal action could then be taken against all those creating external costs through the disposal of toxic waste. Unfortunately, this is not as straightforward as it sounds. The first difficulty is that property rights would have to be negotiated, not a straightforward matter given the international nature of the problem. However, even once the property rights are allocated, legal action could be extremely difficult and costly. For example, just looking at chemical waste indicates the number of different causes, such as motor oils, batteries, solvents, paint, pesticides and others. Thus in order for the system to work a great many contracts would have to be devised. The transactions costs of this could be considerable.

Despite the difficulties, the EC has introduced an ex ante pesticide registration system which sets certain standards which must be met if the pesticide is to remain within the law.

2   Ex Ante Testing and Taxing System

A Pigouvian approach would be to try to test the size of the externality involved and then set an appropriate tax upon the activity of disposing of toxic waste. Thus the negative externality would be internalised. There are various difficulties with this approach. Testing to try to determine the size of the externality is expensive. However, even once testing has occurred, the level of uncertainty remains high. Currently, testing does occur within the European Community, but there is no tax system that corresponds to the testing. Either no action is taken, or the disposal of the waste is banned. The difficulty of introducing an appropriate tax system is principally due to the large level of uncertainty. It would be possible to reduce this level of uncertainty, but this would require further tests which would further increase the cost of the policy. It is unclear whether the benefits of this extra testing would justify the costs. Another concern is that many of these extra tests would have to be conducted upon animals, a policy that may not be deemed acceptable to many.

3   Ex Post Liability System

An alternative version of the Coasean approach would be to wait until damage was caused, and then for a legal system to charge for any damages. This was suggested in a Green Paper in March 1993, with the idea that damage should be determined and then awards made by a judicial system. Once more, there are difficulties with this system. There is a high fixed cost associated with all claims, averaging perhaps £4000 per claim. This is a particular problem given the likelihood of diffusion of toxic waste implying that many parties could suffer a small cost, perhaps smaller than the fixed cost of the claim. The full costs of toxic waste may not be clear for many years because of the accumulative nature of the damage caused. Thus it may be that costs have to be suffered for a long period of time until a successful claim can be made. The situation is complicated further by the problem of synergism: it is difficult to trace and to prove the exact cause and effect of any damage given the number of parties who may have been involved in production and consumption.

CONCLUSION

A review of the environmental problem suggests that it can properly be described as an economic problem: it involves the inappropriate use of the world's scarce resources. The economic concept of externality is particularly helpful in understanding the essence of the problem.

There are two overall economic approaches to devising appropriate policies in this area: the Pigouvian tax system and the Coasean property rights system. It is unclear which has the greater merit. Indeed, upon looking at differing examples of the environmental problem, it is evident that the problems involved are often complex and that there is no ideal policy. The clearest principle appears to be that it is necessary to consider the costs and benefits of different schemes in different circumstances and, in light of that analysis, to pursue what appears to be the optimal solution.

References

Coase, R.H. (1960) 'The Problem of Social Cost', *Journal of Law and Economics*, October.
Meade, J. (1973) *The Theory of Economic Externalities* (Geneva: Sijthoff-Leiden).
Pigou, A.C. (1932) *The Economics of Welfare* (London: Macmillan).

7 Government Provision of Services: Health Care and Education

There are several recurrent themes throughout the history of economic thought. One of them, and one which has moved very much into the limelight in recent years, is whether goods and services are best provided through the free market or whether there is a need for government intervention, perhaps in the form of state provision. It is this fundamental issue that this chapter will investigate, using as case studies the government provision of health care and education. These appear to be particularly apt examples in light of recent discussion over the appropriate way in which to provide and to fund these services and the significant government reforms that are taking place.

There are really two aspects to the debate regarding the desirability of allowing the market to provide goods and services without government intervention. First, there is debate concerning the goals of economic activity, the desirability of the ends that are achieved. Here it is often suggested that the free market may lead to the greatest individual liberty, perhaps a highly desirable goal. Second, there is debate regarding whether the market is the best means of achieving certain predetermined goals. The relative merits of market and government provision of goods and services can be considered in both of these areas, and it is helpful to remember that they can be seen as distinct.

The role of the state in the provision of goods and services has expanded greatly in the twentieth century, moving from the provision of certain basic services (such as the value of the currency and law and order) to a much fuller state role in providing education, health and social security, and in providing macroeconomic management. The role of the two world wars was significant in this as they forced a greater role upon the government, and both times the government did not withdraw to its pre-war level of provision. The fuller role of state provision was cemented in the Beveridge Report (1942), the Education Act (1944), the Employment White Paper (1944) and the subsequent establishment of the Welfare State and the nationalisation of several major industries. This consensus regarding the role of the state in the provision of goods and services persisted throughout the (in retrospect) relatively stable levels of economic growth in the 1950s and 1960s. However, the consensus began to be challenged as the economy hit more turbulent times in the 1970s, and the election of Mrs Thatcher's government in 1979 marked the beginning of a shift in policy regarding the perceived desirable level of government provision of goods and services in the economy. It is against that background that the case for and against the market (or state) provision of goods and services should be understood.

The chapter will divide itself into the following five areas:

1. The general case for the market provision of goods and services.
2. The perceived problems with the market provision of goods and services (and thus the case for the role of the government).
3. The problems involved with government provision of goods and services (government failure).
4. The provision of health care. This section considers both the general case for the role of the government in health care provision and the recent government reforms of the UK health service.
5. The provision of education. As with health care, both the general case and recent government reforms will be considered.

THE CASE FOR MARKET PROVISION

The starting point for the desirability of allowing the free market to provide goods and services in the economy is often taken to be the model of perfect competition. It is worth noting that if this is the be-all and end-all of the case, then it is not much of a case given the lack of real-world examples of such a level of competition. In one sense, it might simply appear to suggest the need for perpetual state intervention. However, as will be seen, there is more to the suggestion than simply the existence of perfect competition. In practice, the case is more to do with a cost–benefit consideration of the desirability of the market in any particular situation.

Part of the general case for allowing goods and services to be provided by the market was given in Chapter 5 on privatisation where it was suggested that the free market in a competitive situation could lead to both technical and allocative efficiency. Here, the emphasis is on a concept known as 'Pareto Optimality'. This concept, named after its founder, Vilfredo Pareto, states that an allocation of resources is optimal or efficient if it is not possible to make someone better off without making someone else worse off. Once this position has been reached, it is impossible to make an unambiguous improvement because if one person is to be made better off, then someone else will have to be made worse off. As it is not possible to measure such things (interpersonal comparisons of utility are felt to be unmeasurable), then it can never be known whether such a rearrangement has improved or worsened the overall level of utility in the economy. The first fundamental theorem of welfare economics suggests that a fully competitive market equilibrium will necessarily be Pareto optimal: it cannot be unambiguously improved upon.

This is logical if one thinks of completely free trade of all goods and services taking place between fully informed individuals. In such a situation, trading will take place as long as both parties involved believe that they are gaining. Thus every trade that takes place can be seen as a Pareto improvement: individuals are being made better off without anyone being made worse off. Trading will cease only when there are no more mutually advantageous trades available, when it is not possible to make one person better off without making a different person worse off. In other words, the free market has led to Pareto optimality. Thus, there is the suggestion that allowing the free market to provide all goods and services in a competitive environment will lead to what is usually judged to be a highly desirable position.

The second fundamental theorem of welfare economics states that if there are no increasing returns (economies of scale) in production, then every Pareto optimal state is a competitive equilibrium corresponding to some initial distribution of purchasing power. The absence of economies of scale is important, for if there are economies of scale, then monopoly situations may be liable to develop in the economy. This theorem is stating something similar to the first statement, but it is making the point that once an initial distribution of resources or spending power has been established, then trade in the free competitive market will lead to a Pareto optimal situation. There are many different possible positions of Pareto optimality, each one corresponding to a different initial endowment of resources. The important implication of this is that if there are concerns regarding the distribution of income (and hence goods and services) between individuals, then this can be tackled by a government simply altering the distribution of spending power within the economy. Thus concerns about equity do not necessarily imply the case for the government provision of goods and services. This can still be left to the market. In fact, this is not quite as straightforward as suggested given the level of information that would be required by the government in order to know what final distribution of goods and services would be achieved from any one starting point of individuals' purchasing power. There is also the problem that a transfer of spending power is likely to involve a distorting of incentives (this is discussed later).

Thus in a fully competitive situation, the case for allowing all goods and services to be provided by the market appears to be a strong one. However, as mentioned earlier, this approach does rely ultimately on the impossible assumption of perfect markets. A different strand of argument in favour of free market provision does not do so. The Austrian approach, particularly associated with Friedrich Hayek, rests upon imperfect competition, and particularly imperfect information. The suggestion here is that the process of the free market provides the dynamic of economic progress. It is as firms strive to make profit that innovation and economic progress take place. Perfect competition would be a situation in which this process had come to an end.

The Austrian approach also stresses how, in a world of imperfect and dispersed information, the market succeeds in achieving an allocation of resources with the minimum of information required. All any individual requires to know is his or her own preferences and the relative prices of relevant goods and services. A firm would have to know its costs and the same relative prices. Given this, the free market will allocate the scarce resources of society, paying attention to both preferences and costs. For the state to be able to do a similar thing would require a vast amount of information because the preferences of all individuals and the costs of all firms would have to be known. Thus the proposition is that the provision of goods and services is best left to the free market.

The arguments thus far considered can be described as instrumental: they suggest that the free market may be the best way to provide goods and services. However, the free market may also be viewed as an end in itself. According to this argument, the economic freedom given by the free market (as it gives the maximum possible choice to individuals) is a prerequisite for political freedom. The philosophy is one of individualism, as the liberty of the individual is judged to be of the highest worth. The argument has very clearly moved into the terrain of strong value judgements at this point. The government's role is seen as providing a framework of law and order within which individuals should then be allowed to do as they please. Thus, individual liberty is maximised and the previous arguments suggest that the best possible provision of goods and services will also be attained for all individuals through this system. There is no role for the government in providing goods and services.

THE PROBLEMS WITH MARKETS AND THE CASE FOR GOVERNMENT INTERVENTION

There are problems with the ideal situation described above. As was hinted at before, the fact that much of the case for market provision appears to rest upon the assumption of a highly competitive situation (perfect competition) might be felt simply to suggest that there must be a strong case for the role of the government in the provision of goods and services in an economy, given that the conditions required for perfect competition are so stringent. The standard economic approach for justifying a role for the government in the process of providing goods and services is indeed to consider significant ways in which the model of perfect competition breaks down in practice, and thus that the free market will not necessarily lead to a situation of Pareto optimality as was discussed above. In this case, there appears to be a legitimate economic role for the government.

There are various ways in which markets are perceived to 'fail'. It is helpful to split these into demand and supply side failures. On the side of demand, a common failure is perceived to be with regard to information. In a fully competitive market, all parties have perfect information. When this is not the case, then problems can arise. Often the problem is that information is 'asymmetric': one party involved in a transaction has more information about the trade than the other one does. This could lead to some form of exploitation by the more informed party or various other problems. In Pareto terms, it could lead to a trade taking place where both individuals believe that they can gain, but subsequently one of the individuals finds that he or she is worse off. A Pareto improvement has not occurred through trade.

A particularly interesting example of the problems caused by lack of perfect information concerns the market for insurance. It is important to consider this because of its relevance to the health care market. If individuals are 'risk-averse' (a common assumption in economics, even if somewhat contradicted by the existence of gambling) then there is a potential for mutually advantageous trade to take place in the provision of insurance. Individuals are prepared to pay in order to receive the utility of not having to worry about the impact of various future events upon their lives. Given some knowledge of probabilities, entrepreneurs can set payments so that there is the potential to earn profit from providing the desired insurance. Unfortunately, due to certain information problems, the market may not function in the way desired. The first problem encountered by insurers is that of 'adverse selection'. The difficulty for insurers is that they lack information regarding the level of risk attached to different individuals. With full information, it would be possible to set an appropriate premium for each individual based on his or her risk. However, there is a clear incentive for those with a high risk not to reveal their true level of risk to the insurer in order to try to reduce their premium. Thus the insurer may not be able to distinguish high risk from low risk individuals and thus may have to set a universal premium. The problem with this is that the premium involved may be too high to make it a worthwhile transaction for low risk individuals: the price is too high given their low risk, and thus they drop out of the insurance scheme. The insurers are then left with just high risk individuals and will find that the premium that they have set will prove too low. Thus the market does not function as desired. The second major problem associated with insurance is 'moral hazard'. Once an individual is insured, there is less incentive to try to prevent the event against which insurance has been taken, thus making the event more likely to happen and leaving the possibility of insurance companies making unexpected losses. The problem for insurers is once again one of lack of information: it is not possible fully to monitor individual preventative activity. There may be other problems involved with the insurance market, but these two information problems alone may be sufficient either to see an under-provision of insurance in the free market, or possibly whole insurance markets to fail. Given this, then there could be a role for the government in certain insurance markets. In general, where there is a lack of perfect information, there may be a role for the government either in improving the information available or in intervening more directly.

There may be a perceived problem of demand in a free market due to inconsistency of preferences or perhaps even irrationality of choice. This is a difficult and contentious area. Suggesting that people may make irrational choices contradicts the commonly used assumption of rationality. The suggestion that society or the state can judge that an individual's action is irrational would also not be compatible with a commitment to a position of individual liberty, as often taken by those supporting the free market. However, there seems little doubt that certain forms of government intervention in the economy are at least in part based on this perceived failing. Examples might be seen in attempts to stop people smoking, insisting that people wear seat-belts, providing free school milk and making school education compulsory.

A further problem may emerge on the demand side through the lack of incentive for individuals to reveal their true preferences in certain circumstances. The case of public goods could provide an example of this. This situation was considered in Chapter 4. Given the two characteristics of non-reducibility and non-excludability, then there is no incentive for an individual to reveal his or her preference for such a good as it should be possible to 'free ride' on someone else's provision of the good. Given this, together with the problem of a firm recouping any of the costs of provision due to non-excludability, it is likely that such goods, which could be mutually advantageous trades, will not be provided by the free market. Thus there is a case for the government to provide such goods, financing their provision through the tax system.

On the supply side, market failure can arise where private costs of production do not coincide with social costs of production. One version of this is where the social value of production is undervalued by the market. This is the notion of merit goods. Examples here might be felt to be such things as the arts where the overall benefit to society may be judged to be greater than that simply gained by the individuals involved. However, it is hard to avoid value judgements of some magnitude here. The desirability of the arts to the general culture of a society is not something that would gain universal assent. Another interesting example could be employment. The benefit to society of someone being employed could go beyond that received by the employer and the employee insofar as the state finances will be improved by the employment and all possible socially undesirable things associated with unemployment may be reduced. In these situations, the problem is that the free market could lead to an under-provision of the good or service. Thus there may be a role for the government in attempting to increase the level of provision.

Another example of private costs diverging from social costs is where the social costs of production exceeds the private cost involved. This is a negative externality. Many problems can arise from this, and Chapter 6 considered in some detail several areas of particular current concern. If the private cost of production is below the social cost, then the market price will be too low and there will be over-production of the good or service concerned. A good whose production involves polluting the environment is seen as a typical example. There is then a role for the government in trying to reduce the level of production to a point nearer to that considered socially optimal. Regulation or taxation of the externality are two commonly suggested actions. For a full discussion, the reader is referred to the chapter on environmental economics.

A further problem on the supply side may arise where economies of scale exist. In this case, there will be a tendency towards monopoly (or at least lack of competition) as firms have to be large in order to minimise costs, but this implies there may be room for only a limited number of firms in the industry concerned (perhaps only one). In this situation, price will be significantly different to marginal cost and firms may lack the incentive to minimise production costs if they wish to pursue other goals. For a fuller discussion of this, the reader is referred back to Chapter 5. Some caution should be employed here since the theory of contestable markets suggests that firms in concentrated markets may still have to behave competitively if they are faced with the threat of entry into the industry. The key thing then is the level of sunk costs. Insofar as industries with large economies of scale may also be industries with large sunk costs, then the worries about lack of competition remain. In these circumstances, there may be a role for the government, especially in the case of natural monopolies. Previously, this was seen as a case for nationalising the industry. Today it is seen as a case for regulating the industry while allowing it to be run through the private sector.

Concerns over equity have been seen as another reason for government intervention in the provision of goods and services. It will be recalled that the second fundamental theorem of welfare economics implied that if there were concerns about the distribution of income in an economy, then this could be overcome simply by affecting individuals' initial purchasing power. However, once there is perceived to be a legitimate role for the government in providing certain goods and services, then this provision in itself is bound to have some impact on the distribution of resources within society. In that case, there can be no clear separation of distributional concerns from the provision of goods and services, and thus the impact on the distribution of resources will become a factor when considering the appropriate level of provision of certain goods and services by the government. This might apply in the cases of both health care and education.

The whole situation regarding the role of the government in providing goods and services could be further complicated if it is believed that the free market could lead to macroeconomic failures. The most obvious example would be Keynes's analysis of how a free market could get stuck in a position of widespread unemployment. If this is so, then it may be felt to be the responsibility of the government to raise employment through increasing demand in the economy. This could include paying people to produce goods and services, an act that would imply government provision.

All the above arguments can be described as instrumental in nature: they suggest that the government may improve the means of attaining the goal of the best possible production of goods and services. However, as with the case for market provision, government provision of certain goods and services may be seen as intrinsic to the goal of personal liberty. This would be so if a 'positive' view of liberty is taken which implies that people are only truly free to function and to fulfil their potential if they are provided with certain important necessities. These would include the provision of some basic health care and education. Thus the argument regarding personal freedom is not clearcut.

The case, then, for government involvement in the provision of goods and services appears strong. However, this is far less clearly so when it is realised that governments as well as markets can fail.

PROBLEMS WITH GOVERNMENT PROVISION: GOVERNMENT FAILURE

The whole discussion regarding the extent to which it is appropriate for governments to be involved with the provision of goods and services in an economy is further complicated by the existence of government failure. This means that when governments intervene, the intervention often either does not have the desired effect, or that it produces undesirable side effects, or both. There are various possible examples of such government failure.

A major difficulty facing any form of government intervention in the provision of goods and services concerns the level of information that the government requires if it is to make optimal decisions. One of the Austrian arguments in favour of the free market was how it imposed minimal informational requirements on the process of resource allocation. As long as individuals knew their own preferences, firms knew their own costs and everyone knew the relevant relative prices, then no more information was required. The same is not true if there is to be state provision. The state would have to have information regarding the preferences of all individuals and the costs of all firms if it were to ensure that the ideal provision were to be made. This is an impossibly high level of information to possess. The result of the requirement is that significant resources will have to be devoted towards the discovery of the relevant information. This can lead to high levels of government bureuacracy and may well be judged to be a poor use of the economy's resources as it does little directly to contribute towards utility. It may also create a class of bureaucrats who pursue their own objectives within the system, implying that the attainment of economic efficiency is not the first priority. The other problem implied is that all of the relevant information will never be fully gathered and therefore there is a significant chance of bad and inaccurate decisions being made. For example, it would be extremely difficult to know what would be the ideal level of provision of any particular public good.

Other failures of government intervention emanate from the perceived self-interest of politicians. Given the assumptions regarding the motivation of individuals usually made in economics, it might be reasonable to suggest that politicians may endeavour to see that all government intervention in the economy is geared to their own utility rather than that of the whole of the society. Given that the principal concern of politicians is often judged to be to ensure that they are re-elected, then the most obvious manifestation of this observation would be the political business cycle whereby the incumbent government attempts to ensure that the economy is in a boom as the nation approaches a general election. The economy may be deliberately manipulated in this fashion. If this is so, then the overriding concern of all government intervention in the economy is no longer whether it will lead to a greater level of economic efficiency, but rather whether it will help to contribute towards the re-election of the government. The two questions may sometimes yield the same answer, but equally they may sometimes give different answers.

Perhaps related to the above point is the tendency of politicians to attempt to embrace too many objectives, to promise too much. The problem is that the objectives may be contradictory, and thus there is no possibility of a coherent policy. There are several examples of this. One might be the impossibility of holding the objectives of simplicity and fairness within the tax system at the same time. This might imply that the tax system devised is not ideal.

Relating to the above point is the problem that in fact it is probably impossible to design an ideal tax system. This issue is discussed in Chapter 8 on taxation. If there is to be state provision of goods and services, then there must be taxation. It is possible to have taxes that do not distort economic behaviour (especially the incentive to work). An example would be a poll tax. However, recent experience suggests that such a tax would not be acceptable on equity grounds. Thus, to have a tax that is acceptable on equity grounds will mean that economic behaviour is distorted. This could lead to undesirable side effects, such as a sub-optimal level of work effort.

A further problem of government intervention is that the public service may be open to capture by interest groups. If this were to happen, then the service concerned could be run solely in the interests of the group concerned rather than the whole of the population. Perhaps the biggest alleged example of this is the capture of the Welfare State by the middle classes in the UK. It is sometimes suggested that the provision of the Welfare State, particularly in the area of health care and education, has become geared to satisfying the desires of the articulate and politically important middle classes. If this is so, then it would certainly make a nonsense of justifying the government provision of certain services on equity grounds.

A final problem with government intervention in the provision of goods and services concerns the existence of legislative rigidities. A quick and flexible government response (as may be required by a change in consumer preferences) is not legislatively possible. Decisions are made and then enacted some time after they may have first been appropriate. This is often felt to have been a problem with fiscal policy used to manipulate the level of aggregate demand. By the time the policy became effective, it was no longer appropriate.

Where then does this leave the debate concerning the relative merits of free market and government provision of goods and services? The answer must be, in a state of some uncertainty. From all of the preceding discussion, the only thing that economic theory can reasonably suggest is that there is a need to look at each particular case and to take some form of cost–benefit approach to deciding whether any particular good or service is best provided by the market or the government. It is highly unlikely that either system will be ideal, and thus it is a matter of choosing the least bad (or best) alternative. The rest of the chapter will look at two important cases in such a fashion: the provision of health care and education.

THE PROVISION OF HEALTH CARE

The correct role for the government with regard to the provision of health care is now a topic for earnest discussion in a fashion that was perhaps unthinkable during the post-war consensus on the Welfare State. Reflecting on the general discussion about the appropriate role of the government in the provision of goods and services, it can be suggested that from an economic perspective, the case for the state provision of health care was based upon the perception of significant market failures within the health care market. On the other hand, recent concern to try to change the nature of government provision owes much to concern regarding government failure. This section of the chapter will consider both the nature of the market for health care (and thus the possible case for government intervention) and recent government reforms in attempting to introduce a quasi-market into the provision of health care in the UK.

THE NATURE OF THE MARKET FOR HEALTH CARE

The first point that needs to be made about the market for health care is that the demand involved is a derived demand. While it may be possible that certain individuals derive utility from the process of health care itself, the principal reason for wanting health care is in order to become healthy. It is a means to an end. It is important to be aware of this from the outset as some of the peculiarities of this market stem from the nature of the demand involved: the market is more complex than it would be with non-derived demand.

It should be remembered that the fundamental theorems of welfare economics suggested that there is no role for the government in providing a service if a fully competitive market exists. Thus the way that the health care market will be investigated will be to look at how it compares with the fully competitive model and to consider how government intervention may be seen as necessary or desirable in order to overcome deficiencies in the market if it is left entirely to its own devices.

The first way in which the health care market may diverge from the fully competitive model is in the fact that people care about other people's health. There could be three possible reasons for this. The first is that individuals are affected by the health of other individuals. This would be most obviously the case with contagious diseases. In this case, an effective vaccine would benefit not only the person concerned but others as well. Thus the social value is greater than the private value and there could be a tendency for the market to under-provide. Therefore the state could have some role in provision. People may also be concerned about others' health simply through reasons of altruism. Thus utility is derived through others receiving appropriate health care. This could be resolved through private charity, but there may be the problem that people try to 'free ride' the charity of others in the hope that they do not have to contribute themselves. If everyone behaves in this way, health care is under-provided and there is a case for some form of government intervention. A final reason why people may care about the health of others concerns a desire for equity. This is by no means a straightforward issue (regardless of the value judgements that are involved). What sort of equality may be desired is unclear. Is it equality of expenditure on all people, equality of access, equality of use, or equality of health that is sought? Studies into the use of the National Health Service in the UK have sometimes suggested that is the middle classes who have derived the most effective use of the health care that is provided, despite the fact that all studies on health indicate that it is not the middle classes who suffer most ill health. Thus justifying the provision of health care by the government on equity grounds has, in practice, not been at all clear.

Various different problems occur in the health care market due to failures of information. Health care can be seen to suffer particularly from the problems involved with insurance markets that were discussed earlier. The state of one's health would seem to be an obvious example against which risk-averse individuals would wish to insure. However, the problems of adverse selection and moral hazard are likely to mean that the market does not function well. There is the further problem in the health care market that the probability of illness for certain individuals may well approach one. Given the transactions costs that are involved in any insurance arrangement, this implies that these particular people (typically the old and those with congenital health problems) will receive no cover. Thus there appears to be an important role for the government in improving the functioning of the market for health insurance, perhaps by taking full responsibility for all health insurance. This may or may not involve providing the health care as well.

The health care market by its very nature is characterised by asymmetric information. A major element of health care provision involves people visiting their GPs in order to obtain information about their health that they do not already possess. In the arena of a private market, consumers can be seen as buying information. Thus the nature of the relationship between patient and doctor is intrinsically one of asymmetric information. This relationship can best be understood within the context of principal–agent relationships. A principal (in this case the patient) delegates actions to an agent (the doctor) that are necessary to achieve certain outcomes (an improvement in the health of the patient). The relationship can become a problem if the principal and the agent have conflicting objectives. It is clear that given the intrinsic asymmetry of information that characterises a patient/doctor relationship, patients should wish to delegate some responsibility for decision-making to the doctor. The question is whether objectives will conflict. This is not entirely clear. Doctors may possess a range of different objectives (including status, income, leisure, satisfaction of a good diagnosis and others) some of which are more likely to clash with the objectives of patients than others. One possibility is that there may be 'supplier induced demand', a situation where there is more demand for health care than if the patient possessed all the relevant information and were to make the decision himself or herself. This could happen if the doctor could increase his or her income by recommending certain treatments and would clearly lead to an over-production of some health care. This is a clear example of a market failure. It will then be necessary to ensure that there are appropriate institutions that guard against this. It might be necessary to monitor the behaviour of doctors or to construct an income scheme that gave no incentive for supplier induced demand. However, the easiest choice is to have a code of ethics that would simply outlaw the possibility of such practice. This could be seen as one of the aspects of having a health service that does not have any goal of profit maximisation within it so that doctors are not encouraged to behave in a way that maximises their income in a fashion that was undesirable for economic efficiency.

A further characteristic of the health care industry is that there is restricted entry of suppliers. There is a form of licensing insofar as medical practitioners are required to have various qualifications. This is designed to protect consumers of health care, but it does confer a certain monopoly power on those who have the qualifications and implies that they do not face full competition. Similarly, there may be some increasing returns to scale in the health care industry. The significance of this probably depends upon the population density of any particular area. If population is not dense, then increasing returns could imply the possibility of local natural monopolies for hospitals and possibly even for GPs. This is another example of market failure and can again be seen as justifying some role for the government in the provision of health care.

The market for health care thus appears to suffer from considerable imperfections and much possible legitimate reason for the intervention of the government in health care. The complication is to know what form that intervention should take. The answer in the UK since the Second World War has been that intervention should take the form of both provision and finance of health care. However, the recent health care reforms appear to suggest that the answer may now lie in the government having a role in financing health care but not necessarily in providing it.

Before turning to the recent reforms to the health service, one final problem concerning the provision of health care needs to be explained. If it is decided that it is not appropriate to provide all health care through the market with resources being allocated according to consumers' willingness to pay certain prices for different treatments, then a different system for allocating health care resources will have to be found. This presents a considerable problem and it is by no means clear that there is a fully coherent system which dictates the distribution of health care resources in the absence of the market (indeed, long waiting lists might be seen as the alternative to market prices). One possibility that has been suggested by economists is the use of QALYs (quality adjusted life years). Without going into great technical detail, this implies calculating the extent to which a treatment is judged to improve the quality of life over however many years. This figure (which is a measurement of the benefit gained through health care) can then be compared with the cost of each treatment, and some judgement can be made about which treatments represent good uses of resources. Such a system could be a way of endeavouring to ensure the optimum use of health care resources in the absence of market prices.

REFORMS TO THE PROVISION OF HEALTH CARE

The pressures for reform of health care in the UK can be seen as emanating from three sources:

1. Concern over the level of expenditure on health care. In 1992, health care expenditure accounted for 6.5 per cent of the UK's GDP. This compares with 4.5 per cent in 1970. The major reasons for this appear to be the cost of ever more complex medical technology, an ageing population, and the continually rising expectations of the population regarding the level and standard of health care. The concern is that without some sort of reform, health care could swallow up an ever-increasing amount of national income and make impossible demands on the economy.
2. Concern that health care was not being provided efficiently. Thus it might be possible to achieve a greater improvement in health care status for a given level of expenditure. Much of the problem was felt to stem from inappropriate incentives, for example the fact that all treatment is free to consumers, implying an incentive to over-use, and the fact that the system could provide incentives to doctors and hospitals to provide too much care in an effort to maximise income. Thus it was seen as necessary to change incentives in an effort to achieve a better outcome.
3. Concern over possible inequitable provision. In the UK, this was particularly expressed over the length of waiting lists in certain areas. The solution was seen as the need to introduce some competition in order to reduce waiting lists (not to increase resources to health care).

Against this background, the government White Paper, *Working for Patients*, was published in 1989. As stated before, it can be characterised as a continuing commitment by the government to finance health care, but not necessarily to be the provider of health care. The new arrangements can be summed up in Figure 7.1.

The system before the reforms was that all NHS finance went through the District Health Authorities and all NHS hospitals were managed by the District Health Authority. The two key aspects to the reforms have thus been to allow GPs with more than 9000 patients to become fundholders and to receive their finance directly and to spend it as they see fit in the provision of health care for their patients, and to allow hospitals to become trusts so that they can govern themselves rather than being managed by District Health Authorities. These measures can be seen as an attempt to create competition for the provision of health care in the belief that this may increase efficiency. Thus the new system

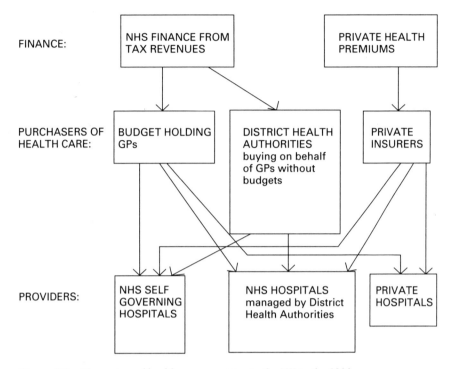

Figure 7.1   *The system of health care provision in the UK in the 1990s*

may be described as the introduction of a 'quasi-market' (sometimes referred to as an internal market).

A quasi-market is exactly as the term suggests. It is an attempt to create a sort of market, but it is one that does not fully correspond to a fully functioning free market. It is a market insofar as it creates some competition in the provision of a particular service. However, it is different from a free market in that on the supply side it is far from clear that the institutions concerned will aim to max-imise profits and the institutions are predominantly owned by the public sector. On the demand side, consumers' purchasing power is represented not directly by money spent but by earmarked budgets that become available to institutions when consumers use their services.

The overall aim, then, of a quasi-market is to introduce competition which will force greater 'x'-efficiency and thus lower costs upon the providers of health care. Those providers of health care that do not minimise their costs will find that they will lose custom to other hospitals who do minimise costs and are thus able to offer the same services at a lower price. The level of allocative efficiency should also be improved insofar as the quasi-market permits greater choice than was previously available. This is simply the classic case in favour of competition discussed earlier in the chapter.

It is certainly too early to be able to draw any clear conclusions regarding the effects of introducing a quasi-market into the provision of health care. However, various observations are possible. It is not entirely clear how much patient choice will actually be increased through the reforms. There are likely to be problems of information and inertia stopping patients from readily changing their GPs. Equally, there is the possibility of providers and purchasers becoming locked into agreements given the possible benefits of a long-run relationship. It is also possible that the result of the competitive process for health care provision could be the development of more local monopolies insofar as there are further economies of scale to be exploited which are currently not being exploited. Thus there is the ironic possibility that the introduction of competition could have the long-run effect of destroying competition.

A further problem with quasi-markets is likely to arise due to the transactions costs of writing and monitoring contracts for the provision of health care. There will be costs involved initially in the negotiation of contracts and then subsequent costs in attempting to ensure that the contract obligations are fulfilled. Given the level of uncertainty and imperfect information that characterises the health care market, this may be a difficult and costly task and may require the use of considerable health care resources in a way that does not directly lead to the provision of health care.

There are concerns that the system created will lead to a two-tier system with the suggestion that patients belonging to GP fundholders will do better than others as they are given preferential treatment on waiting lists and receive a higher level of funding. It is not easy to see how this is intrinsic to the introduction of a quasi-market, and it must be suggested that it has more to do with the rules that have been given to the game which may be skewed in favour of fundholders. This need not be the case. Perhaps of greater concern is the point regarding equity, that the system gives an incentive to GPs to try to select patients that are of low risk since they are likely to need a low level of expenditure relative to the funds that they provide the GP. This would no doubt be considered as unethical behaviour, but there must be a concern that the introduction of a quasi-market may lead to a more profit-maximising ethos within the medical profession (indeed, this can be seen as part of the purpose of the reforms) and that this might make more abuses of the system (as are feasible with a situation of asymmetric information) likely in order for doctors and hospitals to maximise their income. It must be hoped that Adam Smith's 'sense of duty', as described in his *Theory of Moral Sentiments*, in some ways proves stronger than his better-known description of people's regard for their own interest, as mentioned in his *Wealth of Nations*.

The final point that needs to be made about the health care reforms is that they clearly still leave the health care market significantly imperfect. As such, there must be a very strong case for the introduction of an independent regulator. This has been seen as crucial to the possible success of some of the major privatisations, and it should be no less important with the developments in the health care market.

FURTHER EXAMPLES OF THE REFORMS IN THE PROVISION OF HEALTH CARE

The United Kingdom has not been alone in attempts to reform its system for the provision of health care since the 1980s. Two other important cases in point are provided by the Netherlands and the USA.

The Netherlands

The Netherlands provides an alternative example of the possible direction of the reform of the provision of health care within Europe. Here the reforms involve a basic compulsory insurance system for the whole of the population. Income-related funds are paid into a central fund. This central fund then pays risk-related premiums to independent insurers. The purpose of this is to try to ensure that there is competition created in the finance sector involving the insurance against ill health. The central fund gives a voucher to permit individuals to enrol in the insurance scheme of their choice. Thus, regulated competition is created as insurers have to compete in order to gain consumers and consumers are permitted to choose the providers of health care. On behalf of the consumers, insurers draw out a contract with providers of health care. Thus the providers of health care must also compete with each other in order to gain these contracts. The whole system is introduced to competitive forces. The expectation is that this competition should lead to low cost and good quality provision, both by the insurance sector and the provision of health care sector. One interesting point is that it does not need to rely on any provision by the government. If the government were a provider of health care, it would be in competition with private providers. The role of the government is restricted to the payment of risk-related insurance premiums from the central fund to which all make an income-related contribution. Thus, the solution seen is very much market orientated.

The USA

One of the most interesting case histories of the possible reform of health care in a country was Clinton's attempt to reform health care provision in the USA. There is a state system of health care provision in the USA in the form of Medicaid which provides for those on low income through general taxes. Medicare, which is part state funded, also helps to provide for those above the age of retirement, those on renal dialysis and those permanently disabled. The rest of the system relies on private insurance and direct charges by health care providers.

There are problems with the health care system as it exists. About 14 per cent of the population is not insured by either the public or the private system. Health care provision takes up approximately 14 per cent of GDP. These costs have been increasing in real terms for some time. Firms' costs are significantly affected as they often pay the health care insurance premiums of their employees. Workers are thus also reluctant to move their employment for fear of losing these health care benefits. Despite these costs, health care provision cannot be judged to be better than the rest of the world in terms of the USA's relatively high infant mortality rate and low life expectancy.

Why have these problems arisen? There are several perceived reasons. The first is one of the standard problems of any insurance sytem: moral hazard. Once a person is insured, there is no disincentive to use the fullest possible range of health care services that are available. The decentralised insurance sytem also has extremely high administration costs: over 20 per cent of all health care spending is on this administration alone. There is also an element of what may be described as 'cost shifting': the uninsured are effectively paid for by increasing prices to all private patients.

It was to address these difficulties that Clinton's reforms were intended. The proposed system gave a guaranteed universal coverage at a constant premium. There was then to be the formation of regional health alliances to which all individuals would have to enrol. These would then purchase health plans from insurers. The regional health alliances would offer all members a menu of different types of health plans from which they could choose. Members would have the right to change their plans each year. Employers would be expected to meet 80 per cent of the average premium charged by the health alliance, the rest then being paid by individuals. There would be a cap on the total amount that any employer would be expected to contribute: a maximum of 7.9 per cent of the total payroll. Anything above this would be financed by the state. There would also be provision made for those not employed. Costs would be controlled by the market power of the regional health alliances who would force providers of insurance and health care to be competitive. The rate of growth of premiums would also be capped to rise by a maximum of the current rate of inflation. Thus, these reforms were not a clear move to greater marketisation, as in the UK and the Netherlands, but rather a reorganisation, still relying on the power of market forces, to try to make the system work better.

Why then did Clinton's health care reforms fail? Several factors can be distinguished. The first is that there were very powerful political lobbies opposing their progress. The health care insurance business is very strong. The second problem with the scheme appeared to be the suggestion that the employers should pay such a large percentage of the premiums. There is no logical reason why this should be the case: it appears an accident of history that employers currently pay most health care insurance premiums. Finally the cost looked set to be 83 billion dollars in the year 2000: higher than under the current system.

THE PROVISION OF EDUCATION

Having studied the case for government provision of health care, the approach to the provision of education can be very similar. It will be a matter of considering where and how a free market in education may suffer from important imperfections and thus what the appropriate government response may be. Again, recent government reforms appear to be changing the precise role of government intervention, especially through the creation of a quasi-market, and these will be examined.

THE NATURE OF THE MARKET FOR EDUCATION

One of the principal problems in the market for health care concerned lack of information, particularly information asymmetries. It is interesting to consider to what extent this can be deemed to be a problem in the market for education. Perhaps the major difficulty in this area concerns the fact that, with regard to school education, the decision-maker is not the consumer of the education, but is rather the parent who makes the decision on behalf of the child. This could be felt to create difficulties if the interests and objectives of the child conflict with those of the parent. Thus, there may be a role for the government to force a certain level of schooling upon children by force of law and/or free provision. However, this is a difficult argument insofar as it clearly suggests that there is a legitimate paternalistic role for the state and that the government is a better judge than parents of what is required for a child's welfare. This is a strong value judgement and one that would probably not meet with universal accord.

A further problem regarding information may concern a lack of parental information regarding school education. There could be significant incentives for those working in schools to present inaccurate or distorted information regarding the quality of education in order to attract pupils to a school so as to maximise income. It may be very difficult to guard against this given that gathering full information could require significant costs to parents (especially in terms of the time that may be involved). In addition, the decision, once made, may be considered as irreversible insofar as it may be some time after joining a certain school that the initial information is found to be inaccurate, and during this time significant sunk costs are likely to be invested in the school, such as friendships formed and the settling in to a certain routine and style of school. Thus, the consequences of inaccurate information can be very costly. This again suggests a possible role for the government so that undesirable choices are not made. However, whether that role should be one of providing information, compelling attendance at certain schools or some other possibility is not clear.

Probably the biggest market failure that is attributed to the market for education is the size of the external benefits involved in education. The suggestion is that the benefit to society of an individual being educated is greater than the benefits that accrue only to the individual concerned. The private benefits of education might be considered to be any utility that is gained by the individual through the process of education and the future higher level of income that is gained due to the individual's investment in human capital. However, there may be further benefits to the whole of society that go beyond these. Included amongst these external benefits might be the benefits of a more ordered society which required, for example, less resources to be used on crime prevention, and better coordination and cooperation between people which could, for example, be of benefit in team settings within industry. Other possibilities are that democracy should function more effectively if voters are better informed due to their education, and that the general level of utility may be higher if people's potential has been properly realised through education leading to, for example, the production of good poetry and the arts. The problem, then, of leaving the provision of education to the market would be that there would be an under-provision: people would only consider their private benefits when deciding the level of education that they desired. Thus there could be a role for the government to ensure that there is not this under-provision. That role might or might not involve the direct provision of education. One difficulty, however, in this area is the very imprecise nature of the external benefits that are suggested. This is not to say that they are not legitimate, but simply that it is perhaps impossible to measure them and decide how they compare with the private benefits of education. Thus it is extremely difficult to suggest what may be the optimal level of education for a society.

Another potential problem with the market provision of education concerns a possible capital market failure. If people are to increase their human capital through education, and thus to increase their future income, they should be able to borrow against that future income to finance current education. The problem is that the size of the increased income returns due to education is extremely uncertain, and thus financial institutions may be reluctant to lend, or may only lend at high rates of interest. Thus financing desirable education could prove to be more difficult than should ideally be the case. This suggests another possible reason for government intervention of an appropriate form, provision or otherwise.

Economies of scale are unlikely to provide a significant market failure within the education market as long as there are reasonable population densities. There are possibilities of local natural monopolies developing in sparsely populated rural areas, and this could provide a reason for some government intervention, possibly provision.

The most significant argument for the provision of education by the government is probably the non-economic argument of equity. Provision of a certain level of education for all may be judged to be fundamentally desirable in its own right, if people are to be free to do that of which they may be capable. There are complications, however, with this. Equality of educational opportunites could have three meanings:

1. Equal amounts of education for everyone.
2. Education sufficient to bring everyone to a certain standard.
3. Education sufficient to permit everyone to reach their endowed potential.

The third meaning is often taken to be the aim, but then the suggestion is that educational resources should be distributed according to the capacity to learn, and the capacity to learn may often be greater in children from well-educated backgrounds. Thus a meritocracy is created and possibly proves to be self-perpetuating. Whether this would be seen as desirable on equity grounds is unclear.

Thus there may be several possible reasons why there could be a legitimate role for the government in the education market. In the UK, this has led to a system of state provision. Recent concern and dissatisfaction with that system has prompted the government to introduce various reforms into the provision of education in the belief that these will increase the level of efficiency in that provision.

REFORMS TO THE PROVISION OF EDUCATION

The essence of recent government reforms to the provision of education in the UK is similar to that in health care insofar as the key element is an attempt to introduce a quasi-market in the belief that this will lead to greater technical and allocative efficiency. The 1988 Education Reform Act introduced, amongst other things, a system whereby institutions are compelled to compete for state-funded students. Educational establishments were to be funded simply upon the number of students wishing to attend, and the individual establishments were to be given freedom to use those funds as they themselves saw fit. Two further interesting reforms have been the introduction of student loans rather than full government provision for the maintenance of students in higher education, and the use of 'league tables' available to the general public giving various pieces of information regarding all schools in the country.

It should be noted that the market is rightly described as 'quasi', as it lacks various features of a true market:

1. No money for funding education finds its way to private providers.
2. There is no free entry to potential providers of education.
3. Parental choice is limited due to the National Curriculum.
4. Teachers' salaries are set nationally rather than being determined by individual institutions.

The belief is that forcing schools and other educational establishments to compete for funds by attracting students should ensure that the provision matches the desires of the 'consumer' (the student or the parent). Only by providing what is wanted will educational establishments gain funding, and this should help to improve allocative efficiency. In addition, the system provides an incentive to improve 'x'-efficiency, because an ability to provide an educational service at the lowest possible cost will give the establishment the chance to use any surplus funding that may thus be accrued (or a failure to minimise costs will mean that the funding is insufficient to cover the services provided).

The league tables can be seen as attempting to overcome some of the information deficiencies that exist in the market for education. They are designed to allow parents to make a more informed choice regarding schools, and thus to help allocative efficiency. There has been much concern, however, regarding the nature of information that is provided, namely examination results and truancy records. Most research suggests that the fundamental determinants of these factors are the nature of the children who enter the school in the first place. If schools are to be judged by these criteria, then there is a clear incentive for schools to try to exclude 'bad risks' (a known truant) and to ensure that its intake is such that should ensure a good performance in the league tables. Thus the system that has been created is likely to have an inherent tendency to introduce selectivity into the provision of education as schools try to gain candidates of a high ability. This may be seen as either a desirable or an undesirable development of the quasi-market. It has led to suggestions that it would be better to try to measure the 'value-added' (i.e., the level of improvement) gained through attending a particular school. The problem with this is that it is less easy to measure than simple examination results.

The introduction of student loans rather than full government provision of a maintenance grant for those in higher education stems from the suggestion that because there are considerable private benefits to be gained through higher education it is reasonable to expect students to have to pay. As noted earlier, it is extremely difficult to determine the size of the external benefits due to education compared with the private benefits, and thus also difficult to obtain the correct equation. It is also thought that loans may discourage students from higher education because of the uncertainty regarding the precise impact upon future income. It has therefore been suggested that some form of graduate tax might be preferable as this would be payable in proportion to the extra income that was earned following higher education, but would not be paid unless income rose to a certain level.

CONCLUSION

The case for government intervention in the provision of certain goods and services appears clear when considering the nature of the market failures involved. However, this picture is less clear when government failure exists. The discussion is complicated considerably by concerns over equity. In the case of health care and education, concerns over equity and market failure have led to a system of state provision. Recently, dissatisfaction with this system has led to the introduction of quasi-markets for health care and education in the belief that this will help to provide a more efficient provision. The consequences of this can only be judged over a long period of time, but it is important to notice that significant market failures are bound to continue to persist in both markets.

8 Taxation

We all dislike taxes. They are seen as a (perhaps) necessary evil. An ability to reduce taxes is perceived as an important ingredient for any incumbent government wishing to win a forthcoming general election (see Chapter 13 on political business cycles). Lower taxes produce a 'feel-good' factor. It is believed that people do not work as hard as they might due to the existence of taxes. The purpose of this chapter is to look at what economics has to say about taxation. Why do we have to have taxes? Are some taxes better or worse than others? Do some tax systems work better than others? Economic theory has much to contribute on these and other questions relating to taxation.

In particular, this chapter will look at three aspects of taxation:

1. What is the rationale for taxation? Why is it deemed necessary to have taxes, given their evident unpopularity? Certain fundamental economic principles can be used to suggest when, and when not, taxes are needed.
2. What makes a 'good' tax? Given that it may be necessary to have a tax system, what attributes make for better, or worse, taxes? Included in this section is an overview of the arguments concerning the effect of taxation on the incentive to work.
3. How can the principles of taxation discussed in the second section be applied to particular tax issues? Three specific applications will be explored:
    (a) What is the ideal structure for an income tax system?
    (b) What is the ideal way of taxing commodities?
    (c) Should museums charge people to visit them?

It will be seen that the application of some important economic principles can lead to some significant suggestions regarding issues relating to taxation.

WHY TAX? THE RATIONALE FOR TAXATION

It appears to be rather a fundamental question as to why governments force their citizens to pay taxes. Presumably it is not due to any particular sadistic pleasure that those in power may derive from such action. However, much discussion about taxes often by-passes this initial basic question and proceeds to look at issues pertaining to taxation, assuming that they simply exist. So, why tax?

As with most fundamental questions in economics, the answer can usually be found by referring back to first principles. Here, the fundamental theorems of welfare economics appear pertinent (see Chapter 7 on the government provision of goods and services). These can be summarised as:

1. A perfectly functioning free market will lead to a position of Pareto Optimality (a welfare position that cannot be unambiguously improved), given any initial distribution of income.
2. Any desired optimal outcome for an economy is possible, given an appropriate initial distribution of income.

From this, it follows that there are two possible legitimate economic roles for the government:

1. The correction of market failures where there is not a perfectly functioning market.
2. The redistribution of resources and income.

The role of taxation needs to fit within the above framework. Given that a tax is a form of government intervention in the economy, the two possible economic reasons for imposing taxes are firstly to help to correct market failures, and secondly to redistribute income and other resources.

With regard to redistributing resources within society, it might appear that the obvious and best thing to do is to set taxes so that those with higher incomes pay a higher proportion of their income in tax than those on lower incomes. Indeed, taxes are often categorised in three ways, reflecting how they may redistribute income in this fashion. A progressive tax is one that ensures that higher income earners pay a higher percentage of their income in tax in the manner just described. A proportional tax implies that all income earners pay exactly the same percentage of their income in tax. A regressive tax is one where those on higher incomes pay a lower percentage of their income in tax than those on lower incomes. In fact, from an economic point of view, all taxes on actual earned income are not ideal because they are bound to distort the incentive to work in some fashion. It would be better to tax the earning capacity of an individual rather than his or her actual earnings as a redistribution could be achieved in this fashion, but it would not create distortions in the same way since there would be no avoiding such a tax. Unfortunately, such a tax does not appear possible to organise, as will be discussed in the next section of the chapter. Thus redistributive taxes are seen in light of their impact on actual earned incomes.

The other role for taxation may be in correcting, or at least improving, market failures. The easiest way of considering the possible role of taxation here is to consider certain market failures and how appropriate taxation may be used as a means of intervention when compared to other tools that may be available to a government.

A commonly perceived failure of market economies is the anticipated lack of provision of public goods due to the problem of 'free riding'. (For an explanation of these and other market failures, see Chapter 7.) Taxation seems to have no helpful direct role here. Incentives cannot clearly be altered through the tax system in such a way as to make private provision and purchase of public goods profitable. The usual recommendation is that the government needs to intervene by directly providing the good. Of course, taxation can still be seen as having an indirect role here as it is the method through which governments are likely to raise finance in order to provide the public good.

Lack of perfect information is a common market failure. Particular problems can be caused by asymmetrical information where one party to a trade has more information than another. This allows the possibility of a transaction that is not mutually advantageous as one party does not realise that it is not gaining. A purchaser of a second-hand car may be unaware of certain defects that are possessed by the car, and thus embark upon a transaction that appears to be of mutual advantage, but given full information, the purchaser would not have entered into the trade. Thus the market fails. It is not at all clear how taxation could be seen as an appropriate form of government intervention here. Some form of regulation, perhaps via the legal system, is the type of government intervention that could combat the failure. Thus, the role of taxation would simply be to finance any costs involved in the regulation.

The tendency of the free market to create monopolies, for example due to the existence of substantial economies of scale in certain industries, is another source of market failure. Prices are not equal to marginal cost and cost inefficiencies may be generated. It is possible that the tax system could be used to move marginal cost closer to price by subsidising output, and thus raising output and lowering price. However, the information needed to get this equation correct would be considerable, and the usual form of government intervention that is seen as most effective is to regulate any monopolies that may exist, for example by setting pricing rules as in the case of the privatised utilities in the United Kingdom.

Coase's analysis suggested that the failing of markets could in many ways be seen as deriving from a lack of property rights (see Chapter 6). Thus, seas are over-fished because no one has ownership rights of the sea and thus no charge is made for fishing. Fishing thus continues until the marginal utility derived from the activity has fallen to a low level. The response of the government here might be to create an ownership structure through the legal system to ensure that there were likely to be charges for the use of resources. It might then be deemed appropriate to tax the owners for any excessive rents that they were thought to have gained due to selling the right to use the resource. However, the tax here would be being used for redistribution purposes rather than correcting a market failure.

The existence of merit and demerit goods can be seen to create a further failure of the market. Merit goods are under-provided by the market and demerit goods are over-provided. One version of what is viewed as a merit or demerit good is based on paternalism: consumers do or do not consume certain products due to a lack of full information and understanding. If people fully appreciated how cigarettes were not desirable for them, then they would not make the decision to consume them that is currently made. There are several ways that the government could attempt to correct this perceived failure. One of them is clearly to use an appropriate tax which raises the price of cigarettes and thus deters consumption. Here, then, there may be the possibility of a direct role for taxation in correcting market failure.

External costs and benefits cause either an over-production or an underproduction of the product in question. For example, firms do not have to pay directly for the cost of pollution that may be created through the production process that is employed. Thus private costs are below the true costs to society and this will result in the market price being lower than that required for an optimal level of production. Thus demand and supply will be too high. In this situation, a tax can be a highly appropriate form of government intervention. The tax can be used to raise the producer's costs by the value of the negative externality, and thus increase the firm's private costs to the level of the true social cost. Therefore the level of production will be lowered to its optimal level. One particular example of this under serious consideration in several developed nations is the use of road charging, a form of tax on road use. When motorists use roads at peak times, they create external costs on other motorists by contributing to congestion. This is not a cost likely to be considered in the individual decision-making of a motorist. Schemes could be introduced that involved motorists having to pay a charge for road use at peak times, thus taking account of the external cost created when a decision regarding road use is made.

From the above discussion of basic economic principles, three roles for a tax have emerged:

1.   The redistribution of income.
2.   The correction of certain market failures.
3.   The raising of finance for the provision of public goods and the expenses involved in the various types of government regulation used to correct market failures.

However, some economists would suggest a further possible role for taxation within macroeconomic policy. A Keynesian policy could involve the use of taxes to regulate the level of aggregate demand in the economy. Taxes could be cut in order to raise spending in the economy in a time of unemployed resources, or be raised to lower demand when spending is threatening to outstrip the capacity of the economy to produce. This may be seen as a fourth function of taxation, although an inappropriate level of demand in the economy, if it is seen as a theoretical possibility, could be seen as related to certain market failures (see Chapter 3 on microeconomics and macroeconomics).

Given this analysis, there is clearly a legitimate economic case for a government imposing taxes. Then a further important question must be asked: what is the best way in which to levy taxes? Given the unpopularity of taxes, this appears a particularly pertinent question. The next section of this chapter considers it.

THE PRINCIPLES OF TAXATION: OPTIMAL TAXATION THEORY

If a government is to tax, then it may be that there are better and worse ways of doing it. Given the level of taxation in developed countries, a better tax system could be extremely significant with regard to the optimal use of scarce resources than a less effective system. It would seem an important and legitimate area for economic theory to try to investigate. This is what the work of Diamond and Mirrlees (1971) aimed to do, resulting in what is now referred to 'optimal taxation' theory. However, the concern over the best design of taxes is hardly a recent one.

Smith (1776) suggested that four 'canons' of a good tax could be identified:

1. Economy. All taxes should be inexpensive to collect and should not discourage desirable business.
2. Convenience. All taxes should be collected in a manner that is convenient to the taxpayer.
3. Certainty. All taxes should be clear and easy to understand by the taxpayer.
4. Equity. All taxes should be judged to be 'fair'. As far as Smith was concerned, this meant in proportion to their income.

In many ways, the essence of what criteria can be used to judge taxes today has not changed a great deal from this list. All discussions regarding ideal taxes recognise three 'needs' that must always be considered:

1. The need for fairness, however that may be defined.
2. The need to minimise administrative costs involved in taxation.
3. The need to minimise the disincentive effects of taxes.

The ideal or optimal tax is one that can meet all of these needs. If all three needs suggested that the same sort of tax were desirable, then there would be very little to discuss, and the task of finding the optimal tax would be a relatively simple one. However, the essence of the problem is that needs one and three are seen, at least to some extent, to be in conflict with each other. To make a tax 'fairer' may require a greater disincentive effect. To reduce the disincentive effect of a tax may require making it less fair. This is the classic dilemma faced in the design of an ideal tax. It relates to what is seen as the general problem of the conflict between equity and efficiency in any economy.

Initially, it is easiest simply to consider the role of taxation to be the raising of finance for government expenditure. The possible role of taxes in correcting market failures, notably external costs, is not considered. Indeed, the theory of optimal taxation in its narrowest sense does not consider market failures. With this purpose of taxation, the key economic principle would seem to be not to distort the economy from its most efficient allocation of resources. This will mean not affecting the incentives that are present in the free market as these incentives are what are needed to ensure economic efficiency (see Chapter 7 on the state provision of goods and services). Thus, the essence of a desirable tax would seem to be one that cannot be avoided: there is no way that it would be possible to change behaviour in order to avoid payment. If this were the case, then economic incentives would not be affected, as regardless of what was done, the same tax would be paid. On this criteria, something such as a window tax (as once employed in the United Kingdom) would be a poor tax as it would provide an incentive to build houses with fewer windows. What are wanted are lump-sum taxes. There are several possibilities. The most obvious example is a poll tax: everyone (perhaps over a certain age) has to pay a certain level of taxation with no exceptions. This tax cannot be avoided and in no way distorts economic decisions. However, it is possible to think of other such taxes. These might be based on other unavoidable characteristics such as age, race or sex. The obvious question must be why these taxes are not used in practice, given that they are what is required if the market is not to be distorted. The answer is that they are deemed to contravene the other major principle of taxation, that of equity. Lump-sum taxes of the sort mentioned above are not seen as desirable because they are deemed to be inequitable. The most vivid example of this is the brief recent history of the Community Charge in the United Kingdom. The briefness of its existence was principally due to the fact that it was perceived to be inequitable, and thus it received insufficient support from the nation to allow it to be continued.

If such lump-sum taxes as the poll tax are seen to be impossible due to their unfair nature, then other taxes, such as those on earned income have to be considered. The problem with these taxes, however, is that they do distort economic behaviour. For example, an income tax affects the incentive to work and thus may distort behaviour from what is economically most efficient. That is the fundamental problem of tax design: how to devise a tax that is deemed to be equitably acceptable, but at the same time minimises the undesirable distortion of economic incentives. Before pursuing this issue further, it is worth noting that an alternative tax which did not distort incentives and yet might be considered equitable could, in principle, exist. If it were possible to calculate the earning potential of every individual, then a tax could be charged which varied according to that potential. There would be no way of avoiding such a tax by altering behaviour, and such a tax could be deemed equitable as those with higher income potential would pay a higher tax than those with a lower potential. Unfortunately, it is not possible to see how such an ideal tax could be constructed. The information required could not be obtained. Even if it were possible to obtain much genuine data, the calculation would not be simple. However, there is a very strong incentive for people not to provide accurate information and to behave in a way that does not reveal their true earning potential, for by hiding such information, tax paid can be reduced. Thus, there seems little alternative to the use of distortionary taxes by governments.

Before proceeding further with the analysis, two important points need to be made. The first is that the issue of equity or fairness is one with which economists are not entirely comfortable. Many economists like to see the subject as (relatively) free of value judgements (see Chapter 1 on economic methodology). The concept of equity is one that clearly involves value judgements. How equal or unequal we believe the distribution of resources should be within society depends considerably upon our value system. How, then, do economists deal with this issue? The answer is that they provide a range of possible policy suggestions depending on the level of equality that is deemed to be desirable. However, they would not make a judgement as to which should be deemed the most desirable. That is for society, via the political process, to decide. The general assumption that is made regarding society's desire for a tax system is that it should reduce income inequalities when compared with the pre-tax income. The amount by which that inequality should be reduced is for people to exercise their value judgements on. The value judgements made will affect what is considered to be the optimal tax to some extent. However, there are certain principles which it may be possible to apply, regardless of what is deemed to be the ideal distribution of income.

The second point to consider is how the level of distortion introduced by the introduction of a particular tax might be measured. Economists have a concept termed 'deadweight loss' or 'excess burden' which endeavours to measure the loss of economic welfare due to the distortion caused by any tax. Perhaps the easiest way to try to understand this concept is to consider the impact of the introduction of an indirect tax, such as some form of sales tax, as illustrated on a supply and demand diagram (Figure 8.1).

The tax shifts the supply schedule to the left since it is equivalent to an increase in the costs of firms. The value of the tax is measured by the vertical distance between the two supply schedules. Some of this extra cost is passed on to the consumer as the price of the product concerned rises. The net impact is that price rises and quantity sold falls in the manner indicated on the diagram. The problem is that mutually advantageous trades have now been discouraged due to the introduction of the tax. This is the welfare loss or deadweight loss or excess burden. It can be expressed more precisely by the loss of consumer surplus and producer surplus that has arisen due to the tax. The areas concerned are shaded and represent a (potentially) measurable loss of economic welfare. The problem with any tax that creates a distortion in economic behaviour is that it will lead to some form of deadweight loss of the sort illustrated. The objective must be to try to minimise that loss.

The distortion of economic behaviour that is most usually associated with taxation is the incentive to work. This has generally been particularly associated with income taxes, although it is worth noting that expenditure taxes should logically have a similar effect if it is assumed that the general purpose of earning income is to spend that income, either now or in the future. In the 1980s, the deleterious effects of income tax on the incentive to work were considered to be so significant that it was deemed to be vital to reduce marginal rates of income tax. In 1988, Nigel Lawson, the then British Chancellor of the Exchequer, in his Budget Speech summed up the situation thus:

The reason for the worldwide trend towards lower rates of tax is clear. Excessive rates of income tax destroy enterprise, encourage avoidance, and drive talent to more hospitable shores overseas. As a result, far from raising additional revenue, over time they actually raise less.

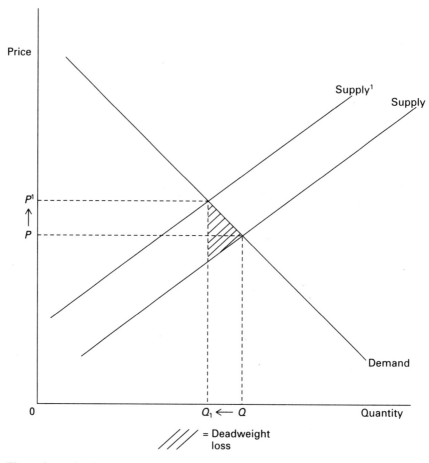

Figure 8.1   *The deadweight loss arising from a sales tax*

These are significant words, not least because the economic beliefs suggested in them guided the economic policies of several western countries during the 1980s. It is thus important to consider what economic theory has to suggest about the probable impact of income tax on the incentive to work.

Lawson's ideas regarding the relationship between the tax rate and tax revenue derives from the suggestion of the Laffer curve. The origin of this simple schedule is the observation by Laffer that if tax rates are set at 0 per cent then there will be no tax revenue. Equally, if tax rates are set at 100 per cent there will be no tax revenue because no one will work as there will be zero payment received for any work done. Given those two starting points, Figure 8.2 must, according to Laffer, be logically true.

The suggestion is clearly that tax revenue will by no means be maximised at high rates of tax because of the disincentive effects that such taxes have upon

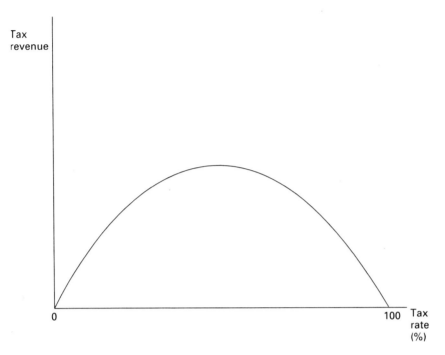

Figure 8.2 *The Laffer curve*

work effort. Unfortunately, Figure 8.2 tells us little of great help, as either of the two shapes of the Laffer curve in Figure 8.3 are just as plausible as the one suggested above.

Thus we still do not know whether very high or very low rates of taxation are likely to be the best revenue raisers. With the Laffer curve, it is still possible that high tax rates will raise most revenue.

The best way to consider the possible impact of an income tax on the incentive to work is to use some simple indifference analysis. This helps to clarify that there are two different types of effect on the incentive to work, due to the imposition of an income tax or a change in the rate of taxation. These two effects correspond to the substitution and income effects that can be identified in economic analysis as arising from any change in price. Consider Figure 8.4.

Several points about this diagram require clarification. The first is that the choice faced by an individual decision-maker is represented as being that between leisure and consumption, both of which are considered to be items that yield positive utility to the individual. This reflects an important assumption behind the analysis, namely that work is considered to be a disutility. People do not enjoy their work (in fact they positively dislike it) and thus the only purpose of work is to earn income with which to purchase consumer goods and services which do yield utility. Thus a decision has to be made between having more

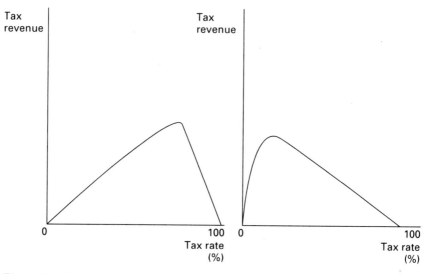

Figure 8.3   *Alternative shapes for the Laffer curve*

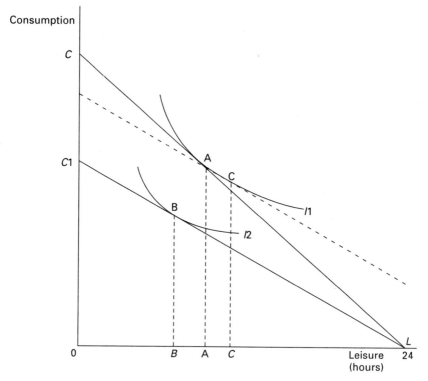

Figure 8.4   *The effect of an increase in income tax on the number of hours worked*

leisure (working less) and having more consumption (working more). The question is how income tax may affect this decision-making process.

It should be noted that the above assumption may not be accepted. Those who are unemployed appear often to want work not simply because it would improve their financial position, but also because there are certain positive attributes associated with being in paid employment which are not solely due to monetary remuneration. The desire to work appears important for feelings of worth and prestige, things that would be identified with positive utility. If this is so, then this analysis would become less clearcut since work as well as leisure could be seen as yielding utility.

With this important point borne in mind, Figure 8.4 shows the following economic analysis. The indifference curves ($I1$, $I2$) illustrate combinations of leisure and consumption that give the same level of utility. The aim of the utility maximising individual is to reach the highest possible indifference curve, given the constraints of the relevant budget line. The amount of consumption possible depends upon the hourly wage rate that is currently paid. Thus, the budget line (such as LC) indicates the different levels of leisure and consumption that are possible, depending on how the individual divides his/her time between work and leisure. Thus, the starting level of leisure (and corresponding work level) is at point A, where the marginal rate of substitution between leisure and consumption is equal to the price ratio between leisure and goods (the wage rate).

The government then increases the rate of income tax from this point. The effect of this is, other things being equal, to pivot the budget line in the manner indicated from LC to $LC1$ so that less consumption can now be afforded as less income is now received, given the higher tax rate. The overall effect of this is to change the level of leisure as indicated to point B. However, this movement to point B consists of two contradictory factors. There is a substitution effect that is shown as the movement from A to C (derived by drawing the dotted budget line parallel to the new budget line back to the original indifference curve, thus eliminating the income effect). This effect is unambiguous. It will always reduce work effort due to an increase in taxation. The individual perceives work now to be less worthwhile, and thus leisure to be comparatively better value. There is a swap from work to leisure for this reason. However, the income effect works in the opposite direction to this, as indicated by the movement from C to B. The effect at work here is due to the possibility that individuals possess a target level of consumption. If this is so, then an increase in tax which reduces the hourly take-home pay will require the individual to work more hours. Thus work effort increases due to the higher tax. In the diagram, this income effect outweighs the substitution effect. However, it is equally possible that the substitution effect is stronger, or that the two effects simply cancel out each other.

The point of the above analysis is that economic theory cannot unambiguously say what will be the effect on work effort of a change in income tax. The studies that have been conducted have proved equally inconclusive. Thus, there appears to be much more to the debate regarding taxation and incentives than suggested by Lawson's words. However, the important point to notice from the standpoint of optimal taxation theory is that there is still a distortion due to the tax, whatever its overall direction may be. It is the substitution effect that is important when considering the deadweight loss of the tax. The substitution effect is the one that is at work at the margin, dictating whether or not an individual decides to work an extra hour. Thus, the tax could discourage a trade that would have existed and been mutually beneficial. This is the deadweight loss of the tax. It is associated with the marginal, as opposed to average, tax rate since it is at the margin that potentially advantageous trades may be discovered.

Given all this, the optimal tax must be one that minimises the deadweight loss. However, it must also be one that reaches the required equity standards set by society (otherwise, lump-sum taxes could be used). The easiest way to think of the problem is to imagine an equity goal set by society for the tax system. The task is then to minimise the deadweight loss, given that equity constraint. If two taxes achieved the desired redistribution of income, but one had a higher excess burden than the other, then there would be no doubting the better tax from the standpoint of optimal taxation theory. However, things may not be quite as clearcut as this. It was stated earlier that the administrative costs of a tax are another undesirable use of scarce resources, not yielding utility, which are associated with the imposition of the tax. These need to be taken into account as well. Thus, a poll tax might have no deadweight loss, but it could be associated with considerable administrative costs. Equally, some taxes can be used in a positive fashion to reduce negative externalities (such as setting a differential tax between leaded and unleaded petrol). This is another factor that may need to be considered when deciding upon what may be a 'best' tax in any particular situation. Optimal taxation theory tends to concentrate on the two issues of equity and deadweight loss.

There do appear to be at least two clear principles that it is possible to establish regarding tax design:

1. It is desirable to tax complements to leisure. If the fundamental cause of deadweight loss arising from a tax is the substitution from work to leisure due to leisure now appearing 'better value', then taxing anything that is complementary to leisure should help to offset this unwanted effect. Thus, all entertainment products could be a target for such a tax. The desirability of such taxes is reinforced by the fact that many products which are identified as being complements to leisure have a high income elasticity of demand. Thus, those on higher incomes would pay proportionately more and the tax could contribute to the equity goal set by society.

2. It is not desirable to tax intermediate goods. There is no distributional argument for taxing any inputs into the productive process as the redistribution can be achieved by taxing the final product. Thus the taxation of inputs can only increase the distortions due to the tax system. In order to achieve productive efficiency, it is preferable that the marginal costs faced by firms for all of their inputs reflect the true marginal cost to society of these inputs. Only if this is so will the action of firms to minimise their private costs of

production achieve the goal of society using minimum scarce resources to produce those goods and services that it demands. Taxing intermediate goods would create an undesirable distortion from this position.

Armed with the principles of optimal taxation, we might consider any important practical implications for tax policy. That is the task of the final section of this chapter.

APPLICATIONS OF OPTIMAL TAXATION THEORY

The theory of optimal taxation can suggest some significant recommendations for government tax policy. This section of the chapter considers three possibilities:

1. What is the ideal structure for an income tax?
2. What is the best way to tax commodities?
3. Should the government charge for entry into museums?

For each of these issues, the approach will be to attempt to apply the important principles emerging from optimal tax theory to suggest some possible answers.

THE IDEAL STRUCTURE FOR AN INCOME TAX

There was a feeling in the 1980s amongst many economic policy-makers that the structure of income tax in many developed countries was not as well designed as it might be. In particular, it was felt to create unnecessary disincentive effects. In the language of optimal taxation theory, it created too high a level of deadweight loss. Thus, a country such as the UK saw the need both to cut the highest level of marginal income tax rates and to reduce the number of breaks in the income tax system where workers could move into a higher income tax bracket. These breaks are clearly important when considering possible incentive effects, as they change the hourly disposable pay for people who may be in a position to receive a higher salary. Can the previous theory suggest how best to structure such income tax systems?

The original work of Diamond and Mirrlees (1971) on optimal taxation theory suggested a structure of income tax that was contrary to the standard patterns of income tax in existence. They asserted that declining marginal rates of income tax for high income earners were desirable. This is entirely different from the standard structure which, certainly in the UK at that time, saw marginal rates of income tax rise as earnings became higher than average. Diamond and Mirrlees' argument relates back to previous points about the effect of marginal rates of taxation on the incentive to work and the Laffer curve. If marginal rates of taxes rise for high income earners, then they may be deterred from earning the higher income. Thus potential production (and hence consumption) and tax revenue is lost. However, if the marginal rate of tax were to fall for high income earners, then they might be encouraged to do the extra work, thus raising desirable production and overall tax revenue. The deadweight loss will have been reduced. The ultimate logic of this argument is that the marginal rate of tax for the very highest earner should be set equal to zero. In practice, this may prove of little interest given the level of information needed and the unlikelihood of setting an individual tax rate for one earner.

The objection to the above suggestion is likely to be on the grounds of equity, the reasoning behind increasing marginal tax rates and why lump-sum taxes were not deemed to be a possibility. However, an important point must be understood here, namely that it is average and not marginal rates of taxation that are relevant for equity. If higher income earners pay a higher average rate of tax than lower earners, then the tax is progressive. This could in general be true of a tax system with declining marginal rates for the highest earners. It is perhaps easier to see how this is true with what is termed a linear income tax system. This is where all taxable income is taxed at the same rate. It is possible to see this as approximating to Diamond and Mirrlees' suggestion for an income tax structure insofar as the decline in the marginal tax rates suggested for high income earners were very gentle. Such a system can be significantly redistributive, depending upon the size of the tax allowance that is permitted. If a considerable amount of income can be earned before any tax has to be paid, then lower income earners will pay a considerably lower average rate of tax than those on higher incomes. The structure can be illustrated simply, as in Figure 8.5.

By altering the point at which income tax has to be paid (A^*), the equity objective of the income tax system can be achieved. The linear nature of all tax on taxable income means that unnecessary disincentives are not created as incomes rise. There is simply one large jump where income becomes taxed, but this is likely to be lower than the vast majorities of incomes, and thus will not enter into the decision-making process for most workers. This system has the further advantage of simplicity and administrative ease, and appears to be the clearest suggestion regarding income tax structure to emerge from tax theory.

THE OPTIMAL STRUCTURE OF COMMODITY TAXATION

There are certain principles that can also be applied to the government's taxation of commodities. The first point was mentioned earlier, namely that there is a strong economic case for taxing products that are complements of leisure higher than those that are not. This is one way of offsetting the undesirable substitution effect of income tax. It is an indirect way of taxing leisure, and thus reducing the size of the substitution effect of taxing the alternative to leisure, paid employment. One can imagine a range of possible goods here: foreign holidays, golf

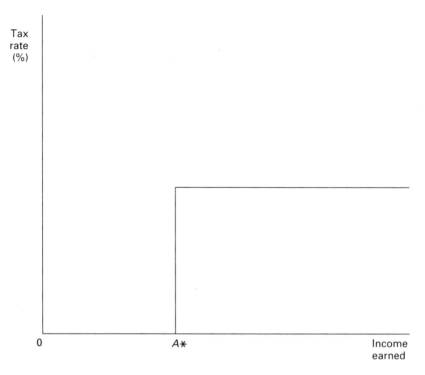

Figure 8.5 *A linear income tax with a tax allowance*

clubs and membership of the National Trust. Some may be judged more politically feasible than others, but that is not the point at stake here. Certainly the case for taxing complements for leisure more highly than other goods is strengthened when the point mentioned earlier is also recalled, namely that many of these products have a relatively high income elasticity of demand and are thus a higher proportion of the budgets of those on higher incomes than those on lower incomes. Such a tax would thus be progressive in nature and could help to achieve the overall equity objective of the tax system.

Another principle which appears to be suggested by this theoretical approach is that there is a good case for taxing goods that have a low price elasticity of demand more highly than goods that have a high price elasticity of demand. This could help to reduce the size of the deadweight loss arising from the tax. This point can be simply illustrated through supply and demand diagrams (Figure 8.6).

In Figure 8.6a, the product has a low price elasticity of demand. The size of the deadweight loss incurred through raising revenue through this tax is less than the deadweight loss incurred through raising the same tax revenue from a product with a higher price elasticity of demand, as illustrated in Figure 8.6b. Another way to understand this is to recognise that less (desirable) trades will be discouraged when there is a low price elasticity of demand.

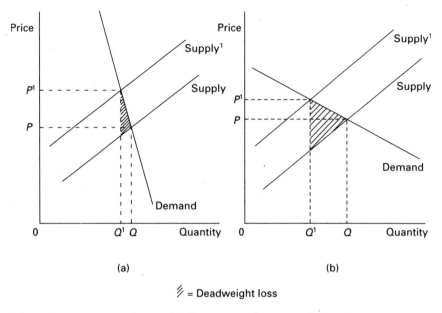

Figure 8.6   *Deadweight loss with different price elasticities of demand*

Unfortunately, the above analysis is not as clearcut as it appears. First it is only clearly true if the products concerned have no cross elasticity of demand. If a cross elasticity of demand with other products does exist, then the demand of those other products will also be affected, thus discouraging further trades. The overall effect on deadweight loss then becomes extremely difficult to calculate. The second problem is that there is often a correlation between products with a low price elasticity of demand and products with a low income elasticity of demand. Thus taxing products with low price elasticities of demand more highly than other goods would be regressive in its overall effect. This would be contrary to the possible equity objectives of the tax system. Given these two problems, the presumption then appears to move in favour of a fixed rate for commodities (with possible exceptions for complements to leisure). This has the advantage of minimising the administrative costs involved. It would also make the system of commodity taxation comparable with a linear income tax system which was seen as desirable in the previous section. This last point is an important one as it would imply that the choice of how much tax to raise through income tax and how much to raise through commodity tax would depend solely on the different effects of the two systems on savings behaviour and the relative administrative costs involved. There would be no other economic issues at stake in the debate over using direct as opposed to indirect taxation.

The final point made above also appears to suggest that there is not a strong case for charging lower rates of tax on products with low income elasticities of demand for distributional reasons. Such a way of redistributing income (as may be the reasoning for exempting such items as food and children's clothing from commodity taxation) is imprecise given the different consumption patterns of different households. A more direct and effective method of redistributing income would be via the use of lump-sum payments to low income households or by altering the size of the tax allowance in the income tax system.

One last point that should be borne in mind regarding commodity taxation is that the existence of externalities could provide a good case for different tax rates on different commodities. There are many possible examples here such as the introduction of a carbon tax to reduce the effects of global warming (see Chapter 6 on economics and the environment).

CHARGING FOR ADMISSIONS TO MUSEUMS

The issue of whether governments should charge for entry into museums has been one to excite considerable discussion. It is possible to see how in many ways it can be acknowledged as an economic issue. However, it is not immediately obvious that it should be considered in a chapter reviewing the possible applications of taxation theory. That it does in fact fit well into such a discussion is indicative of how significant and wide-ranging certain economic principles can be, once identified.

Basic pricing policy would at first sight appear to indicate that there is not a good economic case for charging for entry into a museum. Virtually all the costs associated with running a museum in any given day are fixed. Thus, if price is to be at its most efficient level where price is equal to marginal cost (see Chapter 7 on the state provision of goods and services), then price should be zero if there are no variable and hence no marginal costs. There is, however, a problem with this, namely that such a policy entails the museum making a loss. This may not matter if the loss could be covered by a lump-sum tax, thus avoiding any undesirable distortion. However, as has been discussed before, such taxes are not in practice available to governments and thus a loss has to be covered by distortionary taxes. Given this, it is no longer clear that zero price is the best policy. The principles of optimal taxation theory can suggest what may be the best answer.

One question that the principles considered above lead anyone to ask is what is the relation to leisure of the product being considered. Insofar as visiting museums can be seen as complementary to leisure, then there is an economic case for charging. A further question might be asked regarding the price elasticity of demand for entering museums. If demand is price elastic, then there may be a case for not charging, given the level of desirable trades that would be discouraged through a charge.

Optimal taxation theory suggests the importance of distributional issues when considering any tax. Thus a relevant piece of economic research would be to discover which income groups tend to visit museums most. If there is a tendency for higher income groups to visit museums more than lower income groups, then there is a case for charging for entry on grounds of equity. One significant group who are likely to visit museums are tourists. Not charging would imply a redistribution of income from general taxpayers to this group of people. However, this could open another area for consideration insofar as tourists may be encouraged to visit a country if visiting museums is free and this could have externalities, both positive and negative, for the country. A further possible distributional issue arises with regard to visiting museums since it is possible to price discriminate if a charge is made. Thus children, elderly people and the unemployed could be charged a lower price. This might be seen as a more clearly redistributional policy than, say, exempting food from taxation as food is consumed by all household types. A further form of price discrimination that could be possible and be seen to have economic benefits is to charge different prices at different times of the day and times of the year. Thus, if ever there were congestion problems in the museum (a negative externality) then a higher price could be charged at such times to reflect the higher marginal social cost that visiting at peak times implied.

As with any tax system, there will be administrative costs involved in charging for entry to museums. These would have to be borne in mind. However, perhaps for many people the major issue is that visiting museums is 'culturally desirable', suggesting that it can be seen as some form of merit good (see Chapter 7 on the state provision of goods and services). Thus, not charging for entry to museums may encourage consumption that has positive externalities for a society. The role of value judgements is likely to be important here. However, there is also the same empirical issue that was mentioned earlier, namely the question of who exactly visits museums and who would be encouraged to do so by not having a charge (or discouraged by having a charge). That would help to clarify the issue.

Thus, optimal taxation theory does not give a definite answer to the issue of charging for entry into museums. However, it does help considerably in clarifying what exactly are the issues at stake and what information may be helpful in making the decision.

CONCLUSION

Taxation is unlikely ever to be popular. However, it is possible to devise taxes that are, in economic terms, better than others. The theory of optimal taxation helps to indicate what are the important issues to be considered in the design of any tax system. In particular, the theory indicates the fundamental principle of attempting to minimise the deadweight loss of a tax, while at the same time achieving the equity goal for the tax system that is set by society. From this, some fairly important and clear suggestions regarding how any government might best set its taxes can be made.

References

Diamond, P. and J. Mirrlees (1971) 'Optimal Taxation and Public Production: I and II', *American Economic Review*, vol. 61.

Smith, A. (1776) *An Enquiry the Nature and Causes of the Wealth of Nations* (Oxford: Clarendon Press, 1976).

9 International Trade: Old Theories, New Theories and the Single European Market

Free trade between different countries is a good thing. Few assertions in economics are without controversy, yet the desirability of free international trade for the welfare of all nations has for many years been close to uncontested. During a period in which macroeconomics went through great turmoil and development, the theory of international trade developed little throughout the 1970s and 1980s. The basic model of comparative advantage, first suggested by Ricardo in 1817, was seen as a clear explanation of why it is desirable to encourage full and free trade between all nations. To suggest otherwise might be seen as a lack of perception and understanding of the relevant theory. Any restriction of trade was at best short-sighted and at worse wholly damaging to all concerned.

However, from the 1980s, new theories of international trade have emerged, deriving from some of the perceived inconsistencies of the traditional theory and the unlikely assumptions that are required for its successful operation. Of even greater significance is that these new theories suggest that there can no longer be any automatic presumption in favour of free trade. If there is a case for free trade, then it cannot be derived from the simple prescriptions of the traditional theory.

This chapter will divide itself into three main areas as it considers old and new theories of international trade and their implications:

1. The traditional theories. The first part of the chapter will consider the theory of comparative advantage as suggested by Ricardo and developed by others. This shows how all can benefit from trade. However, the section will also consider some of the perceived inconsistencies and shortfalls of the theory which may have helped to create the pressure for new theories in the 1980s.
2. The new theories. This section will explain the basis of the new theories of international trade that have been developed in the 1980s by Krugman and others. The importance of identifying market imperfections is seen as central. It will be discussed whether these new theories suggest a clear role for government restriction of free trade, or whether the presumption in favour of free trade can be held as before.
3. The Single European Market. Having discussed all the relevant theory, both old and new, the final section of the chapter will look at the development of the single market in Europe within the different theoretical contexts. Do the

138

arguments for (and against) the single market fit more happily with the old or the new theories (or neither)?

TRADITIONAL THEORIES OF INTERNATIONAL TRADE

In 1817, David Ricardo established the theory of comparative advantage. That theory remains the essence of the argument in favour of free international trade as suggested in many introductory economics textbooks.

In essence, the theory is simple. It applies to any specialisation and trade that may take place, not just to trade between nations. Imagine a doctor who employs a gardener to look after his garden as the doctor does not have sufficient time for this, given the demands of his medical work. It happens that the doctor is a talented gardener and is in fact more able at gardening than the gardener that he employs. Why then employ this person? The answer is that although the doctor may be better at gardening than his own gardener, he is far, far better than his gardener at being a doctor. Thus it can be seen to make sense for him to earn his income through pursuing his work as a doctor and employing the other person to work on his garden. This is the essence of the theory of comparative advantage. If everyone, or every country, specialises in what they are 'most better' at or 'least worse' at, then all concerned can benefit through specialisation and trade.

Before pursuing this theory of comparative advantage, it is worth noting that the general case for the desirability of free trade between nations can be seen as emanating from the same case that is given for the operation of the free market, namely the first fundamental theorem of welfare (see Chapter 7 on the state provision of goods and services). This suggests that free trade will maximise welfare. More specifically, it will lead to a position of Pareto optimality as trades will only take place if they are mutually beneficial. Any trade which does not benefit both parties will not take place because one of the parties will not agree to participate. So it is between nations. Any trade that occurs must be mutually beneficial, otherwise one of the nations would not agree to it. Thus free international trade must be desirable. This conclusion relies on the usual assumptions of a perfect market. However, the rather more specific theory of comparative advantage is usually used to justify the case for free trade, and thus this chapter will pursue that line.

As already mentioned, the theory of comparative advantage can be seen as dating back to Ricardo's work in 1817. To illustrate his argument, he used a model involving just two countries, England and Portugal, trading in just two products, cloth and wine. Examples in contemporary introductory textbooks differ little from this original approach (although views as to the cause of differences in comparative advantages have been changed, as will be seen later). The sort of example that can be pursued is shown below.

The production possibilities for Portugal and England in the production of cloth and wine are shown in Table 9.1. If Portugal devotes all of its resources to

Table 9.1   *Production possibilities for cloth and wine in Portugal and England*

	Cloth		Wine
Portugal	110	or	110
England	90	or	70

the production of cloth, it can produce 110 units, or if it devoted all of its resources to the production of wine, it could also produce 110 units. England could produce 90 units of cloth using its resources, or 70 units of wine. If it is assumed that both countries face a straight line production possibility frontier (which it is not necessary to assume, but makes the analysis easier) then the above could also be expressed as shown in Table 9.2.

The first obvious point to make about Table 9.2 is that Portugal is better at producing both products. In other words, Portugal has an absolute advantage in the production of both goods. However, as in the example with the doctor and his gardener, this is not to say that both parties cannot benefit through appropriate specialisation and trade. If both countries specialise in the production of the product in which they have a comparative advantage, then mutually advantageous trade is possible.

The key to determining which country has a comparative advantage in the production of which product is to calculate the opportunity cost of producing each product in each country. This opportunity cost is expressed in terms of how many units of the other good must be foregone in order to produce one unit of the good in question. In this example, the opportunity costs are as shown in Table 9.3. To produce one unit of cloth in Portugal, one unit of wine must be foregone, wheras 7/9 of a unit of wine must be given up to produce an extra unit of cloth in England. The country with the lowest opportunity cost in the production of a particular good is deemed to have a comparative advantage in the production of that particular good. Thus, in this example, Portugal has a

Table 9.2   *Production possibilities for cloth and wine in Portugal and England*

	Cloth		Wine
Portugal	55	and	55
England	45	and	35

Table 9.3   *Opportunity costs of producing cloth and wine in Portugal and England*

	Cloth (C)	Wine (W)
Portugal	1W	1C
England	7/9W	1 & 2/7C

Table 9.4   *Production of cloth and wine in Portugal and England*

	Cloth		Wine
Portugal	15	and	95
England	90	and	0

Table 9.5   *Consumption of cloth and wine in Portugal and England after trade*

	Cloth		Wine
Portugal	57	and	57
England	48	and	38

comparative advantage in the production of wine while England has a comparative advantage in the production of cloth. It can then be shown that if Portugal specialises in the production of wine and England specialises in producing cloth then, after appropriate trading, both countries are able to enjoy a higher level of consumption than if they had attempted to produce all goods for their own consumption. One possibility of this is illustrated in Table 9.4.

Portugal and England produce the amounts of cloth and wine shown in Table 9.4 (which are possible, given their respective production possibilities). Through a system of bargaining, it might then be agreed that Portugal exchanged 38 units of wine for 42 units of cloth. If that were the case, then both countries would be able to consume the amounts shown in Table 9.5.

Referring back to Table 9.2 illustrating the production possibilities (and hence consumption possibilities in the absence of trade), it can be seen that both countries are able to consume a greater amount of both products due to specialisation and trade. This appears to be an unambiguous welfare gain. Perhaps the best way of summing up the point is to show that both countries have been able to consume at a point outside their individual production possibility frontiers due to specialisation and trade. Portugal's gain could be shown as in Figure 9.1.

Portugal is able to consume at point *C* in the diagram due to specialisation and trade with another nation. This is a level of consumption not possible if Portugal produced all of its own goods.

One final point to note from this example is that the terms of trade between the two countries must lie between certain boundaries if both countries are sure to benefit. These are dictated by the opportunity cost ratios calculated earlier. For example, in the case of Portugal, it will be worth trading wine for cloth, as long as it is possible to gain more than one unit of cloth for each unit of wine. If this is not the case, then Portugal would do better simply to stop producing some units of wine and produce its own cloth since it could produce one unit of cloth instead of one unit of wine. Similarly, the situation for England is that it is worth trading cloth for wine as long as it is possible to gain more than 7/9 unit of wine

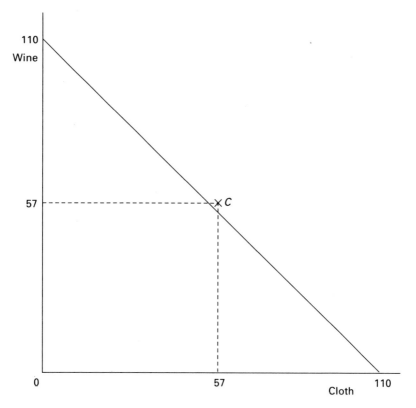

Figure 9.1 *Consumption beyond the production possibility frontier in Portugal due to specialisation and trade*

for each unit of cloth (the amount of wine that could have been produced by England instead of one unit of cloth). Thus, mutually advantageous trade is possible in this example as long as one unit of cloth is traded for something between 7/9 unit and one unit of wine. If this is the case, then both countries can be seen to have benefited through specialisation and trade as compared to self-sufficiency.

The above point does beg the question as to what it is that dictates the precise terms of trade that actually occur. Who will gain the greater benefit out of Portugal and England? The theory provides no answer. It appears likely that some bargaining process will have to occur, the relative benefits gained being dependent upon the strengths of the parties concerned. If this is so, then it certainly suggests the possibility of uneven benefits of international trade. Indeed, it could be taken further still to suggest that if one party is significantly stronger than the other, then one party may not gain at all, or perhaps even lose through trading. A possible example would be a developing country committing itself to the production of a particular cash crop. Such a country is not in a strong position in the international market, unless there is a shortage of the product. It is possible that the country could be offered highly unfavourable terms of trade for its product, but would have little choice but to accept those terms now that it was committed to the production. In retrospect, the country may have been better off not to have indulged in the specialisation, but now it is committed in that direction there is little that can be done, at least in the short run. Such suggestions are the beginnings of concerns surrounding the theory of comparative advantage.

However, before considering the various criticisms of the traditional theory, one important question remains: what is the source of differences in comparative advantage between countries? Ricardo's suggestion was that it was due to the different productivities of labour in different countries (a logical extension of the labour theory of value which suggested that labour costs dictated the value of all products). Thus countries with a high productivity of labour would tend to have a comparative advantage in the production of high technology products (associated with high labour productivity) while countries with low labour productivity would tend to have a comparative advantage in the production of goods and services that required low technology (associated with low labour productivity).

With the development of neoclassical price theory, it was no longer held to be true that labour was the sole factor of production that was responsible for determining the value of products: the other factors of production could also have an influence. Thus, Heckscher and Ohlin (1933) suggested that differing opportunity costs between different countries were the result of different factor endowments in general (not just labour). Thus if one country is well endowed with a pool of unskilled labour, while another country has a large and productive capital stock, then the former will have a comparative advantage in the production of labour-intensive products, while the latter will have a comparative advantage in capital-intensive products. This will dictate specialisation in the world economy and the direction of trade of different products.

CRITICISMS OF THE TRADITIONAL THEORY

Referring back to the example regarding the terms of trade leads into the concerns that have grown up about the theory of comparative advantage. The problem suggested that unfavourable terms of trade for one country could not really happen under the theory since one of the assumptions underpinning the theory is that there is perfect competition. Under the assumptions of perfect competition, no international market would be dominated by any one group involved in trade, and thus a very unbalanced distribution of the gains from trade would be unlikely. Equally, there would be no problem due to a country being committed to the production of a certain commodity as the assumption of perfect factor mobility would imply that the country could immediately swap its production if the terms of trade were found to be unfavourable. Whether such assumptions can be deemed to be appropriate in an international market which is dominated by the operation of large multinational companies and has seen developing countries suffer severe consequences through specialisation in certain cash crops, is clearly open to question. Large multinational companies pose the other problem for the traditional theory that the drive to ever larger international companies sits uneasily with the assumption that there are constant returns to scale (necessary if the assumption of perfect competition, requiring many small firms, is to hold). The drive for ever larger firms suggests the importance of economies of scale.

A related point to the above is that the theory relies on the joint assumptions of constant costs in all industries and full employment. Without these assumptions, then it is possible that the gains from specialisation that are suggested may be offset by unemployed resources because there could be a limit to the possible resource transfer towards activities that have diminishing returns as wages cannot fall below some subsistence level. Thus, it is possible, for example, that not all cloth workers in Portugal may be able to shift into the production of wine in the manner suggested, and thus the theory may not function as suggested and countries involved in free trade which leads to specialisation could suffer from some unemployment.

The assumption of perfect competition is not the only doubt that has been raised concerning the theory of comparative advantage. Certain simple observations about the nature of international trade appear to contradict the suggestions of the theory. One such observation concerns the level of international trade that is in practice 'intra-industry'. This phrase simply means that trade takes place between different countries in the same product. Countries produce and sell cars to each other, rather than one country specialising in the production of cars and then these being traded for another product produced by a different country, as is the pattern suggested by the theory of comparative advantage. Indeed, the majority of world trade appears to take place between developed nations with relatively similar factor endowments. Various suggestions have been offered to explain this. As individuals and nations become richer, so the demand for variety becomes greater. Thus, the products being traded may be differentiated in some fashion, some people preferring Japanese cars to German cars, others preferring French cars to Italian ones. They are viewed as different products. Another possibility is the importance of scale economies which imply that the wider market gained through trading internationally can help firms to reduce their long-run costs, and thus there is likely to be competition between firms from different countries producing the same good in an effort to gain a sufficiently large market to reduce their unit costs as far as is possible. The competition thus implied could be seen as desirable to consumers as it ensures the lowest possible prices.

The important point to note about the explanations offered of intra-industry trade is that they are not part of the theory of comparative advantage. While they still lead to a presumption in favour of free trade, they suggest gains different from those presented in the traditional theory. Wider consumer choice, the gaining of scale economies and international competition may all be viewed as tangible benefits of international trade, but they all fall outside of the theory of comparative advantage. Of particular significance may be the perceived importance of economies of scale, given the implication that this may have for the likely level of competition in the particular industry concerned.

A further contradiction to the traditional theory that has been observed is the so-called 'Leontief paradox'. This emanated from a study by Leontief (1954) which appeared to suggest that US exports were more labour-intensive than US imports. The implication of this is that, if the Heckschler–Ohlin explanation of differences in comparative advantage is accurate, the USA is more favourably endowed with labour than other countries, but less favourably endowed with capital. This is something that does not appear consistent with the USA being a highly developed nation. Various explanations for the observation have been offered, including Leontief's own suggestion that if allowance is made for the greater efficiency of US labour, then in fact it is true that the USA is more favourably endowed with labour than with capital. Thus the observation need not contradict the traditional theory.

There were clearly seen, then, to be weaknesses and possible shortcomings to the theory of comparative advantage as an explanation of the pattern of international trade and a vindication of the presumption in favour of free trade. However, it was not until the 1980s that these concerns generated alternative theories which challenged the previous automatic view in favour of free trade. The next part of this chapter considers the suggestions of these newer theories.

NEW THEORIES OF INTERNATIONAL TRADE

The starting point of the newer theories of international trade (e.g. Krugman, 1987) is the simple but significant observation that perfect competition is not a reasonable assumption with regard to any model of international trade. It was suggested earlier that one of the major benefits of international trade in practice is likely to be the wider market that is available to producers, thus allowing them to benefit from greater economies of scale than if there were no trade between countries. The problem with this is that the existence of significant economies of scale suggests the impossibility of the existence of anything approximating to perfect competition, because the drive to reduce costs, a presumed benefit of competition, will lead to concentration and to the domination of any industry with significant economies by a few firms. These economies can also create barriers to entry into the industry as any new firm can only set up and compete successfully if it enters as a large enterprise. It is worth noting that such reasoning provided the logic behind the so-called 'infant industry' argument for protection against free trade. It was argued that new, smaller firms needed protection for a period of time until they were 'grown up' and sufficiently large to be able to compete on an even footing in the international market.

The overall point of significance of this observation is that fundamental economic theory suggests that where there is market failure (as there is if there is not perfect competition), then it is in principle possible for a government to intervene to improve upon a market equilibrium (see Chapter 7 on the state provision of health care and education). Thus there can no longer be an automatic presumption of the desirability of free trade. It is theoretically possible for a government to intervene in the process of international trade and secure a permanent improvement in the welfare of its citizens. The new theory does not suggest that international trade is undesirable, but rather that there may be a case for government intervention in international trade providing a better outcome than permitting totally free international trade.

The new theories of international trade have all developed from this starting point. In practice, they have boiled down to two specific examples where it appears possible to show that a country's welfare could be greater with government intervention in the trade process than without it. The first example involves the use of what may be termed 'strategic trade policy'. The essence of this is that in a world of increasing returns to scale and imperfect competition, firms in certain industries may be able to earn long-run abnormal profits, or returns greater than the opportunity costs of the resources employed. This is especially so in the extreme example where the economies of scale in an industry are so large that there is only room for one firm to function successfully in the industry. More than one firm would imply that both firms would incur losses. In other words, the industry is a natural monopoly. In such a situation, it is possible to illustrate how strategic government intervention can benefit a particular country.

The clearest way of illustrating the above is to imagine a situation where there are two countries that are capable of producing a particular product for the world market. A particular weapons system could be an example. To make the example as clearcut as possible, it can be assumed that there is just one firm that could make the product in each country, and that all of the product would be exported, thus linking any surplus earned by the firm more clearly with the individual country's welfare. The market will be profitable if just one of the firms enters, but unprofitable if both of them enter. This situation could be represented by the following matrix:

FIRM A

		Enter		Don't Enter	
	Enter	−10	−10	0	250
FIRM B					
	Don't Enter	250	0	0	0

In the matrix, firm A's results are represented first, and firm B's second. Each firm can be seen as representing its country, as suggested earlier. If neither firm enters the industry, then zero pay-off is gained by both firms. If both the firms enter the industry, then both firms make a loss equal to 10 units. However, if one of the firms enters this industry to produce the weapons system while the other firm does not, then the firm entering gains a pay-off, or surplus, of 250 units.

As the example stands above, there is no clear outcome. Thus it is helpful to assume that one of the firms, say firm A, has a head start in the production of the weapons system that allows it to enter the industry before firm B. In that case, firm A would enter and it would not be a rational decision for firm B to enter as that would imply a loss of 10 units. Thus firm A, and country A, gains the surplus of 250 units. In this case, The government of country B would be interested in changing the outcome. It could do this successfully by committing itself to subsidise firm B to the value of 15 units if firm B produced the weapons system. Given this, it would be rational for firm B to enter the market, even if firm A had already done so as firm B could now make a profit of 5 units due to the subsidy from the government. However, if firm A is aware of this situation, then it will no longer enter the market as it now knows that firm B will definitely do so. Given this, firm B is left to gain the surplus of 250 units for country B. Thus, for a subsidy of 15 units, the government of country B has ensured a surplus of 250 units for the country. This appears a clear welfare gain to the country through strategic government intervention as compared to the outcome that would exist in a world of free trade.

The other major case in favour of government intervention in international trade concerns the possible existence of external economies. If certain industries produce positive externalities for an economy, then there is an economic case for government intervention to try to boost the level of production in that industry beyond that which would be produced by a market equilibrium. The benefits to the economy as a whole will be greater than those accruing to the private firms involved, and thus there will be under-production without government intervention. This could provide a rationale for a government intervening in the process of free trade between nations.

Perhaps the clearest example of these external economies is where there are 'overspills' of knowledge from one firm to others. If one firm indulges in the process of research and development, then the new products, production techniques or any other benefits that are discovered are unlikely to be enjoyed solely by the firm which undertakes the research and development. Other firms will also be able to benefit from the discoveries. This is the basis of the economic argument for government intervention in the area of research and development, for without it, there would be a tendency for all firms to try to 'free ride' on the efforts of others, and thus for an under-provision to take place (see Chapter 7 on the government provision of goods and services regarding the problems of public goods). With regard to international trade, it is possible to suggest that governments may increase the welfare of their country by protecting from international competition a firm or industry which is producing such external benefits. If the forces of international competition were to curtail the activities of that firm or industry, then other domestic firms would also suffer. Thus, there is a case for an appropriate government subsidy or tariff to reflect the value of the external benefit to the economy. If this makes the industry viable, then there is a net welfare gain to the nation.

It may be worth noting with this example that the gains through maintaining the production of a firm or industry generating external benefits may not just be gained by the country concerned. Given the nature of the spillover effects, firms from other countries may also benefit. Thus, restriction of free trade for this reason may be less clearly strategically to the benefit of the country involved than the other example that was given.

Does this new theory, then, lead to a new presumption in favour of restricting free international trade? There are a number of reasons for thinking that this is not in fact the case and that free trade may still represent the best economic outcome. A crucial point to recognise is that with a world of imperfect competition, as is suggested by the new theory as characterising the world of international trade, there is likely to be considerable uncertainty. Knowledge will not be perfect. One implication of this is that the examples mentioned earlier which provide a rationale for restricting trade cannot be as precise as suggested. With regard to the possibility of strategic trade restriction to secure an industry for a domestic firm, it is not possible to give definite numbers concerning future pay-offs. There is every chance that both cost and demand conditions could change considerably in the future from those postulated when calculating the pay-offs. For example, an outbreak of peace in a particular part of the world could render the weapons system used as an example as entirely unprofitable. Given this uncertainty, it will be very difficult to calculate the appropriate level of government intervention in the process of free trade. There is every chance that there could be either too much or too little. A similar point applies to the example regarding external economies. By their very nature, such benefits are hard to quantify and to predict. Will a particular piece of research and development lead to considerable external benefits to other firms, or to very little benefit to anyone? By the nature of the process, the answer is probably unknowable. Thus, governments are likely to have to choose 'winners' which receive more government protection than predicted 'losers'. Such government policies are felt to have a poor track record, as with the Concorde project in the United Kingdom. Clearly, the idea of setting a precise tariff exactly equal to the external benefit does not appear a possibility.

Given the level of uncertainty surrounding what would be the appropriate level of government intervention, a further problem presents itself. It is quite possible that particular interest groups may succeed in capturing the government intervention. As the government cannot be certain of the pay-offs involved, it may support those groups that have the greatest political clout and presentational abilities. If the defence industry has a powerful influence upon government affairs, then it may well be that the weapons system has a better chance of receiving strategic government assistance than another industry with the possibility of a similar pay-off, but less political influence.

A further related point here is the fundamental economic principle that all activities have an opportunity cost. Thus, government intervention to support one sector of industry in an economy will draw resources from other sectors. This is particularly true if the favoured sector expands, thus increasing the price of domestic resources and thus raising the costs of other industries. This places a further informational requirement on the government. Not only must they know the beneficial effect upon the industry being protected, but also the costs being imposed on the unprotected industries. In a world of uncertainty, this will be difficult to calculate, but if the wrong industry is protected by the wrong amount, then it is possible that the net impact could be a reduction of welfare in the economy.

If there is a clear case of market failure with regard to the world of international trade, this need not imply that the best form of government intervention is to restrict trade. The general rule is to try to hit the source of the market failure as directly as possible. Another example regarding external economies helps to illustrate the point. The training of labour that will be involved in the establishment of a new infant industry in a country is likely to provide a pool of newly trained labour. Some of this labour is likely to leave the industry and work elsewhere. This represents an external benefit as other industries gain from the skilled labour. Thus, a case could be made for the protection of the infant industry from international competition. However, other forms of intervention might be more appropriate. For example, it might be better for the government to lend workers money so that they can finance their own training up to the point that it is equal to the private benefit that they will receive from it. This could achieve the objective of an optimal level of training without restricting international trade.

A further problem arises with government protection of domestic industries if such protection changes the behaviour of the firms involved. If firms receive protection for strategic reasons, then it is possible that 'x'-inefficiency may arise within the industries concerned rather than the country receiving the full potential profit pay-off. This suggests the importance of competition provided by international trade, an argument for free trade, but a different one from that provided by the theory of comparative advantage.

A final obvious point to make that does not favour the restriction of free international trade is the possibility of retaliation from other nations. Returning to the example of the weapons system, it would be perfectly rational of the other country's government to attempt to outbid the protection offered by the domestic government in an effort to secure the industry for its own firm. This could lead to a whole series of counter bids which leads to ever-escalating levels of government protection: a classic 'beggar-thy-neighbour' situation. The end result is that all concerned become worse off. Even where the protection has the potential not to damage other countries, such as the promotion of external benefits which could benefit all, the level of uncertainty means that other governments could easily interpret such behaviour as strategic and decide to retaliate. This all appears to suggest that the prisoners' dilemma (see Chapter 4 on game theory) may be the best way of understanding the world of international trade. One country can gain if its government alone intervenes, but as soon as all countries' governments intervene, then all are worse off. The best solution is likely to be the establishment of rules which stop this, the simplest being the insistence on free trade.

Thus the approach of the new theory to international trade does not, on balance, appear to present a case for the restriction of free trade. What it does, however, is to present a different case for free trade than that suggested by the traditional theory. Alternative gains may be more important than those presented by the theory of comparative advantage, and the case for the government not intervening may have more to do with government failure than with a lack of market failure.

THE SINGLE EUROPEAN MARKET

A possible case study of the perceived gains available through trade with other countries is the European Single Market. The liberalisation of trade within Europe involved in the creation of a single market has been due primarily to the perceived economic gains available through the increased European trade that will be encouraged. Again, while other aspects of European integration remain highly controversial, there appears to be considerable unanimity over the desirability of increasing trade. An examination of what exactly are seen to be the major economic advantages may further clarify the applicability or otherwise of traditional and newer trade theories.

The objectives of the Single Market were explained in the 1985 White Paper *Completing the Internal Market*. The basic aim was to remove all remaining barriers to trade within the European Community by the end of 1992. As such, it can be seen as principally a deregulation process and an exercise in market liberalisation. It also represents the logical completion of the common market within Europe, a process begun in 1957. There were really four types of trade barriers removed:

1. All forms of fiscal barriers. These included differential tax treatment of domestic goods as opposed to goods produced in other European nations and the taxes and subsidies used in agricultural trade.
2. All forms of quantitative barriers. These included quotas on the production and trade of certain agricultural and other products.
3. All forms of restrictions from entering markets. These especially applied to several of the public utilities.
4. All real costs that are incurred in trade between European Community countries. Obvious examples of these were all the costs involved in the various types of border checks that took place.

The removal of these barriers was to turn the European Community into a single market, encourage trade and thus allow all the nations of the European Community to gain the benefits that would accrue. It is worth noting, however, that certain important trade restrictions remain in place after the process. One example is the different prices of pharmaceutical drugs in different European countries. This will not change as they are part of national health policies, and these are not included in the process of the Single Market. In addition, the true completion of a single market would include not just the goods market (which is where the liberalisation has been aimed), but also the financial and labour markets. It is likely that cultural and linguistic differences will imply lack of a single labour market, at least for the foreseeable future.

There are many important questions and implications for Europe raised by the move to the Single Market. These include the implications for tax policies in different countries. If there is to be no restriction on trade, then it will prove very difficult for governments to maintain different expenditure taxes. If full labour migration is permitted, and the cultural and linguistic barriers are not felt to be too great, then it may also prove to be very difficult for countries to maintain different levels of income tax. With the freer trade rules available, European countries will have to think carefully about what developments are required for competition policy throughout Europe. In general, the whole issue of subsidiarity will need careful thinking through. Which economic policies will now be best handled by individual countries and which will need to be handled on a Community-wide basis? These are all highly significant issues. However, the issue to be discussed in this chapter is what exactly are perceived to be the economic gains of increased trade.

One obvious but important point to make about trade within Europe is that it is principally intra-industry. Many European countries produce similar products and then trade these with each other. Further, the factor endowments of many European countries do not appear to be significantly different when compared with the differences between European and non-European countries. The implication of these two observations seems to be that the gains to be derived through exploiting comparative advantage are not great. This is reinforced when it is realised that the European market in all products is characterised by varying levels of imperfect competition rather than the perfect competition suggested by the theory of comparative advantage.

The gains of freer trade within Europe must then lie elsewhere. Increased competition is seen as one important possibility. Flam (1992) suggests three ways in which the Single Market's completion increases competition:

1. The number of competitors will increase in some markets as prohibitive market access barriers are eliminated.
2. The market power of domestic firms will be diminished as quotas on foreign firms' market shares are lifted.
3. The marginal cost of supply of foreign firms will be reduced, as various border trade costs are eliminated and as products no longer have to be adjusted to different national product regulations.

If it is believed that increased competition leads to greater productive and allocative efficiency (see Chapter 7 on the state provision of goods and services) then there are potential welfare gains for all countries in Europe. However, there are also likely to be some losers, at least in the short run, as less efficient firms are no longer viable in the more competitive market.

The other major economic benefit that is likely to result from the completion of the Single Market is the greater scope that is afforded for economies of scale. As stated earlier, if this is so, it is an indication of an imperfect market as there will be room only for a limited number of firms in the industry. Given the wider market that is now available within Europe following the removal of trade restrictions, firms will be able to produce on a larger scale. If this enables greater economies of scale to be gained, then firms' costs will fall. Coupled with the above point that there is now a higher level of competition, these lower costs should be enjoyed by consumers in the form of lower prices for the same products. Pratten (1988) in a survey of European industry suggested that 'there are substantial scale effects for products and production runs to be obtained in a wide range of manufacturing industries. The sources of these economies are technical economies of scale for production processes and the spreading of product development costs over the output to which they relate.' If this is accurate, then there are welfare gains available from this source.

It may be worth noting that the level of product diversity may also be affected by the Single Market as variety of choice is seen as a possible factor in consumer welfare. However, it is not entirely clear what the effect will be. It is possible that local and national products may disappear in any particular country due to the fiercer competition. However, they may be replaced by alternative products from other countries that can now trade successfully due to the removal of trade restrictions. Whether choice will increase or decrease is thus unclear.

The overall message is that there is scope for important economic benefits to arise through the increased trade afforded in Europe through the completion of the Single Market. However, the most important sources of those gains cannot be found from looking at the theory of comparative advantage, but rather from the benefits of increased competition and greater economies of scale in an imperfectly competitive market.

CONCLUSION

The theory of comparative advantage has been seen as the key piece of economic theory in explaining the benefits that are available from international trade since the time of Ricardo's work in the first part of the nineteenth century. The theory may help to explain certain trade patterns between nations. However, in today's imperfectly competitive world market, the most important gains from international trade are to be found in areas outside of the traditional theory. Indeed, the case today for the desirability of free trade may have as much to do with government failure as with the perfect competition suggested in the comparative advantage model. A brief look at the European Single Market appears to confirm the view that gains other than those suggested by the traditional theory are likely to be the important advantages of international trade today.

References

Flam, H. (1992) 'Product Markets and 1992: Full Integration, Large Gains?', *Journal of Economic Perspectives*, Fall.
Ohlin B. (1933) *Interregional and International Trade* (Cambridge, Mass.: Harvard University Press).
Krugman, P. (1987) 'Is Free Trade Passé?', *Journal of Economic Perspectives*, Fall.
Leontief, W. (1954) 'Domestic Production and Foreign Trade: The American Capital Position Re-examined', *Economica Internazionale*, Feb.
Pratten, C. (1988) 'A Survey of the Economies of Scale', in Commission of the European Communities (ed.), *Research on the 'Cost of Non-Europe'. Basic Findings*, Vol. 2 (Luxembourg: Office for Official Publications of the European Communities.
Ricardo, D. (1817) *Principles of Economics* (Harmondsworth: Penguin, 1971).

Part III

Developments in Macroeconomics

10 Macroeconomic Models

Much of the study of economics involves the use of models. How is it possible to consider the effects of a government policy upon inflation and unemployment? What is the possible impact upon an economy of a central bank raising interest rates? What happens if workers succeed with a particular wage bid? Does it matter if there is a significant increase in the money supply? All of these, and many more, macroeconomic issues are viewed through the lens of a particular macroeconomic model. Such models, simplifications of reality relying on the use of assumptions (see Chapter 1 on economic methodology), provide a framework within which it is possible to discuss pertinent issues. Without such models, analysis would be more difficult and discussion could easily end as description.

The purpose of this chapter is to look at the three main macroeconomic models that are generally used in standard economics textbooks. The particular focus of attention with each of the models will be to consider the key macroeconomic issues and policy dilemmas that it is possible to illustrate through these models. Thus the chapter will consist of the following sections:

1. The 45 degree diagram. The simplest of the macroeconomic models used in the study of economics is explained. It has some clear drawbacks, but can be used to illustrate particular policy issues that might face an economy.
2. *ISLM* analysis. The original interpretation of Keynesian analysis was put in the framework of what became known as *ISLM*. This is a more sophisticated model than the 45 degree diagram, allowing a role for the money market. It can be particularly useful in highlighting international issues when a balance of payments schedule is introduced.
3. Aggregate supply and demand. This has now become the standard model used in many texts. Its advantage is that it can illustrate both supply and demand side effects. It clearly highlights the major disagreements between neoclassical and Keynesian standpoints and their implications for government policies.

However, before embarking upon this survey of macroeconomic models, a major health warning needs to be issued. Such models tend immediately to fall into the trap discussed in Chapter 3, on microeconomics and macroeconomics, namely that the macroeconomic models are considered without reference to their microeconomic foundations. This is the danger in the whole study of macroeconomics: it is too easy to try to study it without a proper integration with the appropriate microeconomic models. Thus each of the three models considered would better be seen in conjunction with the microeconomic models compatible with its assumptions. This needs to be borne in mind during the following discussion.

THE 45 DEGREE DIAGRAM

The simplest of the macroeconomic models here is really a simplified version of what are interpreted by some economists to be some of the important points of Keynes's view of the functioning of an economy stemming from his *General Theory* (1936). Perhaps the most important assumption of the model is that prices will remain fixed until the economy has reached a position of full employment (further implying that it is possible for an economy to remain in a position below full employment). Equilibrium, a position of balance with no tendency for the key variables to change, is at a point where the economy's planned expenditure is equal to its planned income which is equal to its planned output. In such a situation, all withdrawals from will equal injections into the country's circular flow of income, and the level of national income will not tend to vary.

It is from the above equilibrium condition that this model derives its name. The level of national income is plotted along the horizontal axis and the level of expenditure is plotted on the vertical axis. The 45 degree line, starting from the origin, on such a diagram thus plots all the possible points of equilibrium in an economy where income is equal to expenditure. On to this standard graph a schedule giving the level of aggregate expenditure or demand is then added. This total demand comprises all consumer expenditure (C), investment expenditure by firms (I), government expenditure (G) and overseas expenditure on the nation's exports (X). The value of imports (M) is then subtracted from this figure, as consumer, investment and government expenditure will all include spending on imports, but this does not contribute to expenditure on the nation's output. It is assumed that investment expenditure, government expenditure and export expenditure do not vary with income (an assumption that is open to question, as, for example, investment by firms is likely to change as national income changes) and thus these could be represented by a horizontal line on the diagram. However, consumer expenditure is assumed to vary directly with national income as it is anticipated that a certain percentage of any extra income received will be spent on goods and services (the rest will be saved). The exact amount that consumption will increase as income increases is measured by the marginal propensity to consume. Thus, the schedule representing consumer expenditure will slope upwards on the diagram. Putting the different components of aggregate demand together can thus allow the 45 degree diagram to be drawn (Figure 10.1).

Equilibrium national income is at point Ye where the aggregate demand schedule cuts the 45 degree line. At this point, expenditure is equal to income and there is no tendency for national income to change (even if that position were associated with unemployment).

Given that the only schedule on this diagram is the aggregate demand line, then its principal function must be to analyse the possible effects of changes in the level of aggregate demand on the economy. This is best illustrated via a simple example. Starting from a position of equilibrium national income, there

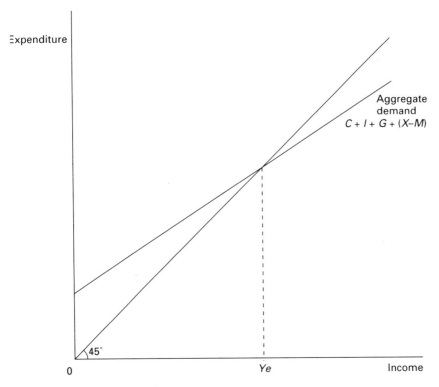

Figure 10.1 *The 45 degree diagram*

is an increase in business investment due to a rise in the level of business confidence. This causes an increase in the level of aggregate demand, the effect of which can be shown on the 45 degree diagram (Figure 10.2).

The increase in aggregate demand has caused the level of equilibrium income to rise from $Ye1$ to $Ye2$. The diagram does not, however, indicate how this has happened. The answer is that national income has increased through the multiplier process, an important part of Keynes's analysis. The rise in investment demand causes firms to wish to produce more investment goods in order to meet the higher demand (given the assumption of fixed prices, firms will not respond to the higher demand by raising their prices). In order to do this, they will need to increase the number of workers that are employed. These workers will receive income, and thus the level of national income rises. However, the process does not end there. Those people in receipt of higher incomes will spend some of that income, thus causing a further rise in the level of aggregate demand. This will stimulate a further rise in output and thus employment. Income will increase again, this in turn creating a further increase in the level of expenditure. This process will continue through several rounds until it has eventually burnt itself out. The implication is that the final increase in national income will be greater

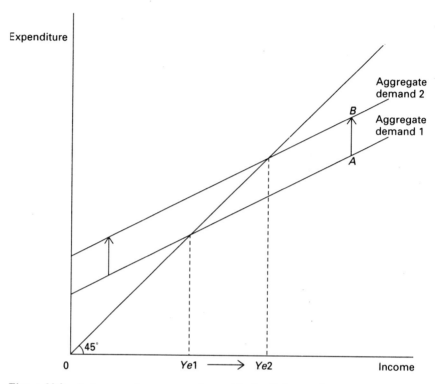

Figure 10.2 *An increase in aggregate demand in the 45 degree diagram*

than the initial increase in investment expenditure, as illustrated by the fact that the distance *Ye*1 to *Ye*2 is greater than the vertical distance between the two aggregate demand schedules, *A* to *B*, which shows the original change in investment. The extent to which the final increase in income is greater than the initial change in expenditure is dependent on the slope of the aggregate demand line. This depends on the value of the marginal propensity to consume, and the value of the marginal propensity to consume (how much of any increase in national income received is spent) thus determines the size of the multiplier effect.

   The model becomes more interesting when the concept of full employment income is added to it. Full employment income is the level of income and expenditure that is just sufficient to induce firms to produce a level of output that requires the full employment of all available resources in the economy. Thus, a specific level of national income can be identified as corresponding to this point and this can be added to the diagram. The important point about this model is that there is no logical reason why the level of equilibrium income in the economy should correspond with the full employment level of income. It might equally be above or below the level required to secure full employment. Again, it is possible to illustrate this on the diagram: see Figure 10.3.

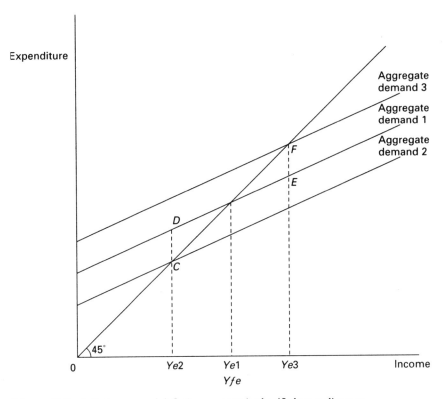

Figure 10.3 *Inflationary and deflationary gaps in the 45-degree diagram*

If aggregate demand is at level 1, then equilibrium national income (*Ye*1) is equal to full employment income (*Yfe*). However, if total expenditure is at level 2, then equilibrium income (*Ye*2) is below that required to secure full employment. In that case, a deflationary gap of *CD* is said to exist. This distance represents the shortfall of aggregate demand below the level needed to guarantee full employment in the economy. A country in this position will be characterised by unemployed resources. The opposite situation is when aggregate demand is at level 3 and equilibrium income (*Ye*3) is greater than the income needed to secure full employment. In this case, an inflationary gap is said to exist, as indicated by the distance *EF*. This is the excess of total expenditure above the level needed to give full employment. Here, the level of demand is too great for the capacity of the economy and prices thus rise as output cannot meet demand. An economy in this position will suffer from inflation. Thus, the principal cause of unemployment is identified as too little demand in the economy and the main cause of inflation is seen as too much demand.

Several important points must be made about the above analysis. The first is that the persistence of an equilibrium in the economy characterised by widespread unemployment is seen by many economists as relying on the assumption of fixed prices, particularly the price of labour. It might be argued instead that, in the face of unemployment, there would be a tendency for the real wage to fall (surpluses causing prices to fall in a functioning market system). This would cause employers to employ more labour, and thus unemployment might fall. Thus, equilibrium with mass unemployment will not persist. Keynes (1936) suggested that there were several reasons why this was not necessarily true. Although a fall in money wages (or the rate of increase in money wages) might be secured by workers, the real wage might not fall as firms might lower prices, or the rate of increase in prices, in response to the changed level of money wages. If workers are concerned to maintain their position in a perceived hierarchy of wages, then the chances of a cut in the rate of increase of money wages will also be hard to secure since any individual group of workers would be concerned that they might lose out in comparison with others. The problem is that wage negotiations take place with individual groups of workers rather than labour as a whole. However, a further point is that even if the desired cut in wages were secured, this will in turn have a demand-side effect according to Keynesian analysis, and the lower level of demand that is created will not be beneficial to employment. Thus the suggestion is made that wages will not adjust in a way that will move the economy away from a position of unemployment.

A further interpretation of Keynes's work is to suggest that he turned the whole process considered above on its head. Rather than seeing the real wage as determining the level of employment and output, it can be suggested that he was asserting that the real wage was not the determining but rather the determined variable. The level of aggregate demand determined the level of output in the economy. This determined the level of employment that there would be, and the level of employment dictated the level of the real wage. Thus, it was inappropriate to look for adjustment in the real wage as a cure for unemployment in the economy.

The use of full employment income in the 45 degree diagram suggests that an economy may suffer either from unemployment or inflation, or if equilibrium is exactly at full employment income then it will suffer from neither. As such, this model appears ill-equipped to cope with stagflation, the co-existence of unemployment and inflation. According to the 45 degree diagram, this is not a logical possibility given that it would require both deficient and excess demand at the same time. Stagflation was experienced by many developed nations in the 1970s, and it is not entirely surprising that this corresponded with a disenchantment with simple Keynesian models such as the 45 degree diagram approach. Either the model was wrong, or there were important factors outside of the model that were important in dictating events within an economy. Again, it may be important to stress that it was not necessarily Keynes's original analysis that could be deemed to be at fault here as he did have some concern for the supply side of the economy. Rather, the fault arises from this particular simplistic interpretation of Keynes's analysis.

In terms of policy prescriptions, the message of the 45 degree diagram for governments is a simple one. If there is widespread unemployment, then the government needs to raise the level of expenditure in the economy in order to reduce the size of the deflationary gap and move equilibrium income closer to full employment income. This could be done through fiscal policy (raising government spending and or lowering taxes) or monetary policy (lowering interest rates). If there is inflation, then aggregate demand needs to be lowered, thus reducing the inflationary gap. Two points need to be made here. The first is that, according to the 45 degree diagram, it would be of no importance how the government raised aggregate demand. Thus the whole issue of how a government budget deficit that was created through an expansionary fiscal policy might be financed, and whether it would be of any consequence, is not considered. The other obvious point to make is that if a government is faced with both unemployment and inflation, then this approach can only suggest tackling one of them by making the other worse. Thus, if inflation is chosen as the most important target, then the cut in demand required will further worsen unemployment. This is a classic policy dilemma (see Chapter 11 on unemployment, inflation and the Phillips curve).

One final policy dilemma that the 45 degree diagram can be used to illustrate concerns a country's balance of payments. It is sometimes suggested that certain countries, such as the United Kingdom, have their employment and growth rates constrained by their trading position with the rest of the world. It is possible to try to show this on the 45 degree diagram: see Figure 10.4.

Full employment income is at *Yfe*. The export line is shown as horizontal, as exports are not seen as varying directly with the level of national income. The import line slopes upwards since spending on imports rises as income rises. It can be seen that there will be a certain level of income where imports are equal to exports, or where there is balance on the current account of the balance of payments, *Ybp*. The fact that *Ybp* is below *Yfe* in the diagram could be perceived as a difficulty for an economy. If it is felt that an economy must, in the long run, achieve balance between its imports and exports (the alternatives are continual sales of the nation's assets or ever-increasing debts with other countries) then in the long run national income cannot rise above *Ybp* because a higher level of income would imply an excess of imports over exports. The problem with this is that a deflationary gap exists at *Ybp* and there is unemployment. Thus there is a balance-of-payments constraint on demand and hence the level of employment and economic growth in the country depicted. This would remain the situation until the export line is shifted upwards and/or the imports schedule is moved downwards. This suggests the need for policies other than those which manipulate the level of aggregate demand.

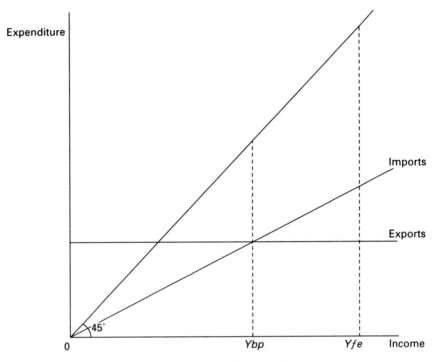

Figure 10.4   *The balance of payments constraint on employment*

THE *ISLM* FRAMEWORK

The original attempt at placing Keynes's macroeconomics analysis into a macro-economic model was made by J.R. Hicks and led to the so-called *ISLM* framework. It is more sophisticated than the 45 degree diagram. In particular, it allows a role for the money market as the money supply and the interest rate are being seen as integral to the functioning of the economy.

The axes involved in the *ISLM* model are not the same as in the 45 degree diagram. National income is still plotted along the horizontal axis, but the interest rate is now plotted on the vertical axis. The *IS* (or investment, savings) schedule illustrates all of the points that give equilibrium in the product market. This is best understood by considering Figure 10.5.

In quadrant number one, investment is plotted against the interest rate. The assumption is that the higher the rate of interest, the lower the level of invest-ment as less schemes are viable than at lower interest rates given the higher level of pay-off required for any investment project. Quadrant number two plots investment against savings. In a simple two-sector economy with no govern-ment or foreign trade, savings must be equal to investment if there is to be equi-librium. Thus, the 45 degree line shows all the points of equilibrium. This would

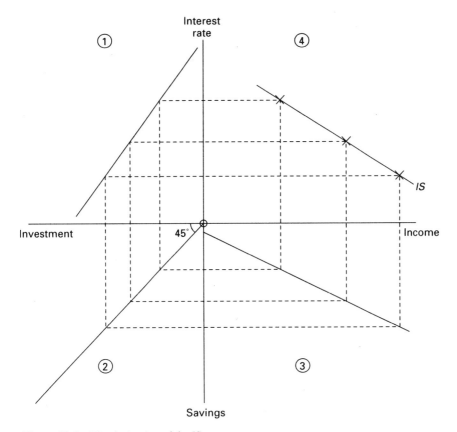

Figure 10.5 *The derivation of the IS curve*

be equally true if the government and foreign sectors were added and government expenditure and exports were added to the investment axis, and taxation
and imports added to the savings axis. Quadrant number three plots savings
against national income. It is assumed that savings rise as income rises, but not
by as much as the rise in income. The exact amount will depend upon the marginal propensity to save. From quadrants one to three, it is now possible to plot
the *IS* schedule in quadrant four, as indicated. This results in an *IS* schedule that
slopes down from left to right. It indicates all the different combinations of
national income and the interest rate that give equilibrium in the product market.
To put it another way, if the rate of interest is given, then the level of income is
determined by the point at which savings are equal to investment.

The *LM* (or liquidity preference/demand for money, money supply) schedule
gives the combinations of the interest rate and national income that are compatible with equilibrium in the money market (i.e. where the demand for money is

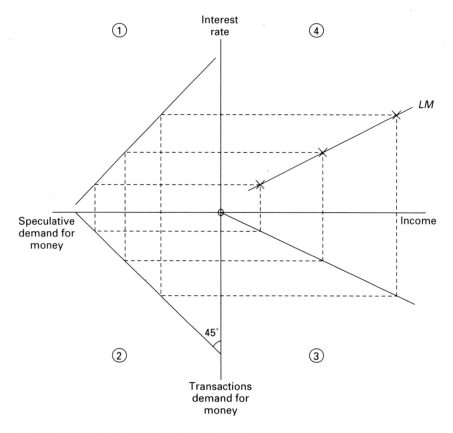

Figure 10.6 *The derivation of the LM schedule*

equal to the supply of money). The derivation of this schedule is best understood by considering Figure 10.6.

In the derivation of the *LM* line in Figure 10.6 it is assumed that the money supply is fixed and is determined outside of the system by the actions of the central bank. Quadrant one shows the relationship between the speculative demand for money and the interest rate. The suggestion is that the higher the rate of interest, the lower the speculative demand for money. This requires some explanation. It is assumed, for reasons of simplicity, that speculators choose between holding wealth in the form of money or in the form of government bonds. Being profit-maximisers, they will wish to hold bonds when the price of bonds is anticipated to rise, and money when the price of bonds is anticipated to fall. The relationship between the price of bonds and the interest rate is an inverse one due to the fact that holders of bonds receive a fixed annual money payment, regardless of the current market price of the bonds. Consider the following example. A bond is originally sold for £100 with an annual £10 payment associated with it. This is the equivalent of an interest rate of 10 per cent. Now suppose that the market price of the bond were to fall to £90. The annual payment received on this bond would still be £10. However, this would now be the equivalent of an interest rate of approximately 11 per cent. Equally, if the price of the bond were to rise to £110, then the £10 repayment would be equivalent to an interest rate of approximately 9 per cent. Thus, there is an inverse relationship between the price of bonds and the rate of interest. If the interest rate is high, this implies that the price of bonds is low. The suggestion then made is that speculators work with some idea of a 'normal' rate of interest or an average price of bonds in their minds. Thus, if bond prices are perceived as low, then the expectation is that they will rise. In that case, speculators will wish to hold their wealth in the form of bonds rather than money as this should soon increase the value of their wealth. The speculative demand for money is low. However, if interest rates are low, then the price of bonds is high and is expected to fall. Thus, the demand for bonds is low and the speculative demand for money is high.

Quadrant two in Figure 10.6 indicates that the supply of money can be used either for speculative purposes or for the purpose of conducting transactions (in fact, it is also used for precautionary reasons, but this demand for money could be added to the speculative or transactions demand axis without affecting the analysis). The 45 degree line shows all the possible splits between speculative and transactions purposes, given the money supply. Thus, if there is a large demand for money for speculative purposes, then there is less available for transactions purposes. Quadrant three indicates the relationship between national income and the transactions demand for money. The suggestion is that as national income rises, then so the transactions demand for money will rise as more money is required to facilitate the higher level of transactions associated with a higher level of income. Thus it becomes possible to derive the *LM* schedule as shown in quadrant four. It slopes upwards from left to right and gives all those combinations of income and the interest rate where the supply of money will be equal to the demand for money. To put it another way, given the level of income, the interest rate is determined by the point at which the supply of money is equal to the demand for money.

The *IS* and *LM* schedules can now be put together on Figure 10.7.

This diagram suggests that there is a unique point of national income, *Ye*, and rate of interest, *re*, which yield equilibrium in both the money market and the product market. This is the point to which the economy will tend to move. It is important to note that these schedules have been drawn with the assumption that the price level is fixed. If the price level changes, the position of the schedules would be affected.

The framework can now be used to consider changes in the economy emanating either from the product market or the money market. Consider first the same example as that used in the 45 degree diagram framework, namely an increase in investment due to an increase in business confidence. This would be represented by an outward movement of the *IS* schedule: see Figure 10.8.

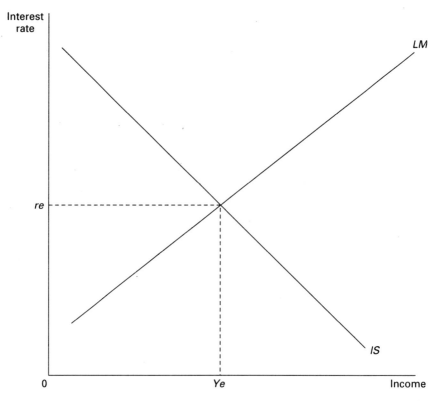

Figure 10.7 *Equilibrium in the ISLM model*

The *IS* schedule moves outwards to the right (*IS* to *IS*1) because at all interest rates, firms now wish to invest more than was previously the case. Looking at the original derivation of the *IS* schedule, this creates an outward movement of the schedule in quadrant one which causes the *IS* line to move. The effect is to increase equilibrium national income (*Ye* to *Ye*1) and the equilibrium rate of interest (*re* to *re*1). However, the process through which this occurs needs some consideration. Without any interest rate effect, income would move to *Y*2 through the multiplier process when using the 45 degree diagram approach. However, as the economy moves towards that point in this analysis, the interest rate will rise because the higher level of national income will create an increase in the transactions demand for money to facilitate the higher level of transactions associated with the higher income. This increase in the interest rate will moderate the increase in investment as less projects will appear viable than was initially the case with the lower rate of interest. Thus the final increase in the level of national income (to level *Ye*1) is not as great as it would have been if there had been no interest rate change. The size of the multiplier effect has been reduced compared to the 45 degree diagram approach because the effects of a

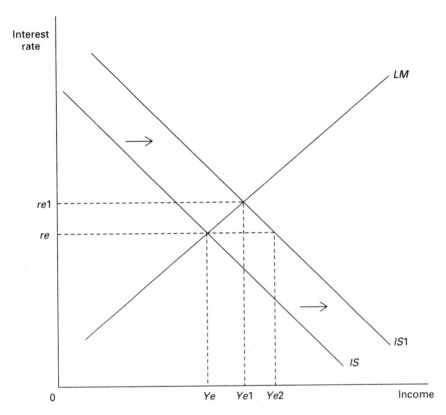

Figure 10.8 *A movement of the IS schedule*

change in aggregate demand have had an impact on the money market and this is taken into account in the analysis.

It is also possible for the equilibrium position of the economy to change through a movement of the *LM* schedule. This will tend to be due to changes in the money supply, and thus associated with government monetary policy. However, there is one important way in which the real money supply could be affected without a deliberate change in money supply by the government. If the general level of prices in the economy rises, then this is equivalent to a reduction in the real money supply if the nominal supply of money is unchanged. The same nominal money supply will be capable of facilitating fewer transactions. This will cause the *LM* schedule to shift to the left and cause an increase in interest rates and a fall in national income. In terms of monetary policy, it is important to understand that monetary policy that leads solely to a movement of the *LM* schedule must be associated only with the buying and selling of bonds by the government. If the government were to pursue an expansionary monetary policy, then it would buy bonds on the financial markets. This would cause the money supply to rise as people's money balances rise due to their sales of bonds. At the same time, the interest rate would fall as the increased demand for bonds due to the government's actions forced up bond prices. This would be represented by a rightwards movement of the *LM* schedule as illustrated in Figure 10.9.

In terms of the diagram illustrating the derivation of the *LM* schedule, the line in quadrant two has moved outwards due to the larger money supply. This causes the *LM* curve to move to the right. The movement of the *LM* line has led to a lower equilibrium interest rate (*re* to *re*1) and a higher level of national income (*Ye* to *Ye*1). However, how this is achieved needs explanation. The initial fall in interest rates due to the purchase of government bonds is represented by the fall in interest rates from *re* to *re*2. However, the effect of this is to stimulate investment demand as more investment projects now become viable to firms. As investment rises, so the level of national income starts to rise via the multiplier process. This increases the transactions demand for money and raises the interest rate above the level to which it had originally fallen. This is how the final equilibrium is achieved.

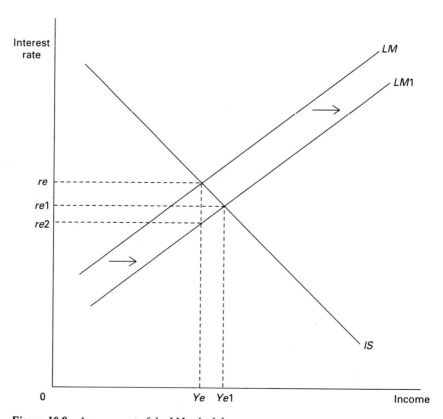

Figure 10.9   *A movement of the LM schedule*

One point worthy of note here concerns what different economists mean by monetary policy. In this framework, it must only be the 'sale and purchase of government bonds. There was some argument in the 1970s, when debates between Keynesians and monetarists were at their strongest, that said an expansionary monetary policy was the equivalent of dropping money from a helicopter on to an economy, and in turn, this was bound to create inflation. Two points can be made here about that suggestion. The first is that according to *ISLM* analysis, such an action is not pure monetary policy. For example, if the money were to land directly upon an old people's home, then this would be the equivalent to the government raising the state pension for the people concerned. As the money was spent, this would be represented by a rightwards movement of the *IS* schedule. Thus this is in fact a mixture of monetary and fiscal policy as both the *IS* and the *LM* schedules would move. The second point to make is that this model could not tell us whether such an action would be inflationary. That relies upon assumptions concerning the flexibility of prices and whether the economy could be at a level that corresponded to some definition of full employment. As with the 45 degree diagram, a different model is needed to consider this.

It was mentioned above that fiscal policy in the *ISLM* framework was represented by a movement of the *IS* schedule. Thus a reduction in the rate of taxation would cause the *IS* schedule to move to the right as some of the increased disposable income received by tax-payers was spent. This must be financed by the sale of government bonds so that there is no accompanying expansion of the money supply, as would be the case with an expansionary fiscal policy financed by borrowing from the nation's central bank. What effect will this have on the economy? The answer appears to depend upon the slope of the *LM* schedule, as indicated in Figure 10.10.

The movement in the *IS* schedule will have a large impact on the level of national income if the *LM* schedule is interest elastic as with schedule *LM*1, but will have only a small impact on national income if the *LM* schedule is interest inelastic as with schedule *LM*2. It is possible that fiscal policy could be highly ineffective if something similar to *LM*2 exists in the economy. In this case, interest rates rise considerably and little happens to national income. This was the argument behind the suggestion that expansionary fiscal policies simply led to a 'crowding out' of private expenditure.

The debate can be taken further by considering the effectiveness of monetary policy with different *IS* schedules: see Figure 10.11.

If the *IS* schedule is interest elastic (*IS*1), then monetary policy has a large impact on national income. If the *IS* schedule is interest inelastic (*IS*2), then monetary policy is relatively ineffective. In this way, the debate between monetarists and Keynesians concerning the effectiveness of monetary and fiscal policy, as characterised at the time, became a case of a semi-empirical argument over the relative slopes of the *IS* and *LM* schedules. However, this appears a barren debate. Any concerns could simply be overcome by an expansionary fiscal policy financed by the government borrowing from the central bank and

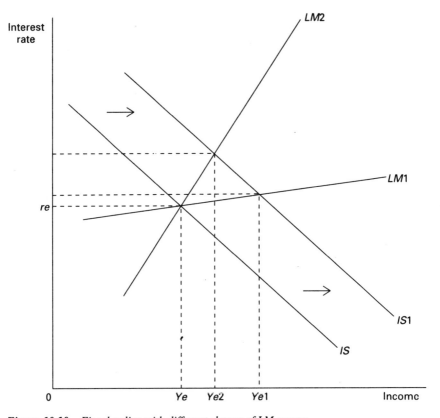

Figure 10.10   *Fiscal policy with different shapes of LM curves*

hence causing an expansion of the money supply. The effect of this would be to shift both the *IS* and *LM* schedules to the right in the manner shown in Figure 10.12.

This diagram suggests that the slopes of the *IS* and *LM* schedules do not really matter if a government is prepared to use both fiscal and monetary policy to achieve its desired goal. National income can be increased. The real issue is whether this increase in national income will be due to an increase in output and employment or an increase in the general price level. In the diagram as it stands, it must result from an increase in output due to the fixed price assumption. If the price level were to change, then there would be a further movement of the schedules. However, in principle, there is nothing that clearly states that it will automatically be only output that changes with changes in the level of national income. It could equally be the price level that moves. This is the same question regardless of whether fiscal or monetary policy is seen as responsible for the expansion. This model does not clarify this fundamental point: it relies upon the assumptions made about the flexibility of prices and the tendency of the

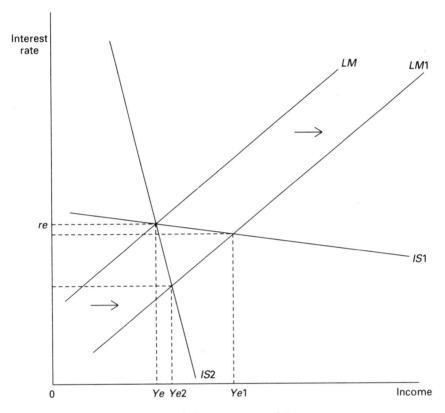

Figure 10.11 *Monetary policy with different shapes of IS curves*

economy to move automatically towards full employment which appear to be the real fundamental issues in macroeceonomics.

One further feature that can be added to the *ISLM* model is the so-called *BB* line. This indicates all the permutations of national income and interest rates that are compatible with balance in the overall balance of payments for the economy. Generally the slope of this schedule might be expected to be as shown in Figure 10.13.

As national income increases, then so will expenditure on imports. This will move the country into deficit with other nations. In order to offset this, the interest rate needs to rise in order to attract money capital from overseas into the country, as the return to be gained on such money capital is now higher. The slope of this *BB* schedule will depend upon the mobility of money capital through the world: how quickly and easily international investors can switch their wealth from one country to another. The very high level of money capital mobility in today's developed economies suggests that the slope of the schedule is likely not to be very steep for many countries. A small rise in interest rates

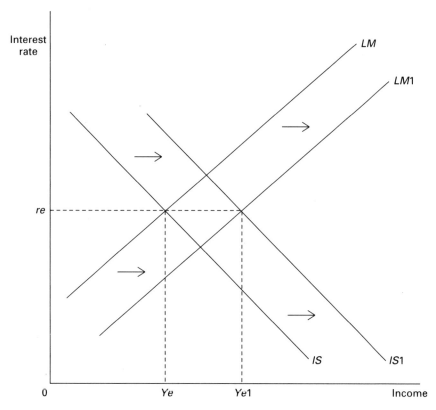

Figure 10.12 *The effect of expansionary fiscal policy financed by borrowing from the central bank*

can lead to a large movement of money capital. This has implications for the effectiveness of a government's fiscal and monetary policy.

Consider the extreme example of perfect mobility of money capital. In this case, the *BB* line would be horizontal: the slightest move in interest rates would bring an infinite movement of money capital. The effectiveness of fiscal and monetary policy in this situation can be shown as in Figure 10.14.

An increase in government expenditure will shift the *IS* curve to *IS*1. This leads to a temporary equilibrium at point *B*. What happens now depends upon the exchange-rate regime used by the country. There will be a surplus in the external balance due to the higher interest rate attracting large amounts of money capital into the country. With a fixed exchange rate, this will cause an increase in the money supply and thus cause the *LM* schedule to move to the right to *LM*1. Thus the final equilibrium will be at point C with a large increase in national income. If a flexible exchange rate is used, then the value of the currency will rise. This will cause the nation's products to become less price com-

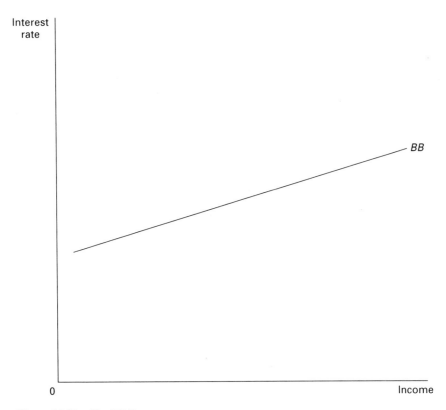

Figure 10.13 *The BB line*

petitive and thus reduce expenditure on these products. This will cause the *IS* schedule to move left and back to its original point. Fiscal policy would be ineffective. With monetary policy, a purchase of bonds by the central bank causes the *LM* schedule to move to *LM*1. This creates a temporary equilibrium at point D. This implies an external deficit. With a fixed exchange rate, this causes the money supply to fall and thus causes the *LM* line to move back to its original point and the monetary policy to have no effect. With a flexible exchange rate, the deficit will cause a depreciation in the value of the nation's currency which will increase the level of the nation's international competitiveness. This will increase expenditure on domestic goods and services and thus shift the *IS* schedule to *IS*1 and cause the final equilibrium to be at point C. Thus the effectiveness of monetary and fiscal policy depends upon the type of exchange rate employed by a country. This is of particular interest to the discussion over Europe's decision to adopt a single currency (see Chapter 12 on economic and monetary union). Given that a single currency is the most extreme form of a fixed exchange rate, this analysis confirms the view that European countries will be left with no effective monetary policy with a single currency. However, it also

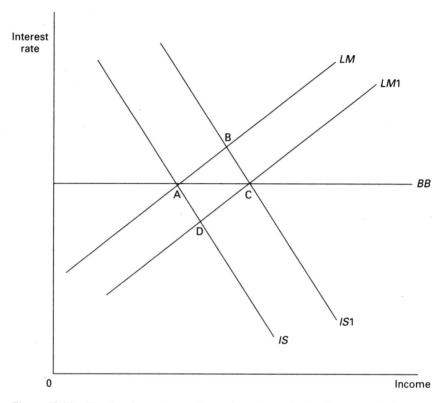

Figure 10.14   *Fiscal and monetary policy with perfect mobility of money capital*

suggests that fiscal policy could be a weapon still available to national governments.

AGGREGATE SUPPLY AND DEMAND

The third of the macroeconomic models is now the most popular in many economics textbooks. Its great advantage over the other two models discussed thus far is that it gives overt consideration to the supply-side as well as the demand-side of the economy. It is also more clearly identifiable with the principal microeconomic model and thus offers a better prospect of integrating macroeconomics with the relevant microeconomics.

In this model, output (which will be the same value as national income in equilibrium) is on the horizontal axis and the price level is on the vertical axis. The derivation of the aggregate demand schedule bears similarities with the *LM* schedule in *ISLM* analysis. Figure 10.15 helps to explain this.

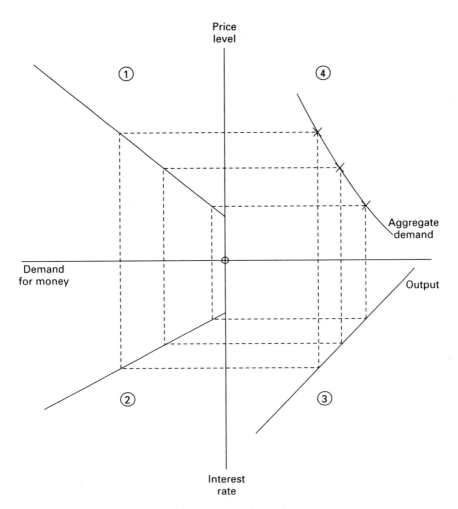

Figure 10.15   *The derivation of the aggregate demand curve*

In quadrant one, total demand for money is shown as rising as the price level rises. This is due to the transactions demand for money. As the price of products rises on average, so more money is required to finance the same level of transactions. In quadrant two, the money supply is assumed to be fixed in the same fashion as with *ISLM* analysis. Thus, as the demand for money rises, then so will the price of money or the interest rate. Quadrant three suggests that the lower the rate of interest, the higher the level of output and vice versa. This is due to the effect of the interest rate on national expenditure. A low interest rate stimulates a high level of spending which will cause a high level of output. A high interest rate will induce low expenditure and a low output. Given this information, it is possible to derive the aggregate demand schedule in quadrant four. It will tend to slope down from left to right.

There is no agreed shape of the aggregate supply schedule. There are various different possibilities depending upon the flexibility of prices, notably wages, that is assumed. This helps to go to the heart of genuine macroeconomic disagreements between economists. The easiest starting point is to consider the shape of the aggregate supply curve that is suggested from the 45 degree diagram. Here, it was assumed that output and employment would respond to any change in the level of aggregate demand up to the point of full employment. If total expenditure were to rise above this point, then there would be inflation as the price level would rise, given that output could not respond. Thus in Figure 10.16 the shape of aggregate supply is effectively assumed.

If aggregate demand were to rise from *AD*1 to *AD*2, then output would increase, as there would be unemployed resources in the economy. However, if aggregate demand were to rise from *AD*2 to *AD*3, then there would be inflation, as the economy would be at full employment. In practice, it is suggested that the

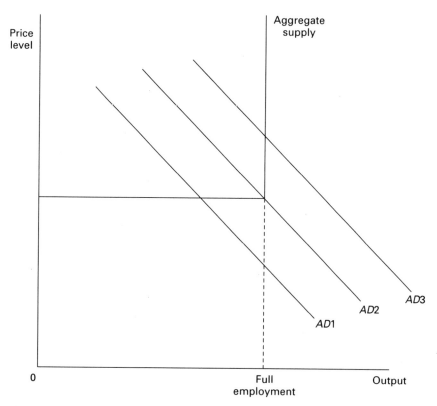

Figure 10.16   *The aggregate supply schedule suggested by the 45 degree diagram*

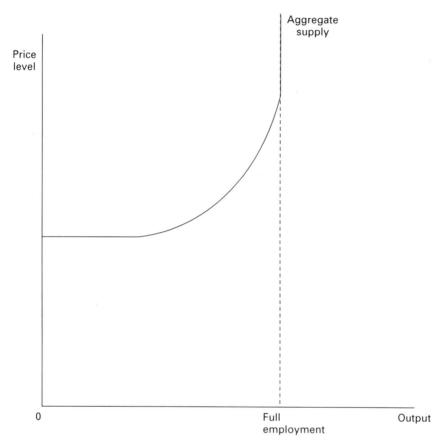

Figure 10.17   *The aggregate supply schedule allowing for gradual rises in the price level*

actual shape of the aggregate supply schedule is more likely to be as indicated in Figure 10.17.

As the economy begins to approach full employment, there will be a tendency for the price level to rise before full employment is reached, as bottlenecks and shortages develop in some areas of the economy, thus pushing up some prices. Thus, an increase in aggregate demand could lead to some inflation before the economy has reached full employment.

From a neoclassical standpoint, the aggregate supply schedule suggested thus far could not be accurate in the long run. It assumes the possibility of an economy being stuck in a position of having significant unemployed resources. For the neoclassical economist, this could only happen if prices, particularly wages, are inflexible. This is possible in the short run, but is not the case in the long run in a market economy. In the long run, prices do adjust so as to clear shortages and surpluses. Thus if there is a surplus of labour, then the price of labour, the real wage, will fall until that surplus has disappeared. In other words, real wages adjust so that unemployment does not persist. In other words, the economy will tend towards full employment in the long run. If the economy is at full employment, then any increase in aggregate demand can only have an impact on the price level, in other words lead to inflation, as output cannot increase in response to higher demand. Thus the shape of the long-run aggregate supply schedule must be as indicated in Figure 10.18.

Changes in aggregate demand have no impact on output and employment. It is still accepted that an economy could be stuck in a position of unemployment in the short run because prices usually cannot adjust immediately. Thus, the short-run aggregate supply curve may not be vertical, and increases in aggregate demand can have a short-run effect on output and employment. However, this effect will not persist into the long run when prices can vary as fully as required in order to allow the market to clear.

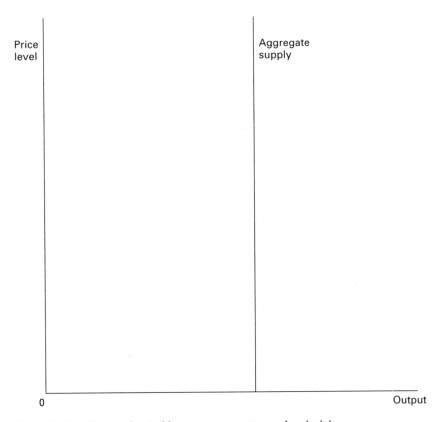

Figure 10.18   *The neoclassical long-run aggregate supply schedule*

Here, then, can be seen the importance of the argument concerning the possibility of the persistence of unemployment in the economy. This is why Keynes's points mentioned earlier regarding the inefficacy of changes in the rate of money wages in reducing unemployment are felt to be significant. If wages cannot alter to clear labour surpluses in the way suggested by neoclassical economists, then the aggregate supply schedule could remain less than vertical over a long period of time. This is not simply a barren academic debate. It has fundamental policy implications. If the aggregate supply schedule is similar to the shape suggested by the 45 degree diagram, then it is a legitimate, indeed required, policy response of the government to raise aggregate demand in the economy in the face of significant unemployment. Thus an increase in government spending, a cut in taxation or a reduction in interest rates would be sensible policy responses: output could rise and unemployment fall. However, if the long-run aggregate supply schedule is vertical, then an expansion of demand by the government must be deemed as foolhardy in the long run. Much as it could stimulate an output response in the short run, in the long run it can only lead to inflation. Manipulating aggregate demand could still have a role in government policy, but only in terms of reducing aggregate demand which leads to a lowering of the rate of inflation (or perhaps eventually a fall in the price level). Given the significance for policy, disagreements over the shape of the aggregate supply schedule must be seen as a macroeconomic theoretical difference of real importance.

The belief in the vertical long-run aggregate supply schedule by neoclassical economists, and the increasing sway that these economists began to have on many developed nations' economic policies from the middle of the 1970s, make it easy to understand the rationale for the development of so-called 'supply-side' policies. Given the impotence of the government to increase output through demand management policies, what then could governments attempt to do of benefit for the economy? According to the aggregate supply and demand framework, the logical alternative is to try to shift the aggregate supply schedule to the right. This will lead to higher output in the economy, in other words economic growth. This is a possibility that could not logically have been suggested through the other two models. The effect of such a policy can be simply shown: see Figure 10.19.

The rightward movement of the aggregate supply schedule causes an increase in output and a fall in the price level, a highly desirable result. The sorts of policies that have characterised several western economies, such as the USA and the UK, during the 1980s can be seen as supply-side policies which attempt to move the aggregate supply schedule to the right. Thus, within the labour market, attempts to reduce trade union power, reduce welfare benefits and abolish any minimum wage legislation are efforts to make the market function more effectively. A more efficient labour market will allow all forms of unemployment to fall and entrepreneurs to raise output profitably: the aggregate supply schedule will move to the right. Similarly, attempts to

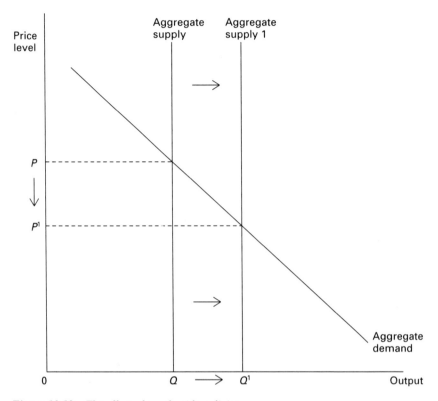

Figure 10.19   *The effect of supply-side policies*

increase enterprise in the economy, such as cutting the top marginal rates of income tax and providing a greater reward for high earners, are seen as stimulating new business ventures and employment opportunities, thus moving the aggregate supply schedule. Equally, privatisation was expected to stimulate competition and encourage more efficient production, once more moving the aggregate supply schedule.

Before leaving this framework, it is worth pointing out how it can also help to explain one of the problems that appeared beyond the 45 degree diagram approach: stagflation. Approaches which rely exclusively on movements of demand could not explain the co-existence of inflation and unemployment as it would require both too much and too little demand at the same time. However, allowing the supply-side of the economy to have a role can help to explain situations. Some economists have suggested that inflation may be caused not by too much demand but by the build-up of cost pressures in the economy which cause firms to raise their prices. If workers then attempt to maintain their real wage against these price increases, then further labour cost increases occur, and there

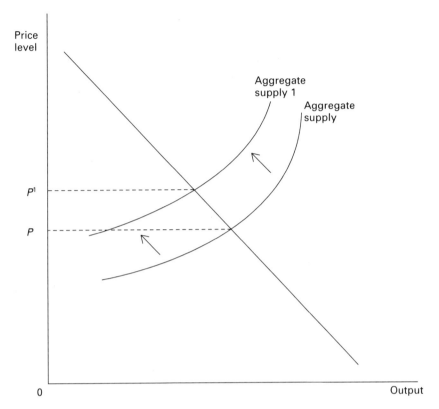

Figure 10.20   *Cost-push inflation*

is an inflationary process. This can be illustrated on the aggregate supply and demand framework: See Figure 10.20.

The increase in costs causes the aggregate supply schedule to move to the left. This causes a rise in the price level, even though the economy has unemployed resources. If the rise in costs is persistent, then there is inflation over a period of time. In similar vein, the framework can help to explain the stagflation that arose from the oil price rises in the early 1970s. The increased price of oil caused a significant increase in the costs of developed nations, thus shifting the aggregate supply schedule to the left. At the same time, aggregate demand fell because the oil-producing nations were not able to re-process the much larger spending power that they now had, and many governments responded to inflationary and balance-of-payments problems by cutting demand in their economies. This shifted the aggregate demand schedule to the left and produced the outcome shown in Figure 10.21.

The price level has risen and the level of unemployment has risen. The conditions for stagflation have been created.

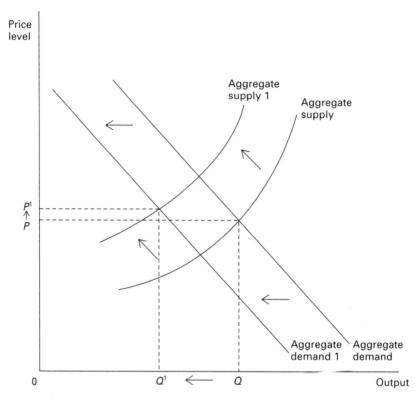

Figure 10.21   *Stagflation due to large increases in the world price of oil*

CONCLUSION

The three different macroeconomic models in use in standard economics textbooks can help to illustrate some of the key issues in macroeconomics. The 45
degree diagram has restrictive assumptions and ignores the money market and
the supply-side of the economy. *ISLM* analysis incorporates the functioning of
the money market and can also introduce an international aspect to the analysis.
However, it still does not deal with the supply-side of the economy. Aggregate
supply and demand analysis does have the advantage of being able to deal with
movements in the economy due either to demand or supply forces. It also illustrates the fundamental importance of the shape of the aggregate supply schedule
for government macroeconomic policy. One concern that has not perhaps fully
been addressed, however, is how well it accords with microeconomic models of
supply and demand with which it might be thought to have some compatibility.
As with the other two models, it is an example of how the two sides of economics have often been separated.

Reference

Keynes, J.M. (1936) *The General Theory of Employment, Interest and Money* (London: Macmillan).

11 Unemployment, Inflation and the Phillips Curve

How do we judge the performance of any economy? How can we say that one country's economy is performing better than another's? There are various measurements that can be taken, but the rate of unemployment and the rate of inflation are certainly two of them. Economists and governments may debate much over the appropriate economic policies required for any country, but there is little or no dissension about the fact that low rates of unemployment and inflation (probably linked with a high rate of economic growth) are the appropriate targets. This, then, is the heartland of macroeconomics, both in terms of theory and of recommended government policy.

Theories concerning unemployment and inflation have existed as long as the study of macroeconomics. The debates that have raged over the past two decades in developed economies concerning causes and cures are not new ones. They also constitute part of the fundamental question in economics, namely how well does the market function if it is left to its own devices? The purpose of this chapter is to outline the suggested causes and to take note of any recent theoretical contributions that may be seen as significant. These may have implications for policy. It will also be necessary to look at the possible relationship between unemployment and inflation, another classic area of macroeconomics study. This is best done within the framework of the so-called 'Phillips curve'. Thus, the chapter is divided into the following three sections:

1. Unemployment. It is easy to explain what is undesirable about unemployment, but not so straightforward to define it. This is considered. The traditional theories of unemployment are outlined, and then new contributions are discussed. The implications for policy are noted, in particular the controversy concerning the desirability of reducing unemployment benefit levels.
2. Inflation. Definition is once more a problem with inflation, but the undesirability of inflation is nowhere near as obvious as is the case with unemployment. This requires careful consideration. The various suggested causes of inflation are discussed, including the limited recent insights. The implications for policy are also discussed.
3. The Phillips curve. The possible relationship between unemployment and inflation was originally formalised by Phillips (1958). This is explained, as is the important challenge made by Friedman (1968) which led to the so-called 'expectations-augmented' Phillips curve. The phenemenon known as 'hysteresis', an apparent worsening of any possible trade-off between

inflation and unemployment, is also considered. Implications for policy arising from the different models are suggested.

UNEMPLOYMENT

No one disagrees that unemployment is undesirable. Politicians of all political hues will admit the need to keep the rate of unemployment as low as is reasonably possible (whatever that might mean). If the essence of economics is to consider how best to use a nation's limited economic resources to try to meet its infinite desires and wants, then the thought of not making use of all available economic resources (in this case, labour) can be seen as little short of economic insanity. The fundamental economic problem is worse than it needs to be if there is unemployment. This is not the only concern about unemployment. Unemployment is seen to have social and personal costs. A feeling of worth is often associated with paid employment. If paid employment is not available, then nor is the feeling of worth. Many people suggest that there is a strong link between unemployment and criminal and delinquent behaviour. Unemployment implies inequality between the 'haves' with paid jobs and the 'have-nots' who are unemployed. Unemployment also creates difficulties for governments. All unemployment reduces a government's income (due to lower tax receipts) and increases its expenditure (in the form of unemployment benefit). Insofar as unemployment is not liked by the electorate, then a government which presides over a significant level of unemployment might be in danger of losing an election. From every perspective, unemployment is undesirable.

Given the concern with unemployment, it is important that its meaning is understood. This is not as straightforward as it might at first appear. For example, how do we measure the number of people that can be considered as unemployed in a nation? Is it all of those without paid employment? Clearly not, as some are disqualified by age. Is it, then, all of those of working age who do not have a paid job? Again, clearly not, as many people choose not to be in paid employment for good reasons, such as pursuing an educational course or wishing to be fully employed in bringing up a family. Given this, the easiest and most sensible definition, then, seems to be that it is the number of those who register themselves as unemployed, as recorded by the government. This would suggest a number that represents those who are available for work but do not currently have any form of paid employment. For various reasons, this figure may not, however, be seen as fully satisfactory. This figure could underestimate the level of unemployment. If there are people who would like a job if it were available but are not eligible to receive unemployment benefit (as they would be the second earner in a household) then they may not register as being unemployed. There are various other reasons for an underestimate depending upon the system that is operated in any particular country. For example, in the United Kingdom, it is no longer possible to be considered as unemployed if under the age of eighteen as there are training schemes available for all sixteen and seventeen year olds. Non-working males over the age of sixty are unlikely to register themselves as unemployed since it is not necessary to be registered as unemployed in order to be given free contributions to the National Insurance fund. It is also possible that official unemployment figures could overestimate the level of unemployment. If people register as unemployed in order to receive unemployment benefit, but at the same time are in paid employment, then there will be an overestimate. Those who are spending a brief period of time between two different jobs are not unemployed in the same way as those who are unemployed with no prospect of another job. This suggests that measuring the duration of unemployment may be as important as measuring the level. There may be those who are registered as unemployed who have no intention of taking up paid employment. Such people would not seem to be in the same category as those who are actively seeking paid employment. Thus, it is very hard to say how many people are unemployed in a country.

The final point made above opens up another classic difficulty in considering unemployment, namely who is voluntarily and who is involuntarily unemployed? Is a fully qualified doctor who loses his or her job and then immediately turns down a job that is available on a factory production line voluntarily or involuntarily unemployed? In one sense, the answer must be that the person concerned is now voluntarily unemployed. However, whether it would be desirable for society for the doctor to take this job, given all the training that has been gained to handle a diverse and highly skilled job for which there is likely to be continuing demand, seems unsure. Many such other examples could be cited. In general, economists tend to work on the following definition. If someone is willing and able to work at the going wage, but is unable to secure paid employment, then he or she is deemed to be involuntarily unemployed. Someone who is not in employment but is not prepared to work at the current wage must thus be deemed to be voluntarily unemployed. This appears to give a clear working definition. Unfortunately, it still does not answer the original conundrum concerning the doctor. The problem is that the definition is a generalisation which attempts to cover the whole of the labour market. In practice, there will be many different going wages in many different parts of the labour market. Thus, it is likely still to be necessary to examine individual cases.

One final problem remains: what is meant by 'full employment'? Again, this appears a relatively easy question at first sight. Presumably, it is when there is no involuntary unemployment (whatever exactly that may be deemed to mean). However, in practice, full employment has always tended to be equated with a certain level of unemployment. There will always be a number unemployed for various reasons, such as those who are simply between two forms of paid employment. For these reasons, Beveridge (1944) suggested that something around 3 per cent of the labour force being unemployed could be deemed to be a state of full employment. More recently, a different version of what might be seen as full employment has emerged and termed the 'natural rate of unemployment' (see the discussion of the Phillips curve later in this chapter). This is a level of unemployment where the rate of inflation does not tend to vary. Estimates of this level for many developed economies have suggested that it could be consistent with rates of unemployment considerably higher than that suggested by Beveridge.

Given all of these caveats, it is now possible to consider the various suggestions regarding the causes of the level of recorded unemployment in an economy.

TRADITIONAL THEORIES OF UNEMPLOYMENT

There will always be a certain level of unemployment within a country. The most obvious reason is that there is unlikely to be perfect synchronisation between someone finishing one job before taking up another. There may be a period of time during which a person who has finished one form of paid employment has to search for another. Economists call this type of unemployment 'frictional' unemployment. Every market economy should expect to have this as people move from one job to another in response to market demand and technological developments. The situation only really becomes a cause for significant concern when such people become stuck between jobs. They may find that they do not have the skills and qualifications required to secure the forms of employment that are available. This severe form of frictional unemployment is referred to as 'structural' unemployment. There are other types of unemployment that are likely to exist in any market economy. Some industries, such as building, tourism and agriculture, suffer from seasonal movements in supply and/or demand. People who work in such industries are likely not to be fully employed at all points of the year, and thus any such unemployment created in particular months is referred to as 'seasonal' unemployment. Government unemployment figures are usually adjusted in order to take account of this. Other possible types of unemployment include 'residual' unemployment which refers to a part of the workforce which has extremely limited skills and thus is unlikely to secure employment.

The focus of this analysis is not on the types of unemployment referred to above, important as they may be for the individuals concerned. Our interest here is on large-scale and persistent (perhaps referred to as 'mass') unemployment. Why might a large number of people be involuntarily unemployed over a significant length of time? It is possible to identify two major explanations for this which can reasonably now be referred to as 'traditional'. The first of these is the classical, or today, neoclassical, explanation.

The neoclassical approach to economics suggests that, if permitted, markets work in order to allocate scarce resources. Further, they work in such a way as not to allow shortages or surpluses to persist. The price of the commodity concerned will adjust in the face of the forces of supply and demand to remove any shortage or surplus. This is relevant when one thinks of unemployment. Unemployment represents a surplus of the commodity of labour. As in the case

of any surplus, the price of the commodity would be expected to fall until the
surplus cleared. In this case, the price of labour, in other words the real wage
rate, could be expected to fall until unemployment disappeared. Neoclassical
theory thus suggests that both the supply of and the demand for labour are functions of the real wage (the real value of the money wage, taking account of the
impact of changes in the price level). This is best understood through a simple
supply and demand diagram for labour: see Figure 11.1.

If the real wage is at $W1$, then there is a surplus of labour equal to $L1–L2$.
This distance represents the level of unemployment at this real wage. According
to this approach, such unemployment could not, strictly speaking, be described
accurately as 'involuntary'. People are unemployed because they will not accept
a lower real wage. They could obtain employment if they were prepared to offer
their services for a lower real wage. They are not prepared to do so, and to that
extent can be described as 'voluntarily' unemployed. There are $L2$ workers who
would be willing and able to work at real wage $W1$, but there are only $L1$ jobs
available at this real wage. This situation will not persist. Given the surplus,

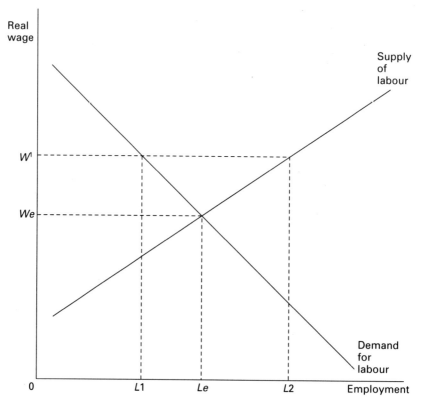

Figure 11.1   *Unemployment in the neoclassical model*

some unemployed workers will now offer their services at a lower real wage than *W*1, as suggested would be required above, in an effort to secure paid employment. Thus the real wage starts to move downwards. As the real wage falls, then so employers are prepared to employ more workers, and more workers are no longer prepared to offer their services. This process continues until the real wage has fallen to *We* and there are *Le* workers employed. At this point the supply of labour is equal to the demand and the surplus has disappeared. There is now no unemployment because all those who wish to secure paid employment at the going real wage have succeeded in doing so. There are still people who do not have jobs who could have, but this is because they are not willing to offer their services at the going real wage: they are voluntarily unemployed. Thus, the concept of 'involuntary' unemployment is alien to this approach, as is the possibility of persistent large-scale unemployment. It should be noted that there will still be unemployment for frictional, structural and seasonal reasons, as suggested earlier.

This analysis appears to suggest that there will not be persistent large-scale unemployment in a properly functioning market economy. It must thus be asked why we have observed such unemployment during the twentieth century. According to this analysis, the answer must be that it is because the real wage rate has got stuck at too high a level and has not been able to fall to the appropriate level. In terms of Figure 11.1, the real wage has got stuck at *W*1 and has not been able to fall to *We* and thus unemployment of *L*1–*L*2 has persisted. This begs the question of what prevents the suggested process of unemployed workers undercutting current real wages and thus forcing down the general real wage rate. There are various explanations that are offered. One is that trade unions prevent real wages from falling to their equilibrium level. Insofar as trade unions have power to set wages in anything less than a perfect market, then they may wish to try to maintain a real wage of *W*1 for all their members and to prevent this from falling. If such action is successful, it is responsible for unemployment. Another favoured explanation for the failure of the real wage rate to fall to the required level is that the level of unemployment benefit that is available to those without work is too high. The suggestion is that unemployment benefit prevents workers being prepared to offer their services at a real wage level that would succeed in clearing the surplus of labour that exists. Thus, the surplus persists.

An alternative version of the above analysis suggests that it is not an inappropriate real wage level in itself that creates unemployment, but rather inaccurate expectations of the real wage rate that cause the unemployment. To understand this possibility, it must be emphasised that the wage rate that concerns actual and potential workers is the real wage rate. It is the real value of the wage, after allowing for the effects of changes in the price level, that is of concern. This can create complications. It is possible to imagine a situation where the rate of increase of nominal wages falls (more likely in modern economies than a fall in the actual level of wages). The consequence of this is that workers perceive this as a fall in their real wage rate, given the rate of inflation. Therefore less workers are prepared to offer their services and recorded unemployment rises. However, this is probably due to a misperception. In fact, the fall in the rate of increase of money wages is likely to be associated with a fall in the rate of increase of all prices, probably due to a reduction in aggregate demand in the economy. Thus, the real wage has not in fact fallen. Once workers realise this, then they will be prepared to offer their services once more. However, until they do so, the unemployment will persist. This is an argument which will be encountered again when considering the Phillips curve.

Some observations can be made about the neoclassical analysis of unemployment. The first is that the sort of diagram used in the above explanation is only really appropriate in a highly competitive market. Only then will the forces of supply and demand set prices with individual agents powerless to affect the outcome. This is not the typical case in most markets, and is certainly not the case in the labour market. Indeed, the suggestion of trade union activity gives one important example of how the labour market does not function in a fully competitive way. The strength of employers in various industries is another important imperfection. In various professions, there are significant barriers to entry, such as social status and qualifications, which prevent full competition from occurring. These factors affect how the labour market will function and thus how it may or may not react in the face of unemployment. At the very least, it implies that there is likely to be much more to consider than the simple mechanism suggested in a competitive situation.

A second point that needs to be made concerns the social objectives of a country. It might be that for the labour market to clear in the way suggested in Figure 11.1, the real wage had to fall to a very low level. A question would have to be asked as to whether this could be deemed to be socially acceptable. This is part of the discussion over the desirability of introducing a minimum wage. From the standpoint of neoclassical analysis, such a minimum wage must create unemployment if it is set at a level above *We*. However, what if society judges that *We* is too low to give an acceptable standard of living? Perhaps unemployment will be the price to pay, or perhaps alternative approaches will have to be sought to try to ensure that the surplus of labour can be cleared without the wage falling to such a low level.

In Chapter 10 on macroeconomic models, it was pointed out that Keynes saw problems in suggesting that the real wage would adjust downwards in the face of unemployment. Even in the competitive situation described above, the problem facing workers is that they can only succeed in forcing down money wages. The fall in the rate of increase of money wages may simply lead to a proportionate fall in inflation as there is a fall in the rate of increase of firms' costs. Thus the real wage is unaffected and there is no movement in unemployment. There is no workable mechanism for reducing the real wage. This is a highly significant point insofar as suggesting the idea of 'involuntary' unemployment. It may be, according to this analysis, that unemployed workers are willing to offer their services for employment at a lower real wage but have no mechanism by which they are able to achieve such a desire. In this case, such unemployed workers can reasonably be described as 'involuntarily' unemployed. The problem is compounded as workers are sufficiently concerned about their position on the wages' hierarchy to resist any possible reduction in the rate of increase of money wages which could see them lose their position in that hierarchy.

Keynes's scepticism over the classical analysis led him to suggest his own explanation of widespread and persistent unemployment. We can now consider this to be the second traditional explanation of persistent involuntary unemployment. Keynes suggested that the focus of attention should not be upon the level of the real wage, but rather upon the level of aggregate demand in the economy. From a different standpoint, the problem was not that the real wage was too high but that the level of spending in the economy was too low. Indeed, Keynes's analysis can be interpreted as suggesting that the real wage depends upon the level of employment rather than the other way round, as neoclassical analysis suggests. In some ways, this was similar to a type of unemployment that had always been identified as existing, namely 'cyclical' unemployment. The business cycle was admitted as a reality of all market economies, and thus there was a certain level of unemployment that was acknowledged as being associated with the downturn of the business cycle. From a neoclassical position, this is due to the misperceptions of workers as wage and price inflation slow down in the face of lower demand. However, Keynes went further. He suggested that a shortage of demand could not only lead to involuntary unemployment, but that that situation could persist indefinitely if the level of demand did not change. The argument is simply illustrated on the 45 degree diagram: see Figure 11.2.

The full employment level of national income (Yfe) is the level of income and spending that is required to ensure that firms will produce the level of output required to make it worth their while employing all available labour. The problem for this economy is that the equilibrium level of national income, where planned expenditures are equal to planned incomes, is at national income level Ye. This is below the level required to secure full employment and thus there will be unemployment. Moreover, the economy will remain stuck in this position until there is a change in the level of aggregate demand in the economy. Thus, anything that causes a significant fall in aggregate demand in an economy can be seen as responsible for causing unemployment. From this perspective, the simplest explanation of the widespread unemployment in much of the western world from the 1980s is the anti-inflationary economic policy stance of many western governments. In an effort to reduce inflation well below the levels of the 1970s, interest rates and other policies have been used to reduce the demand pressure on prices. The result has been unemployment.

Another way of thinking of the situation is that the economy is in some form of vicious circle from which the market system cannot engineer an escape. There are people without jobs who would like to work in return for the going

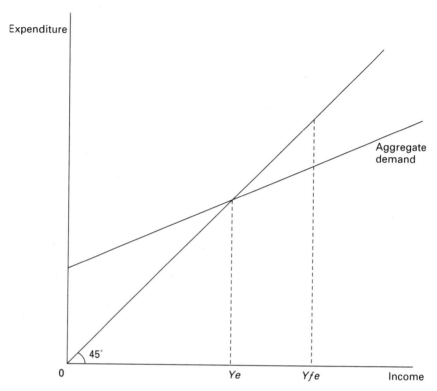

Figure 11.2   *Unemployment due to a shortage of aggregate demand*

wage. There are firms who would like to produce goods and services if they believed that these would be bought. The unemployed workers would happily spend their wages they received if employed upon the goods and services that would be produced by firms if they believed that a market existed for them. Thus, the system could work. The problem is that there is no mechanism for moving from the current position to one where the new wages are earned and the new goods and services produced and bought. Thus, the unemployment persists.

The idea that the economy could become 'stuck' in the position shown above is an important aspect of Keynes's analysis of the unemployment problem. Following Keynes's original analysis, there was much discussion concerning the various mechanisms through which the economy would in fact move itself back to a position of full employment. One of the best known was the so-called 'real balance effect'. This suggested that if unemployment in an economy were to lead to falling wages and prices then this would increase the real value of the monetary balances possessed by citizens. This would create an increase in the level of aggregate spending and thus cause unemployment to fall. As long as prices were flexible, unemployment would not persist. In general, for the classical or neoclassical economist, a position of unemployment as shown above could arise due to the operation of the trade cycle and the possible misperceptions about the real wage described above that might occur. However, the situation would not persist because the real wage would adjust, and the surplus of labour would clear. Thus, some economists see the debate between the interpretations of unemployment as all to do with how flexible prices, particularly the real wage, is likely to be. The more inflexible are prices, the greater the possibility of a Keynesian-style explanation being accurate. In many ways, the newer theories of unemployment to be discussed below tend to concentrate on this issue of reasons for lack of wage flexibility and how it may help to explain unemployment in modern economies. It should, however, be noted that some economists suggest that flexible or inflexible prices were not the issue for Keynes. Certainly, it has already been discussed how he suggested that the necessary fall in real wages could not be achieved in a market economy. However, there is also the suggestion that other factors, such as the somewhat intangible nature of business confidence and its influence over investment decisions by firms, coupled with the role of money in a modern economy, were considered by Keynes to be the issues that were at the heart of unemployment problems. This should be borne in mind during the review of newer theories of unemployment.

NEW THEORIES OF UNEMPLOYMENT

In many ways, the newer theories of unemployment can be taken in tandem with the work of the so-called 'New Keynesians' described in the Chapter 3. There are various suggestions that have been put forward recently which may help to explain the persistence of large-scale unemployment, the issue with which we are principally concerned here. One such example is the increasing returns explanation. This makes the observation that if an economy tends to be characterised by increasing returns to scale (unit costs tend to fall as the scale of production increases), then new small businesses will not be in a position where they are able to compete with established older businesses. The implication of this is that one of the suggestions for those unemployed, namely that they could always set up in business themselves in some way, thus by-passing the problem of having to be employed and paid a wage by a firm, is not in fact available. Such an unemployed person would not be able to produce at a level which allowed him or her to be price-competitive with firms already in existence. Unemployment persists. However, this newer explanation is not typical. The usual nature of these newer explanations is that they tend to give reasons why prices, particularly the real wage, do not tend to change, even in the face of unemployment. Implicitly, they do thus tend to make the assumption that in some way persistent unemployment is associated with too high a real wage. Either, from a classical standpoint, the real wage has become too high and will not adjust downwards, or, from a Keynesian position, the problem of unemployment created by a lack of aggregate demand cannot and will not be overcome by any adjustment in the real wage.

There are several different explanations available for the likely lack of movement of real wages and hence the persistence of unemployment. One type of explanation tends to stress the significance of costs that are associated with changing prices. For firms, there may be a benefit to be derived from establishing a reputation for stable prices which allows consumers to reduce their search costs between different brands of a product. In terms of wages, this could mean workers without employment being able to reduce their search costs by sticking with the firm whose wage is known. It is not certain whether this effect can be deemed important. A greater possibility must derive from the fact that changes in wages have tangible costs associated with them in terms of the adjustment process. In most developed and democratic economies, changes in wages tend to be achieved through some form of bargaining procedure. There are then the required administrative changes when the new wage has been achieved. Depending on the exact procedure adopted and how quickly it achieves the aim of adjusting wages in the manner desired, there could be considerable costs associated with the process. This certainly explains why wage rounds in most countries tend to occur no more often than annually. Of course, the implication is that the opportunities for employers and employees to try to change the real wage are not frequent.

It has been suggested that 'implicit wage contacts' may often exist, and that these are another important source of wage rigidity and hence persisting unemployment. The essence of this theory is that workers tend to be risk-averse, risk-aversion being a common assumption in economics. Risk-averse workers would prefer a stable wage to a fluctuating wage, even if the average of the fluctuating wage were the same as or even slightly higher than the stable wage. Employers may be willing to give the guarantee of such a stable wage, especially if they can secure some premium such as concessions in terms of work practices. The implication of such implicit wage contracts is that the wage is not free to vary, and thus if the economy is in a position of unemployment, the wage cannot be expected to move downwards to clear the surplus of labour.

'Efficiency wages' offer a further possible explanation of real wages persisting at a level that might be considered to be above the market-clearing level. The starting point for this theory is the observation that employers are likely to know less about the productivity of the workers that they employ than the workers themselves do. Employers can only judge productivity by observing actual production. This need not be a totally accurate picture of potential productivity and only allows a judgement to be made on those workers already employed by the firm and not of any potential recruits. There are then various different implications of this, all of which suggest the persistence of wages at a higher level than if the productive potential of each worker were truly known by employers. The first is that firms will tend to offer high wages in the anticipation that this will help to attract high productivity workers to the firm. Workers with a high productivity are in a position to secure a higher wage than those with a lower productivity, and thus such people are more likely to try to secure a job with the firm if it offers a higher wage. A higher wage will also increase the costs for a worker of being sacked as it is unlikely that such a worker would be able to secure as high a wage in alternative employment. Thus the worker is provided with an incentive to work to his or her full productive potential in order to avoid being sacked. A similar sort of point is that the higher wage offered reduces the likelihood of quitting by higher productivity workers as it will not be straightforward to secure a higher wage elsewhere. This helps to reduce the costs of recruitment for a firm which arise when quitting occurs. Related to this is that not only may there be less quitting by those employed by the firm, but there should also be less search activity involving looking for alternative employment taking place amongst the firm's employees. Such activity tends to reduce the productivity of workers as their energies are directed to searching rather than current employment. A further and slightly different possibility is that higher wages may be beneficial to worker motivation. Either due to a pay rise or simply to comparison with similar workers in different firms, workers may feel better motivated. This in turn could lead to a higher level of productivity from a group of workers than the productivity that would be associated with a lower wage.

The efficiency wages explanation of persistently high real wages can be integrated with dual labour market theory to provide a more general model. A dual labour market can be characterised as consisting of a primary and secondary sector. The primary sector tends to be characterised by high wages, good working conditions, stable employment and chances for advancement. In contrast, the secondary sector is characterised by low wages, poor working conditions, high labour turnover and little chance of advancement. Movement between these two sectors of the labour market is limited, because institutional rules tend to prevent entry into the primary sector and the feedback effects of the secondary sector upon its workers mean that they become less capable of entering the primary sector. In terms of efficiency wages, the suggestion is that where the link between wages and productivity is perceived to be important and wages are used to recruit, retain and motivate workers, then the wage is likely to be above the market-clearing level. The demand for employment is thus greater than the supply as not all those who seek jobs will be able to find them. This is a description of the primary sector. In the secondary sector, either it is easy to monitor the productivity of workers or the link between wages and productivity is not seen as important. Here, efficiency wages will not be paid and the wage will equal the market-clearing wage: anyone can obtain a job at the going wage rate. Workers who seek employment in the primary sector are unlikely to accept employment in the secondary sector. They have a greater chance of securing employment in the primary sector by having the time that is available in unemployment to search for jobs. Equally, a willingness to accept a job in the secondary sector could act as a signal to employers in the primary sector that the worker has low productivity. Workers who are unemployed in this fashion can be described as involuntarily unemployed in the sense that they are willing to work at the going wage in the primary sector but cannot secure employment there.

A new theory that has aroused much interest and credence is the 'insider–outsider' model. This starts from an observation that is similar to one of the suggestions made in efficiency wages, namely that there may be considerable turnover costs to firms of replacing current workers ('insiders') with workers not currently working for the firm ('outsiders'). These costs include advertising, negotiations, contracts and training. Insiders are then able to exploit this knowledge by demanding at least some of these turnover costs as part of their wage. A firm would be better off paying the higher wage than making the workers redundant and then having to face the turnover costs of replacing the workers. The greater the turnover costs, the greater the premium that workers are able to claim above the market-clearing wage. Indeed, trade unions could endeavour to raise these turnover costs by threatening industrial action in the face of any suggestion of redundancies. In this way, the real wage could become established and persist at a level above the market-clearing wage, and thus unemployment can persist. The likelihood of unemployment persistence is strengthened by the fact that according to this analysis, unemployed workers will have little if any impact upon the wages of those in work. They do not represent a threat to those currently in employment (due to the turnover costs faced by firms in changing its workforce) and thus high real wages can persist even at high levels of unemployment. This analysis can once more be further refined by considering it in the context of a dual labour market. Here, the power of insiders is considerable in the primary market, and workers may remain impervious to the pressure of outsiders. However, in the secondary sector, the turnover costs of changing workers are much lower (for example, little training is required) and thus outsiders are a real threat and the wage is forced much nearer to the market-clearing level.

POLICIES FOR UNEMPLOYMENT

The practical significance of considering different possible causes of unemployment is in drawing some conclusions regarding appropriate government policy to try to counter the unemployment problem. Clearly, the suggested policy will depend upon the perceived cause of the unemployment. Structural unemployment will need some form of training which could be provided by or subsidised by the government. From the classical or neoclassical position, the essence of the problem of large-scale unemployment is the real wage becoming stuck at an inappropriately high level. The only cure is to secure a fall in this real wage. Thus attention needs to focus upon things that may impede the necessary fall. Attempts to reduce the power of trade unions could, thus, be seen from this standpoint as an attempt to lower unemployment, if trade unions are seen as an important source of maintaining the real wage at a level above market clearing.

From a Keynesian position, the focus of attention must be the level of aggregate demand. The problem is that this is too low. Even if it is associated with a real wage that is in some sense 'too high', this is not the appropriate focus of attention as it will not be flexible downwards. Thus, the appropriate government policy to involuntary unemployment must be anything that will increase spending in the economy. Specifically, this is likely to mean fiscal policy (raising government spending and/or lowering taxation) and/or monetary policy (lowering interest rates).

What of the new theories of unemployment? Do they suggest further possible policy responses? In some ways, the new theories can be taken two ways. From a neoclassical position, they might be seen as identifying possible further sources of real wage rigidity which will need to be tackled if unemployment is to be lowered. But it is not entirely clear how, for example, the persistence of high real wages created through efficiency wages can be tackled by government policy, given that firms voluntarily offer these wages for their own purposes. From a Keynesian point of view, the theories simply strengthen and explain the rigidity of the real wage which means that a shortage of demand can lead to persistent unemployment. The case for an expansion of aggregate demand at first sight remains. However, this is not entirely clear, as the 'insider–outsider' model could lead to a suggestion that an increase in spending may lead current workers to use their insider power to induce firms to raise prices and pay higher money wages rather than to expand output and raise employment. Thus the result of higher aggregate demand is higher prices, not lower unemployment.

One possible implication of the new theories appears to be that reducing unemployment benefit could have a beneficial effect on the level of unemployment. This is a suggestion that accords with a neoclassical approach insofar as unemployment benefit could be seen as a factor in maintaining the real wage at a level that is associated with a surplus of labour. From the standpoint of the 'insider–outsider' model, a cut in the level of unemployment benefit would raise the pressure of 'outsiders' upon 'insiders' as they would now be prepared to accept lower wages to work and would seek harder for all job opportunities. This could force 'insiders' to accept lower real wages and thus could cause the level of employment to rise (if that is the mechanism that is seen as necessary to raise employment). Similarly, from the point of view of efficiency wages, employers now have less worries about individuals quitting to search for a new job, and the threat of sacking becomes a more powerful one. Both of these effects could enable firms not to have to offer a real wage so far above the market-clearing level and thus may raise the level of aggregate employment. This is likely to be a contentious issue and cannot be seen in isolation from any social objectives with regard to minimum standards of living that a society may have. However, Atkinson and Micklewright (1991) have attempted to review the different arguments with regard to the links between unemployment benefit and the level of unemployment. Their most important conclusion appears to have been that it is not the level of unemployment benefit that is likely to be the most important characteristic of different possible unemployment benefit systems in dictating the system's impact upon the level of unemployment. Rather, it is the other characteristics of the unemployment benefit that tend to have a greater impact. These include the duration of the unemployment benefit available. A high rate of unemployment benefit that is only available for six months could be associated with a lower level of unemployment, other things remaining equal, than a lower level of unemployment benefit that is available for a longer period of time. The shorter the period of availability, the greater the incentive to search to find employment during the period in which unemployment benefit is available. A further important characteristic of unemployment benefit systems is the extent to which they insist upon reasonable proof of search activity in order to qualify. If a system can ensure that recipients of unemployment benefit must be involved in active work search (through signed agreements, evidence of job applications and other means) then this may be more significant in reducing unemployment and putting pressure on those in employment than the level of the unemployment benefit.

Thus, the 'right' policy for unemployment must depend upon the perceived cause. However, using unemployment benefit as a case study also suggests that generalisations about such policies may not be as important as specific characteristics. It is necessary to look at the microeconomics as well as the macroeconomics.

INFLATION

Of all the changes that took place in macroeconomic theory and the associated macroeconomic policy of governments of developed countries from the middle of the 1970s and into the 1980s, there is one that can perhaps be seen as having the greatest impact. In some ways it need not necessarily have been associated with important movements in beliefs about economic theory (although in practice it probably was), but could be seen as a reassessment of social goals and priorities. That change was the apparent altering of the priorities within the macroeconomic policies of many of the governments of the western world: inflation, and not unemployment, should now be given the greatest priority when it came to the design of macroeconomic policy. Of course, this might be perceived as simply force of economic circumstance with the large increases in inflation in the middle of the 1970s associated with the oil price rises at that time. However, it represented a truly significant movement. It was most clearly summed up by the adage in the UK of governments since the middle of the 1970s that 'Inflation shall be the judge and jury of our economic policy'. Together with such statements could have been perceived the dropping of any commitment to some version of full employment. If a choice between unemployment and inflation had to be made, then unemployment would come second.

The slightly peculiar thing about this apparent re-ordering of economic policy goals is the lack of clarity in the minds of many as to what precisely is the problem with inflation. The costs of unemployment are plainly seen and listed earlier. Yet ask the so-called 'man in the street' why inflation is such a bad thing, and a range of less than entirely coherent responses might be anticipated. Clearly, an issue of such perceived importance needs investigation. However, before that, inflation itself needs defining. Once again, there may be more to this than at first appears to meet the eye.

The definition of inflation is simple insofar as it is either an increase in the general price level or a fall in the value of money within a country. The value of money falls by exactly the same amount as the general price level rises. However, there are two important points which further qualify this. The first is that inflation needs to be seen as a process rather than simply a one-off increase in prices. A once and for all increase in prices, for example the rise in oil prices in the middle and the end of the 1970s, is not really an inflation of any concern or interest. Prices rise once and then not again. Inflation is rather to do with the continuing raising of prices over a period of time. Thus, when we come to look at inflation, we must look at the whole process and why it persists, rather than consider a one-off price rise. The second point about a general price rise is that measuring it is not as straightforward as it might seem. In every developed country, it requires constructing an index of representative products which are weighted depending upon their importance in the average household budget. The rate of inflation then becomes how much on average these prices have risen, allowing for the weightings that have been given. The rate calculated is thus an average for a country, and the actual inflation rate faced by different individuals in a country could vary considerably. However, the problem goes further than this insofar as there is disagreement over what should or should not be included within the price index. For example, a classic example in the UK concerns the mortgage rate. The price of mortgages (in other words the rate of interest that has to be paid on a mortgage) has traditionally been included in the price index. This is entirely sensible if the reason for constructing the price index is to measure the extent to which the cost of living has risen and thus how much money wages may have to rise in order to compensate. However, there are clear concerns if the purpose of constructing a price index is to compare the inflation performance of different countries. This is a particular issue within Europe where one of the needed conditions to achieve a successful movement towards a single currency is the convergence of inflation rates. Given that there is considerably less home ownership in other European countries than in the UK and that other European nations often exclude mortgage rates from their calculations, then the UK should not include the movement in this price. Thus, it is not clear how inflation should be measured. Indeed, the UK has now been forced to a position where it declares two inflation rates each month for this reason.

The obvious problem with inflation is that average prices rise. However, it becomes rather less clear why this should be perceived as a problem if average incomes also rise by the same amount, as is usually the case. In this case, real incomes do not change and there is no immediate problem to be seen. One has to start thinking harder to discern the economic costs of inflation.

In a world of perfect markets with perfect information, full indexation (meaning that all relevant variables are changed in line with inflation) and flexible exchange rates (which can adjust so that changes in a nation's price level need not affect its international competitiveness), there is only one cost associated with inflation. This is the so-called 'shoe leather' cost caused by the need to keep money in an account which bears interest so that the value of money wealth is not eroded by inflation. This means that there is more activity required by individuals in terms of transferring money in and out of the relevant accounts as it is received and required for transactions than would be the case if there were no inflation. The shoe leather that is lost in the process represents the cost. Although some estimates have suggested that this can be a large cost, it is hard to believe that our concern with inflation would be so great if that was all there was to the issue. Of course, we do not live in the world just described, and thus there may be further costs that are associated with inflation.

One problem comes from the fact that we do not live in a world of complete indexation. Although the inflation experience of the 1970s has led to more indexation than was the case before, there are areas where the lack of full indexation can cause a redistribution of income and wealth in societies that may be deemed to be undesirable (although a value judgement is required to be sure of this). One potential example of this is the redistribution that inflation may cause towards governments. It is for this reason that inflation is sometimes referred to as the 'hidden tax'. If income tax thresholds are not raised in line with the rate of inflation, then higher money incomes which simply keep pace with increases in the cost of living will drag people up into higher income tax brackets. Hence the term 'fiscal drag'. Rising prices cause the value of firms stocks of unsold products to appreciate, and this can have implications for taxation. Capital allowances tend to be calculated on a historic cost basis (that is on last year's costs) and thus in times of inflation firms may not receive the true value of capital allowances that the tax system appears to be giving. The suggestion is that governments tend to receive a higher real tax revenue, other things being equal, in times of high inflation than in times of low inflation.

Other redistributions that are suggested are away from those on fixed incomes (such as pensions) and away from lenders to borrowers (as the real value of a borrowed sum of money is diminished by the effects of inflation). Clearly, the importance of these and other possible effects depends entirely upon the level of appropriate indexation that exists in a society. One important suggestion that has been made here with regard to the effects of inflation on savers is that it could cause a nation's savings ratio to rise. If savers have a target real value for their savings (if for example they are aiming to purchase something in the future with these savings) and if the interest rate does not fully compensate for the rate of inflation, then savers may have to save more of their income in order to maintain the real value of their savings. This could lead to a suggestion that inflation can cause unemployment if the fall in the propensity to consume causes firms to cut their output and employment.

In theory, a flexible exchange rate can compensate for an inflation that is above the relevant average by allowing the value of a country's currency to decline so that there is no loss in international price competitiveness. However, exchange rates are often not fully flexible. In that case, a rate of inflation that is above the average of the nation's competitors will cause a loss of competitiveness, a loss of demand and a reduction in output and employment. With regard to Europe, a single currency would represent the greatest possible level of a fixed exchange rate and no available outlet for higher inflation than a reduction in demand for the nation's products. Even with a flexible exchange rate, there may be difficulties. It may be that a fall in the exchange rate does not moderate the movement in prices relative to overseas prices as there may be inflexibility arising from various sources. The most common suggestion is real wage resistance. This is when any increase in prices results in an equivalent increase in money wages (and hence firms' costs) as workers aim to maintain the value of their real wage. In this situation, the inflationary effects cannot be offset. Equally, the value of a flexible exchange rate is not affected solely by movements in a nation's price level. There may be factors in the capital account that have a powerful effect on the exchange rate and tend to move it in the opposite direction from that required to compensate for the competitiveness effects of inflation. An obvious example would be a high interest rate causing flows of money into the country seeking the high returns available. This will tend to force up the value of the exchange rate and could offset the downward effect of rising product prices.

The world is also not one of perfect markets and perfect information. As such, there are concerns that inflation may cause the price system to be less effective than it might be. In particular, economic agents become confused between movements in relative prices and the general price level. Whilst an increase in the relative price of something might cause producers correctly to respond by producing more of that product, given the increased profit opportunities now represented, an increase in a price of a product that was simply part of a general increase in prices should not provoke such a response. Confusion could thus lead to an inefficient allocation of resources. This problem is likely to be more severe if the inflation is unanticipated. An inflation that is expected is less likely to lead to a confusion of the signals than an inflation that was not expected. Although difficult to quantify, this suggests that high, variable and unanticipated inflation could have considerable costs for an economy. Whether high inflation alone would produce such costs is less clear.

OLD AND NEW THEORIES OF INFLATION

It would not be right to describe developments in theories concerning the causes of inflation as 'new'. Rather, they would be better seen as resuscitating (with possible amendments) old theories. In essence, there are two types of explanation of inflation, the difference between which is best exemplified through the aggregate supply and demand framework.

The first general cause of inflation is seen as emanating from the demand side of the economy. Any increase in the level of aggregate demand in the economy is capable of causing an increase in the price level if there is not an increase in output that exactly matches the rise in spending. This can be shown in Figure 11.3.

The increase in aggregate demand (*AD* to *AD*1) has caused an increase in the price level because output has not responded fully to the increase in demand. Clearly, it matters what is seen to be the correct shape of the nation's aggregate supply schedule (see the discussion on this topic in Chapter 10 on macroeconomic models). The more vertical the aggregate supply schedule, the greater the effect on the price level of any increase in demand. Thus, it will be seen as relevant to consider whether the economy can be deemed to be at or near to full employment.

According to the above analysis, it would not matter what was the source of the increase of aggregate demand. It could equally be an increase in the spending of private consumers or of the government. It might not be so clear if it were due to an increase in investment as this may affect firms' costs and thus could also produce a movement of the aggregate supply schedule which could confuse the possible effect on the price level. However, it is not certain that what is illustrated above represents inflation in the manner described earlier. What is shown is a one-off increase in the price level of the economy due to the increase in demand. There is no suggestion of a process that will lead to a continual increase in prices that is the nature of inflation. Thus we have not really explained inflation. To do this, we would need to see continual increase in the level of aggregate demand leading to persistent increases in the price level. Only then would there be an inflationary process caused by an increase in aggregate demand. Reasons as to why this might happen need to be considered.

Although Figure 11.3 suggested that the source of the increase in aggregate demand may not be of interest, the classical quantity theory, or newer theories of monetarism, assume that the source of the increase in aggregate demand responsible for inflation will always be an excessive increase in the nation's supply of money. Thus, 'Inflation is always and everywhere a monetary phenomenon.' Although there are various different versions of this suggestion, they all differ little from the original quantity theory of money as most simply explained. This revolves around the following identity:

Money supply (*M*) multiplied by the velocity of circulation of money (*V*) is equal to the price level (*P*) multiplied by the number of transactions (*T*). In other words, *MV* equals *PT*.

This equation is true by definition. The value of total transactions over a period of time will be the same as the amount of money in the economy multiplied by the number of times that that money supply circulates through the

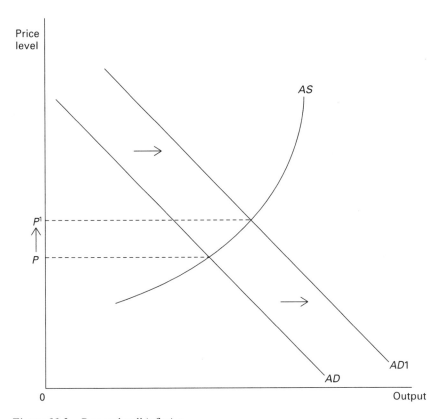

Figure 11.3   *Demand-pull inflation*

economy in that time period. The quantity theory concerns the nature of the assumptions that are made about the equation. The first assumption is that the level of transactions during the time period is fixed. This is essentially the same thing as saying that the level of output is fixed, which again is the same as saying that the level of employment is fixed. In other words, the economy is assumed to be at full employment. Thus the quantity theory of money, or monetarism, is the natural companion of classical, or neoclassical, macroeconomics. A classical view of the economy suggested that full employment was the general tendency of an economy left to its own devices. Thus, the assumption of a fixed level of transactions. The second assumption is that the velocity of circulation of the money supply is fixed. It is assumed that this is determined by institutional factors such as the nature of financial institutions, the nature of salary payment and other factors that are unlikely to change in the short run. Given these two assumptions, it can then be seen that movements in the money supply and movements in the price level will be associated with each other. The third assumption that is then made is that it is changes in the supply of money that will lead to changes in the price level rather than the other way round. Given that, there is then the theory that increases in the money supply lead to increases in the price level, or inflation. Again, this could be a one-off movement in the price level rather than a full inflationary process. However, the line of causation often suggested by monetarists does give a possible process rather than a simple one-off movement. The suggestion is that the usual source of an expansion of the money supply is a government macroeconomic policy aimed at reducing the level of unemployment. This may work initially, but soon simply leads to inflation. In an effort to reduce the level of unemployment, the government may thus increase the money supply further still, leading to yet higher inflation. However, even if this is not done, the higher rate of inflation has entered into people's expectations. Thus, if there is not to be higher unemployment, the government must allow the money supply to continue to rise at a level compatible with the rate of inflation. This idea is discussed further in the consideration of the Phillips curve below. There are, though, two important suggestions being made about how an increase in the price level can develop into an inflationary process. The first is expectations. If an increase in the price level leads to the expectation that there will be further increases in the price level, then this can create behaviour that is likely to lead to further increases in the price level. Although this is a point that is particularly associated with a monetarist view of inflation, it can be equally applied, with equal significance, to all other theories of inflation. The second point is that the government may pursue a policy of permitting monetary growth in the economy because of the fears of the effects on the real economy of not doing so. This accommodating policy could be an important part of allowing a one-off increase in the price level to turn into an inflationary process.

Before moving on, it is worth noting that the various criticisms of monetarism can equally well be seen through the simple quantity theory of money. If the economy can be stuck in a position of involuntary unemployment (the Keynesian suggestion), then an increase in the money supply could equally well lead to an increase in the level of transactions as the price level. If the velocity of circulation is not in fact fixed in the short run (a matter for empirical investigation which has produced conflicting results) then a change in the money supply may have no impact on the value of transactions since it could be offset by movements in the velocity of circulation. Even if velocity and transactions are fixed, the line of causation could lead from changes in the price level to the money supply rather than the opposite. Indeed, this might be another important possibility in the development of an inflationary process, suggesting that the money supply will always tend to accommodate inflationary movements. Even if all three assumptions are held to be true, there still remains the problem of how the money supply is to be defined and measured, and if this is possible whether it lies within a government's powers to control in a modern credit-based economy.

The other type of explanation of inflation that can be derived from aggregate supply and demand analysis emanates from the supply side of the economy. Any

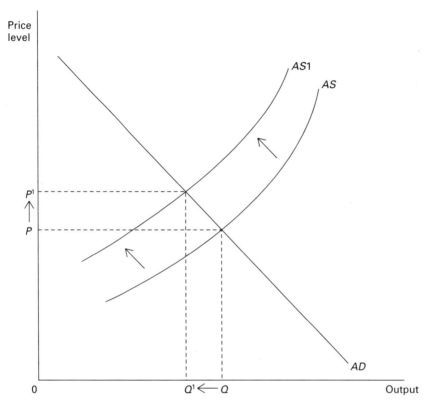

Figure 11.4 *Cost-push inflation*

increase in costs is likely to lead to an increase in the price level, as illustrated in Figure 11.4.

The increase in the costs of production within the economy have caused the aggregate supply schedule to move to the left (*AS* to *AS1*) and thus cause the price level to rise. Once more, the source of the cost increase does not matter: its effect will be to cause an increase in the price level. The costs of raw materials, imported inputs, labour machinery and land could all have had the the same effect. However, once more, all that is shown is a one-off increase. There is no process that could lead to inflation over a period of time. 'Cost-push' inflation can only be deemed a possibility if it can explain how increases in costs can set off a whole inflationary process.

One possible source of an inflationary process can be seen from what has happened to the level of output in Figure 11.4. The increase in costs has not only caused an increase in the price level, but has also led to a fall in the level of output with the likely associated increase in the level of unemployment. This is a source of concern for any government. Thus, there is the possibility that the government will raise the level of aggregate demand (perhaps through an accommodating monetary policy) to try to offset this. This in turn would cause a rightward movement of the aggregate demand schedule which would further raise the price level. An extra element can now be added to the story. The usual source of cost-push inflation is seen as an increase in the costs of labour, not least because this forms the largest part of firms' costs. One significant possibility is that workers demonstrate what is termed 'real wage resistance'. This means that any increase in the price level will provoke an equal attempt to raise money wages to offset the effects of this price level movement upon living standards. This will cause a further leftwards movement of the aggregate supply schedule which will again raise the price level. This can quickly develop into the expectation of continually rising prices which will have to be continually resisted through wage increases. Combined with a government monetary policy which is reluctant to see a rise in the level of unemployment, it is possible to see how a powerful inflationary process could develop.

A further source of a possible inflationary process is seen as arising from workers' concern over their relative wage rather than simply their absolute wage. If workers are concerned about their position in some perceived wages hierarchy, then a wage increase secured by one group of workers is likely to provoke further attempts at raising wages by other groups of workers in an effort to maintain their position in the hierarchy. This could provoke further wage demands, and so the process continues. If this is further combined with real wage resistance, there is a very strong inflationary process. The problem is clearly seen through the lens of game theory (see Chapter 4). Probably the best solution for all groups of workers in a country is to agree to moderate wage increases which lead to low levels of inflation and thus avoid the problems of inflation described above. However, the temptation for any individual group of workers is to try to go for a higher wage increase, either to try to steal a march on other groups or through the fear that other groups may be trying to steal a march on them and this must be resisted. The result is that all groups of workers go for higher wage bids, no one has stolen a march on anyone else and the economy suffers from a high rate of inflation. In this sense, the problem appears to be the decentralised nature of the wage-making decisions. Individual groups of workers behave in a certain way because of how they fear other individual groups of workers may behave.

POLICIES FOR INFLATION

As with unemployment, the suggested policies for inflation will depend upon the perceived cause. Thus, for the monetarist, there is no alternative to the need to control the growth of the money supply. For the cost-pusher, the rate of increase in money wages will have to be controlled. However, the emphasis in the preceding discussion was on the importance of identifying inflationary processes rather than one-off increases in the price level. Four particular suggestions were made regarding what may turn an increase in the price level into an inflationary process: an accommodating monetary policy, expectations of future price increases, real wage resistance, and workers' resistance to any threat to their position on the wages hierarchy. If a policy for inflation is to be truly successful, it must attack the problems caused by these factors. This was the logic behind monetary targeting in the 1980s which announced money supply growth targets for several years. The hope was that this would reduce inflationary expectations. Equally, the insistence of some economists on the need for a workable incomes policy can be understood. It would help to reduce inflationary expectations, eradicate the problem identified from decentralised wage bargaining and cut into the issue of real wage resistance. Designing an incomes policy that works and that still allows some relative movement of wages (important for the proper functioning of any market economy) is another issue. There are various possibilities, such as a tax-based system which does not disqualify any wage increase, but taxes firms for all increases above a certain level. However, given the four factors mentioned above, it is easy to see the logic of Meade's proposal (1982). The level of inflation is dictated by the permitted growth of the money supply (thus eradicating an accommodating monetary policy). The level of employment is then dictated by the level of wage agreements reached. The lower the level of wage settlements, the lower the level of unemployment. This clear link would be important in helping towards a consensus on the need for general wage moderation. The suggestion is further bolstered by the idea that when employers and employees cannot agree on a wage increase, the two bids will be referred to arbitration which will decide on the bid that is deemed to be in the best interests of the economy. This could help to move to the best solution of the prisoners' dilemma described above as it cut out the possibility of high wage bids. Unfortunately, the theory of 'insiders' and 'outsiders' discussed earlier suggests that those in work may be more concerned with their own fortunes than with the employment prospects of any other group of worker. The result could be higher unemployment.

THE PHILLIPS CURVE

Given the emphasis on the importance of unemployment and inflation in the study of macroeconomics, it is perhaps not surprising that there should also be so much discussion concerning the relationship between the two. The framework for this discussion is the so-called Phillips curve.

The history of the Phillips curve dates from a now famous article written by A.W. Phillips in 1958. In this article, Phillips set himself the empirical task of plotting the rate of change of money wages against the rate of unemployment over a period of years. Gathering the relevant data, Phillips then plotted the

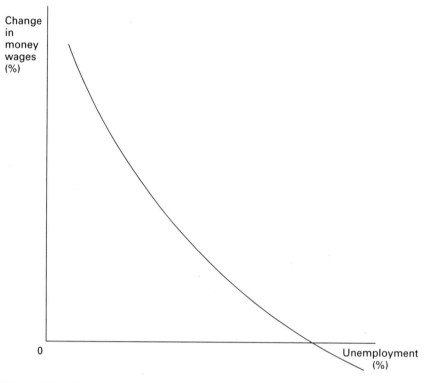

Figure 11.5   *The original Phillips curve*

points for the years in question and found a remarkably stable relationship over time that is illustrated in Figure 11.5.

There was an inverse relationship between the rate of change of money wages and the rate of unemployment. This was also seen as the equivalent of an inverse relationship between the rate of inflation and the rate of unemployment, given that changes in money wages and changes in prices were and are closely associated.

It is worth noting that the original Phillips curve was simply an empirical observation. It was not derived as the logical outcome of any particular economic theory, but rather was a simple graph drawn on the basis of the available data. However, the Phillips curve was soon to be seen as part of economic theory. In particular, it was incorporated into Keynesian versions of the workings of the economy. The Phillips curve was seen as slotting neatly within the Keynesian picture. It is easy to see the closeness between the Keynesian suggestion regarding the shape of the aggregate supply schedule of the economy (see Chapter 10 on macroeconomic models) and the original Phillips curve. The Keynesian suggestion was that at times of widespread unemployment, increases in aggregate demand could lead to increases in output (and employment) without price increases. However, the closer the economy moved to a position of full employment, the more increases in aggregate demand would tend to produce price as opposed to output (and employment) responses. This is very close to suggesting an association between high unemployment and low inflation, and low unemployment and high inflation. If demand in the economy is low, then there will be demand-deficient unemployment and little or no price increases as firms struggle to sell their products. If demand in the economy is high, then there will be little unemployment and prices are likely to rise as there are shortages and firms feel able to raise prices. An alternative way of interpreting the mechanisms at work is to put the emphasis upon wage-push inflation. In that case, high unemployment puts workers in a weak bargaining position since employers may be able to replace their services with those currently out of work. Thus wage demands are low and the rate of inflation is low. Conversely, when unemployment is low, workers are in a strong position and can secure larger wage increases and thus inflation is higher.

As well as being seen within a theoretical framework, the Phillips curve could also logically be interpreted as a possible policy menu for economic policy makers. According to the logic of the Phillips curve, the fundamental choice concerning economic policy that had to be made by any government concerned the desired mix of unemployment and inflation rates. In principle, a position of maximum economic welfare for the nation in terms of the 'best' mix of unemployment and inflation could be identified, probably by the election to government of the political party that represented the electorate's preferred choice. An alternative use could be made by governments of the Phillips curve relationship in an effort to maximise chances of re-election (see Chapter 13 on political business cycles). If governments could correctly perceive what were the current electorate's views concerning the relative importance of unemployment and inflation, then the economy could be manipulated, through the appropriate demand management policies, to the position on the Phillips curve most likely to maximise votes.

THE EXPECTATIONS-AUGMENTED PHILLIPS CURVE

With the stagflation of the mid-1970s, many of the post-war macroeconomic certainties were challenged. The most fatal challenge appeared to be to the Phillips curve. As originally drawn, the Phillips curve could not admit the possibility of both the rate of unemployment and the rate of inflation rising simultaneously. The empirical relationship had clearly broken down and the Phillips curve in its original state could no longer be accepted. Equally, the Keynesian macroeconomics theory that had become intertwined with the Phillips curve was also now seen as clearly flawed. The scene was set for a new theory and a new Phillips curve.

The word 'new' is perhaps not appropriate: 'return to former' theory might be more accurate, as was suggested in the theories concerning inflation. The movement towards an alternative version of the Phillips curve was particularly associated with the work of Friedman (1968). Friedman suggested that the focus of Phillips's work had not been correct. The key focus should not have been the money wage, but rather the real wage, as this is what workers are truly concerned about. Following from this, the key suggestion made by Friedman was that there was not in fact any trade-off between the rate of inflation and unemployment in the long run, and that the true long-run shape of the Phillips curve was vertical. The correct depiction was as shown in Figure 11.6.

This requires some explanation. Central to the understanding of this version of the Phillips curve is the notion of the 'natural rate of unemployment'. This is

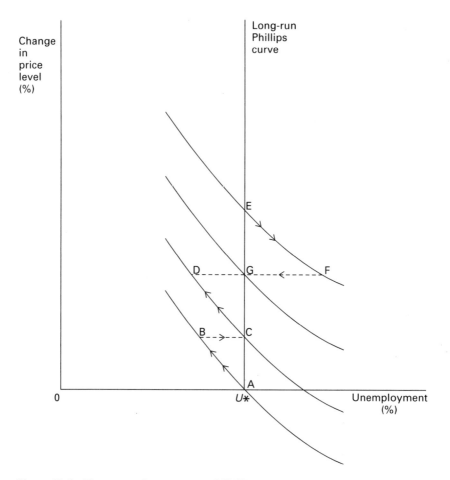

Figure 11.6   *The expectations-augmented Phillips curve*

shown as U^* in Figure 11.6. The natural rate of unemployment is the level of unemployment that arises when there is equilibrium in the nation's labour market, where demand for labour is equal to supply of labour at the ruling real wage. In other words, it can be seen as the equivalent of full employment. The important point about this is the implicit assumption that the economy will, left to its own accord, tend towards this point of full employment through the necessary adjustment of prices and wages. In other words, it is based on a classical or neoclassical view of the economy. The natural rate of unemployment in Figure 11.6 is also the only level of unemployment at which there will be no tendency for the rate of inflation to change. This does not imply a zero inflation rate, simply a stable one. As such, it has also been dubbed the NAIRU (the non-accelerating inflation rate of unemployment). How this suggestion is arrived at needs careful consideration.

Let us suppose that we start in the diagram at position A. There is no inflation at this point, and the economy is at its natural rate of unemployment, U^*. However, the government now decides that this rate of unemployment is unacceptably high, perhaps because there is a general election pending, and there is a fear that if the rate of unemployment is not reduced, then the election may be lost. Given this, the government decides that it will boost spending in the economy, having in mind the model of the original Phillips curve that implies that unemployment can be reduced at the expense of a higher rate of inflation. However, with the expectations-augmented Phillips curve, the outcome of such action is ultimately clearly undesirable. The expansion of the economy will certainly raise prices as the expectations-augmented Phillips curve holds a quantity theory of money version of the cause of inflation. Thus, the increase in the money supply associated with the demand expansion in the economy will lead to inflation. At first, this also leads to a fall in unemployment, as illustrated by the movement from point A to point B in the diagram. However, the reason for this is all to do with misperceptions by economic agents. A double coincidence of misperceptions is postulated. Workers are aware that the wages on offer have risen. They are not so similarly aware that prices are rising. Thus, there is a view that the real wage is rising, and more workers are therefore prepared to offer their services for paid employment. On the other hand, firms are more aware of rising prices than they are of rising money wages, and thus have a view that the movement of the real wage is in the opposite direction. Therefore firms are prepared to employ more workers. Given this, the level of unemployment falls. However, this cannot be a permanent position. At some point, both workers and firms will realise that they were in fact mistaken and that the real wage had not changed. Thus, the level of unemployment will then rise back to its original 'natural' level. The only difference from the starting position is that this point, point C in the diagram, will be associated with a higher rate of inflation, as firms and workers now have this rate of increase in prices ingrained within their expectations of the economy. The only thing that the attempted expansion of the economy has achieved is to raise the rate of inflation.

If the government wishes to persist in its efforts to hold down the rate of unemployment below the natural level, then it will need to engineer a further expansion of the economy. This will bring about a further rise in the rate of inflation which will at first induce the same misperceptions regarding the real wage as before and thus cause unemployment to fall once again and the economy to move to point D. However, a recognition of the mistakes being made by economic agents will again lead the economy to move back to the natural rate of unemployment in the long run. Thus, the only way for a government permanently to be able to hold the level of unemployment below its natural level is to engineer a constantly accelerating inflation rate. Insofar as this is not seen as a viable long-term possibility, then unemployment will always have to rise back to its natural level where the rate of inflation remains stable.

A further implication of the so-called expectations-augmented Phillips curve is that if governments wish to reduce the rate of inflation, then a temporary increase of unemployment above the natural rate may have to be endured, but this will not persist in the long run. Imagine that the government wishes to reduce the rate of inflation from the rate that is associated with point E in the diagram. In that case, it will have to reduce the growth of the money supply. This will begin to secure a lower increase in the level of prices in the economy. However, this will create the same sort of misperceptions that occurred with an expansion of the economy. Workers will now believe that the real wage is falling while employers will see the real wage as rising. Thus there is an increase in unemployment and the economy moves towards point F in the diagram. However, once workers and firms realise that the real wage has not in fact changed, then unemployment will fall back to its natural level at the lower rate of inflation and the economy will be at point G. The government could continue this process, accepting short-term unemployment, until it reduced inflation to as low a level as it desired.

In 1977, Friedman went further in his development of the above process by suggesting that the long-run Phillips curve might in fact be positively sloped, rather than simply vertical. This was because, as suggested when discussing the possible costs to the economy of inflation, significant price increases could cause the market economy to function inefficiently as economic agents became confused between changes in relative prices and changes in the price level. This sort of problem was already suggested in Friedman's earlier work on the misperceptions of firms and workers in the face of changes in the rate of inflation. Therefore, higher rates of inflation would cause increasing misallocations of resources and thus higher rates of unemployment, presumably as the nation lost competitiveness. In this case, it would be true that the best way to reduce unemployment would be to reduce the rate of inflation.

Friedman's analysis was then taken further by other economists in what became known as 'new classical' macroeconomics. The model described by Friedman was effectively relying on what may be termed 'adaptive' expectations. Economic agents base all their current decision-making simply on what happened in the previous time period. They then only change this pattern of behaviour if that expectation proved to be wrong. Therefore if inflation was at a certain level in the previous time period, then that rate will be expected to persist into the next time period. Thus workers and firms could make mistakes if inflation changed, even if inflation showed a persistent tendency to change. New classical economists suggested that this contravenes the rationality assumption at the heart of economics. Economic agents will in fact learn from the past and will not persist in their mistakes: in other words, they will have rational expectations. The implication of this is that if the government attempts to expand the economy, firms and workers will realise that this will not have an effect on the real wage, and so there will be no mistakes causing a change in the level of unemployment. Thus the only effect of changes in the level of aggregate demand in the economy will be on the rate of inflation. The Phillips curve becomes vertical at the point of the natural rate of unemployment in the short run as well as the long run.

The ultimate implication for the conduct of government economic policy is significant. There is no point in the government trying to change unemployment through demand management. The only target that this can affect is the rate of inflation. Rather, the government should concentrate on policies which may shift the natural rate of unemployment to the left. These will be the same policies as those required to reduce unemployment from a neoclassical standpoint discussed earlier in the chapter.

THE PHILLIPS CURVE TODAY

What relationship between unemployment and inflation are we left with today? Do any of the new theories of unemployment discussed earlier help to understand the relationship more clearly? Several observations need to be made in light of recent experience in western developed economies.

The first important point to make is that there appear to be asymmetries in the whole process. The effect of increases in aggregate demand does not appear to be the mirror image of decreases in aggregate demand. It appears clear that while an increase in the level of aggregate demand is likely to provoke an upward response in the price level, a reduction in the level of aggregate demand is more likely to induce a fall in output and employment than a significant movement in the rate of inflation. The implication of this is that it is easier to create inflation than to remove it and thus that it is important to try not to allow inflation to rise in the first place. However, what might explain this observation? The 'insider–outsider' model discussed under the new theories of unemployment appears promising. If there is a rise in the level of aggregate demand, then workers who are already employed will recognise that their services are now more valuable to their employers who will not want to lose workers at a time of higher demand. Thus, they may be able to use this position to secure higher wages. Similarly, from the point of view of efficiency wages, firms may now offer higher wages in an effort to stop workers searching for alternative employment that could be available now that spending has risen in the economy. Equally, the higher wages may be needed to recruit workers with high productivities. Thus wages and prices rise. However, a fall in demand does not work in the opposite direction. Implicit contracts imply a lack of flexibility in the possible reduction of real wages, and thus employment falls. Equally, those 'inside' work do not feel especially threatened by those 'outside' work as they know firms will wish to retain their services rather than recruit others. This enables them to maintain a certain real wage, even in the face of falling demand. Inflation is not readily reduced.

A further important observation linked with the above point is that it may be the rate of change of unemployment rather than the absolute level of unemployment that is the relevant variable in terms of any possible impact on the rate of inflation. Those inside work are not threatened in their position by any particular level of unemployment, be it great or small. However, they may feel their position to be affected by changes in the rate of unemployment. High unemployment is not a threat, but rising unemployment may be. With rising unemployment, there may be workers with appropriate skills who have only just finished working and who could be seen as relatively easy replacements for those inside work. This could be especially true if there is unemployment arising from the primary sector of the labour market, as appears to have happened in many western economies in the 1990s. This threat could cause a change in the wage demands of those in work as they realise that there is less of a premium to be gained from employers given the possible alternatives. Similarly, from an efficiency wages perspective, there is not the need to pay a wage so far above the market-clearing level. If this is so, then the Phillips curve diagram would need re-drawing with the rate of change of unemployment rather than simply the rate of unemployment on the horizontal axis.

However, perhaps the most important observation concerning the Phillips curve, regardless of which version is seen as most accurate from a theoretical standpoint, is that it has shifted to the right over the past two decades. If there is some trade-off between inflation and unemployment, then it has severely worsened. If the Phillips curve is vertical, then it has shifted a long way to the right. This is a phenomenon known as 'hysteresis'. There are various comments that can be made about this. One observation has been that the idea of a permanent vertical Phillips curve is less convincing, or at least less useful, if it is continually shifting. Indeed, the difference between some long-run non-vertical trade-off between inflation and unemployment and a constantly moving natural rate would empirically probably be impossible to distinguish.

The Phillips curve could have moved to the right for various reasons. One possibility is that unemployment breeds unemployment. This is partly explained by the asymmetry mentioned before which implies that once unemployment is created, there is a likelihood that it will stick, as future increases in aggregate demand may have a greater impact on the price level than the rate of unemployment. A further possibility is that once workers are unemployed, they are increasingly unlikely to be able to secure future employment the longer that they remain unemployed. Employers perceive such people as having lost important skills related to the ability to be productive workers. Such people become discouraged from seeking employment, given the amount of search activity that yields no positive result. Thus, a large number of the workforce could come close to being rendered as 'unemployable'. It is possible to see how this could happen if the government opted for a policy of reducing inflation over a significant period of time, as has been the case with many western governments since the beginning of the 1980s. This would, even according to the expectations-augmented Phillips curve, lead to a period of high unemployment while inflation was reduced. The problem is that if the process lasted too long, then the people affected could not receive jobs at the end of the process and the Phillips curve would have moved to the right. In terms of the insider–outsider model, this would mean that a large number of those outside work could be deemed totally irrelevant in terms of applying any pressure upon those inside work, and thus many workers could persist in securing a real wage above the market-clearing level even if there is high unemployment. A further reason why any creation of unemployment could lead to a rightward movement of the Phillips curve is if reductions of output and employment are associated with the scrapping of capital by firms. If firms do not replace machinery, or even sell or scrap working capital, in the face of falling demand, then any future increase in the level of aggregate demand cannot yield an increase in output, despite the high rate of unemployment. Firms do not now have the capacity to increase output, and thus the response to higher demand will be higher prices.

The above discussion does appear to suggest a policy priority, regardless of the model of the Phillips curve that is deemed to be accurate. The key thing appears to be the need to shift the Phillips curve, whatever shape it might happen to be, to the left. From the above discussion, one of the priorities would have to be to ensure that discouraged, perhaps 'unemployable', workers are able actively to re-enter the workforce. This seems to suggest the importance of good retraining programmes. Perhaps it might imply the need to subsidise any employer who takes on such workers because the most important thing in employers' perceptions regarding employability appears to be how recently someone was employed. If such people can once more become viable members of the workforce, then not only may the number of registered unemployed fall, but the pressure on those inside work may increase, thus helping to moderate real wages. It may be that changes are deemed necessary to the system of unemployment benefit in order to encourage search activity. If that is the case, the conclusions of Atkinson and Micklewright (1991) concerning the design of such systems as opposed to the absolute level of unemployment benefit need to be borne in mind. It may be that a workable incomes policy is seen as an absolute priority if a moderate or low increase in money wages is to be compatible with low levels of unemployment. Whatever it is, it is hard to escape the logic that efforts should be directed at moving the Phillips curve to the left.

CONCLUSION

Where does this overview of some of the fundamentals of macroeconomics leave us? There are perhaps two points that can be especially stressed. The first is that insofar as there are genuine and fundamental differences in macroeconomic theories, they revolve around whether market economies, if left to their own devices, tend towards a position that can, in some sense, be described as 'full employment'. This in turn appears to rely in many ways upon the extent to which prices, notably the price of labour, are believed to be able to adjust in an appropriate direction. The second is that regardless of any theoretical difference over macroeconomics, the priority for macroeconomics policy for western governments seems to be the need to attempt to shift the Phillips curve to the left.

References

Atkinson, A.B. and Micklewright, J. (1991) 'Unemployment Compensations and Labor Market Transitions: A Critical Review', *Journal of Economic Literature*, no. 29.

Beveridge, W. (1944) *Full Employment in a Free Society* (London: Allen & Unwin)

Friedman, M. (1968) 'The Role of Monetary Policy', *American Economic Review*, no. 58.

Friedman, M. (1977) 'Inflation and Unemployment', *Journal of Political Economy*, no. 85

Meade, J. (1982) *Wage-Fixing* (London: George Allen & Unwin).

Phillips, A.W. (1958) 'The Relation Between Unemployment and the Rate of Change of Money Wage Rates in the UK, 1861–1957', *Economica*, November.

12 Exchange Rates and Economic and Monetary Union

Must a country possess its own currency? Would a nation be less of a nation if it shared a currency with other neighbouring nations? Strong opinions are expressed regarding this issue throughout the countries of the European Union and the proposed Economic and Monetary Union, involving the creation of a single currency for member states. A whole host of motivations and values gives rise to these differing opinions. The purpose of this chapter, as elsewhere in this book, is to look at the appropriate economic theory and to consider how that may help to inform the debate.

A longstanding economic debate concerns the relative merits and demerits of fixed and flexible exchange rate systems. This seems fruitful ground for considering the arguments regarding a single currency, as a single currency can be seen as the most extreme version of a fixed exchange rate between countries that can be designed. A less-often discussed area of economic theory, but one that would seem particularly pertinent with regard to this issue, is that of optimum currency areas. Can Europe be considered an optimum currency area well-suited to having just one currency? This chapter will outline these areas of theory and then endeavour to apply them to the issue of Economic and Monetary Union within the European Union. The chapter will thus be divided in the following fashion:

1. The theory of fixed and flexible exchange rates. What are the principal arguments for and against these two exchange-rate regimes?
2. The theory of optimum currency areas. What are the criteria that can be used to judge whether any particular area is best suited to one or to several currencies?
3. How can the above theories be used to inform the debate regarding Economic and Monetary Union? The theories can be used to identify the major likely costs and benefits and indicate where there may be legitimate ground for disagreement and the need to gather empirical information.

Before embarking on an investigation of the relevant theory, it is helpful to put current European currency developments within some overall world history of exchange rate orders. McKinnon (1993) identifies the existence of an exchange rate 'order' when there are certain agreed 'rules of the game' by which the participants involved abide. Using this criteria, the first clearly identifiable order that he suggests is the operation of the international Gold Standard between 1879 and 1913. The principal rule under this order was that all countries fixed an official gold price for their currency and then permitted the free conversion of domestic money for gold at that price. No order can be identified for the inter-war period, characterised as it was by various attempts to re-join and leave the Gold Standard. In 1945 the Bretton Woods order was introduced. The rule here was to to fix a value for a country's exchange rate in terms of gold or a currency that was tied to gold. This value was fixed to within one per cent of its par value with changes in the par value possible. McKinnon suggests that the order then changed in 1950 to the Fixed-Rate Dollar Standard, the difference being that all currencies now fixed their values in terms of the dollar rather than gold. This order lasted until 1970. The period 1971 to 1974 saw the floating of currencies with no agreed set of rules following the breakdown of the Fixed-Rate Dollar Standard. From then, there has been no single world exchange-rate order. From 1973 until 1984 a 'Floating-Rate Dollar Standard' can be identified where the main rule was to endeavour to moderate short-term fluctuations against the dollar without being committed to any particular par value. This was succeeded in 1985 by the Plaza-Louvre Intervention Accords which set broad target zones for exchange rate fluctuations between the dollar, the mark and the yen. In the meantime, the European Monetary System was established in 1979, the principal rule for participants of this order being that currencies should be fixed in par value against the European Currency Unit with 2.25 per cent fluctuations permitted around the par value, and a change in the par value being possible.

Perhaps there are two key points to note from this brief potted history. The first is that the swapping between fixed and flexible exchange-rate systems that has occurred suggests that there are likely to be important theoretical differences concerning the possible merits and demerits of fixed and flexible exchange rates. The second point is that the establishment of a single currency within Europe would be something without precedent in terms of world exchange-rate orders. It would be a radical step, and hence the strength of the opinions that are expressed on the issue.

FIXED VERSUS FLOATING EXCHANGE RATES

In the following discussion, a fixed exchange rate is taken to mean an exchange rate for a country's currency, as valued in terms of other countries' currencies, that is set by the central authority of the country and is not free to fluctuate with the day-to-day movements in the foreign currency market. A flexible exchange rate is taken to mean an exchange rate whose value is determined daily by the forces of supply and demand for the currency in the foreign currency market. In practice, there are many versions of exchange-rate systems and it is easiest to picture them as some sort of spectrum with totally fixed rates at one end and totally flexible rates at the other end: see Figure 12.1.

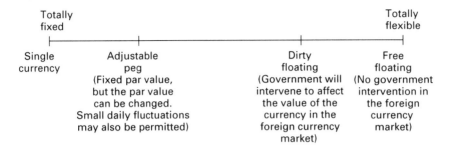

Figure 12.1 *A spectrum of different exchange-rate systems*

Both fixed and floating exchange rates have a claim to be able to secure any necessary economic adjustment that a country may have that arises from its trading with other nations. This is easiest to appreciate with an example of just two countries, A and B. Let us suppose that there is a change of tastes of consumers in both countries away from products produced in country A to those produced in country B. What will happen? With a completely fixed exchange rate, say a version of the Gold Standard, there would be a flow of money from country A to country B as more of A's and less of B's products are purchased. With the Gold Standard, this might be an actual flow of gold. The effect of this is, *ceteris paribus* (particularly, output levels remaining constant), to raise prices in B, as demand rises, and to lower prices in A, as demand falls. This will then have an impact upon consumer preferences causing demand for A's products to rise and the demand for B's products to fall. This process would continue until the trading imbalance between the two countries was resolved. Of course, if the assumption of fixed output levels is relaxed, then it is possible that the adjustment may occur through output rather than prices. This could mean large costs to an economy which would not occur in the same way with price adjustments.

How would a floating exchange rate deal with the same situation? This time, as the demand for B's products rose and the demand for A's products fell, the two countries' exchange rates would alter. In order for consumers in country A to be able to buy more products from B, they must obtain B's currency. Thus, the demand for B's currency rises on the international currency market forcing up the value of B's exchange rate. At the same time, there is less demand for A's currency and a greater supply of A's currency (as consumers try to use it to purchase B's currency). Both of these effects cause a fall in the value of A's exchange rate. The effect of these exchange rate movements is to cause prices to rise in B and prices to fall in A. This causes a movement in demand from B's to A's products, a process that continues until the trading imbalance between the two countries has been resolved.

Thus both fixed and floating exchange rates can be seen to perform the functions that are required of them. How then might a nation, or group of nations, decide between the two possible systems? In attempting to inform such a choice, we can identify various perceived strengths and weaknesses of both systems. This section will concentrate on the different costs and benefits of a fixed exchange rate, given that Economic and Monetary Union concerns a possible move to a totally fixed system. However, the arguments for and against flexible exchange rates are virtually the same, but opposite, to those discussed below.

BENEFITS OF FIXED EXCHANGE RATES

The fundamental point about fixed exchange rates is, of course, that they are fixed. The obvious advantage for both producers and consumers from this attribute is that fixed exchange rates provide a level of certainty regarding the price of exports and imports in the future that a flexible exchange rate could never provide. Insofar as certainty is felt to enhance economic welfare, then this can be seen as a possible advantage of fixed exchange rates. This is easiest to consider by looking at the ways in which uncertainty regarding future prices may be an economic cost. A trade which could provide mutual benefit to both consumers and producers may be deterred if, for example, there is felt to be a possibility that the price could rise or fall, thus implying that one of the parties would not gain from the trade. If producers and consumers are assumed to be risk-averse, a common assumption in economics, then the safe option is not to risk going ahead with the trade. Overall, the effect may thus be to reduce the level of international trade below the level that would allow all the potential gains suggested by the theory of comparative advantage, and the other gains from trade (see Chapter 9 on international trade), to be attained. Economic welfare would be higher under a system which provided greater certainty regarding future prices. Of course, profit-maximising producers and utility-maximising consumers may seek to overcome this problem by insuring against future price movements (exchange-rate future markets allow for this). However, there will be a premium to pay for this, and the price of this premium is still likely to discourage mutually advantageous trades at the margin.

A related point to the one above is that a fixed exchange rate ensures that there are no unnecessary and unhelpful fluctuations in the exchange rate which could cause undesirable dislocations within the economy. Much of this point revolves around the way that speculation may or may not affect the value of a currency. There is a view that speculators help to reduce the likely fluctuations of any price, for example the exchange rate. The explanation for this is that speculators tend to sell when they believe that prices are rising above the long-run average and buy when prices fall below the long-run average. By behaving thus, a profit can be made. The effect will be to moderate all price fluctuations. However, it is also suggested that speculators may rather accentuate, or even create, price fluctuations. If some version of a 'herd mentality' combined with Keynes's 'animal spirits' best describes the behaviour of currency speculators, then a rise in the exchange rate may arouse optimism about its future value and cause speculators to buy the currency and thus force up its value further. If speculators behave in this fashion, then their role is a fundamentally destabilising one and will cause unnecessarily large swings in flexible exchange rates. This increases uncertainty regarding future prices and may lead a country's products in certain areas to become internationally uncompetitive for reasons that have nothing to do with any economic fundamentals, such as comparative advantage. If this is so, then the activities of speculators in affecting the value of a flexible exchange rates are undesirable to an economy. These costs would be avoided by having a fixed exchange rate.

In fact, there are various ways in which speculation about a currency can cause its value to move in a perverse fashion with speculators behaving in an entirely rational manner (perhaps doing no more than pre-empting what would happen without the existence of speculation). Imagine the situation where an increase in a country's inflation rate was announced. Theory would suggest that the value of the exchange rate would tend to fall as the country's products became less internationally competitive and the demand for the currency fell. This fall would offset the effect of the rise in inflation on the nation's competitiveness. However, it is quite possible that speculators may immediately cause the price of the currency to rise rather than fall. This could happen if the expected response of the national authority was to raise interest rates significantly in an effort to reduce the inflation rate. Such a rise in interest rates would induce purchasing of the currency as international investors wished to put their wealth in the country's financial institutions, given the large rise in interest rates. Of course, all of this will further weaken the country's international competitiveness, the opposite of the effect originally anticipated with a flexible exchange rate.

A further perverse movement in a nation's flexible exchange rate may be created by the value of the currency 'overshooting' from what might be its 'ideal' value. It has been suggested that this was the fate of the UK in the early 1980s when there was a large rise in the sterling exchange rate. A significant rise in interest rates led to an expectation of a falling inflation rate over a period of time. Sterling assets thus became attractive to investors as the real rate of return (allowing for the lower inflation anticipated) would become high. In order for equilibrium to occur, the exchange rate needed to appreciate to the point where it was anticipated that its next movement would be downwards, thus stemming the demand for sterling assets. This rather peculiar situation thus implied the exchange rate rising beyond the level dictated by inflation and interest rates, in other words 'overshooting'. This reduced the competitiveness of the UK's products to an unnecessary level. The point is that there are therefore several reasons why a flexible exchange rate may depart from the level that would occur if it were determined solely by economic fundamentals. The problem is that the relative prices thus created may not lead to an optimal allocation of resources. A country may be better opting for a fixed exchange rate.

A further benefit of a fixed exchange rate suggested by some economists is that it exerts a necessary discipline upon economies. The problem with flexible exchange rates is that they allow, or appear to allow, governments, firms and workers to 'get away with' reckless behaviour. If a mixture of expansionary government economic policy, unreasonable trade union wage demands and weak behaviour on the part of employers (the sort of picture that is often suggested as a possibility) leads the country to have an inflation rate above the world average, then a flexible exchange rate can compensate for that by allowing the value of the currency to fall and thus maintaining the country's international competitiveness. In such a country, the depreciation may not be successful because the trade unions pictured are likely to resist the impact of the higher import prices (created by the depreciating currency) on their real wage, and demand higher wages which, backed by a lax monetary policy by the government, will lead to more inflation and further depreciation. Thus a flexible exchange rate can be seen to engender attitudes which, in the long run, breed a weak economic position. A fixed exchange rate would not permit such a scenario. If one country inflated faster than the rest of the world, the safety valve of a falling exchange rate would not be available. Instead, the country would suffer from a lack of international competitiveness leading to lower demand for its products and thus recession and unemployment. Only once inflation was reduced to the world average or below could the situation be improved. This is likely to be a painful process. Knowing this, governments, workers and firms will perceive the foolishness of reckless economic behaviour and will be more likely to behave in a way conducive to the long-run international success of the economy.

COSTS OF FIXED EXCHANGE RATES

If an obvious point about fixed exchange rates is that they are fixed, then an equally obvious point is that they are not, in their strictest sense, flexible. This represents their first disadvantage. A fixed exchange rate removes from an economy a possible means of adjustment to any external shock. For example, suppose that an oil-exporting country was suddenly faced with a large fall in the world price of oil. This would rapidly reduce the foreign earnings of that country and imply the need for an adjustment if balance was to be restored in that economy's trade dealings with the rest of the world. With a flexible exchange rate, this adjustment could occur through an automatic depreciation of the country's currency. As demand for the currency fell due to less being required to buy the same amount of the nation's oil, then so its price against other currencies would fall. This would make the nation's products more internationally competitive and help to earn the extra foreign earnings lost through the lower revenue now received through oil sales. The falling exchange rate would have achieved the required adjustment. If, however, the country's exchange rate is fixed, then there will have to be an alternative channel to achieve the adjust-ment. Instead of the exchange rate depreciating, the fall in spending on oil may cause prices to fall (or at least the rate of inflation to slow down) throughout the economy due to the lower level of demand. This will help to improve the nation's competitiveness and thus achieve adjustment. However, if prices are inflexible, at least in the short run, as is seen to be the case in many developed economies, then the fall in demand will cause output to fall rather than prices. This will also eventually lead to the necessary adjustment since the lower level of economic activity in the economy will mean that there is less spending on imports than previously and hence there is a renewed trading balance. The problem is that this method of adjustment is only achieved at the cost of falling output and rising unemployment. This could be the cost of having a fixed exchange rate.

A fixed exchange rate does not only remove the adjustment mechanism possi-ble through a flexible rate: it also removes the possibility of a government using its monetary policy to target domestic ends. The easiest way of understanding this is to think of monetary policy in terms of the government influencing or setting interest rates. In a situation of deflation (demand having fallen in an economy, for example through a fall in business confidence leading to a reduc-tion in investment by firms), the government may wish to try to stimulate demand, raise output and lower unemployment by reducing the rate of interest and thus encouraging firms and consumers to increase their spending. The problem with having a fixed exchange rate is that this policy may not be possi-ble. If the government cuts interest rates in the economy, then the demand for the country's currency will fall as less people wish to hold their wealth in the nation's financial institutions due to the lower interest now received. This will put downward pressure on the exchange rate. However, the value of a fixed exchange rate is not permitted to fall. Thus, unless the government is able and prepared perpetually to prop up the value of the currency through using foreign currency reserves to buy the nation's currency, the lowering of interest rates is not a policy weapon available to the government. Similar problems would occur in the opposite direction if interest rates were raised in an effort to dampen inflationary pressures within the economy. The interest rate now has to be set at a level that is compatible with the maintenance of the currency's fixed value: it cannot be used for domestic means. However, before leaving this point, it is important to ask just how much monetary policy independence most countries truly have, even with flexible exchange rates. If a government were to lower interest rates in an effort to reflate its economy, then this would cause a fall in the exchange rate as international investors sought to move their wealth to coun-tries which now had higher interest rates. The lower exchange rate would cause the price of imports to rise, an effect that could spread to all prices, especially if imports represent an important part of a country's inputs to its production and its workers tend to demand higher wages in an effort to compensate for the higher prices. Thus inflation rises. If this then threatens any inflation target that the government may have, then it is, in effect, constrained in the extent to which it can use monetary policy to target domestic policies due to the effect of a changing exchange rate on its target variables.

A point mentioned above was the possible use by a country's central authorities of foreign currency reserves to try to maintain the required exchange rate. This could be considered another cost of a fixed exchange rate, namely that a nation will need to possess large foreign currency reserves if it wishes to keep the value of its currency fixed. Given the mobility of international money capital in today's economies, and the reduction of restrictions on money capital movements that have happened recently, for example in Europe, then the level of reserves that may be required by a country to preserve its exchange rate could be vast, perhaps impossibly large. This problem could become an insurmountable problem with varieties of fixed exchange rates that do allow for a change in the fixed value of a country's currency in the face of 'fundamental disequilibrium' in the country's trade with other nations. As soon as international speculators believe that there is a good chance that there will be a downward adjustment in a country's currency, due to the fundamental trading problems faced by the country, then it must be the profit-maximising decision to sell the currency and then to re-buy it at a lower rate once the devaluation has occurred. Therefore if everyone feels that this is likely to occur, there may be an unstoppable selling of the country's currency, thus forcing the government to change the value of its currency, whether it believed that was the best decision for the nation's economic welfare or not. In today's economies with little restriction upon the international movement of money capital, this may suggest that any fixed exchange rate systems that allow for the possibility of adjustments in the value of the exchange rate simply are not viable.

The lack of insulation from world inflation or deflation that is given by a fixed exchange rate is also considered to be a cost. With a flexible exchange rate, an increase in world inflationary pressures will lead to a rise in the price of a country's imports. This would have inflationary effects were it not for the fact that this rise in prices is likely to lead to a fall in demand for imports, which will cause a rise in the value of the country's currency (less of the currency is supplied on the international market since less foreign currency is demanded because of the fall in demand for imports). This will have the effect of lowering import prices and thus moderating any inflationary effects. The exchange rate would move in the opposite direction in the face of world deflation. This cannot happen with a fixed exchange rate. World inflation would cause a rise in domestic prices with no compensating rise in the exchange rate possible.

These, then, are seen as some of the important costs and benefits of fixed exchange rates (and thus of flexible exchange rates). In principle, they are arguments that, to a lesser or greater extent, could be applied to the decision of the European Union to have a single currency. It is worth noting two points before proceeding. The first is that several of the arguments both for and against a fixed exchange rate relate to the possible effect on the country's inflation rate. As a generalisation, the balance of the arguments seems to suggest that countries with higher inflation rates than the world average may find their inflation rate moderated by the discipline of a fixed exchange rate. On the other hand, countries with an inflation rate below the world average may find their inflation rate forced up through a fixed exchange rate due to the lack of insulation that it offers a country from world inflationary pressures. The second point is that many of the arguments in favour of both fixed and flexible exchange-rate systems are couched in terms of the problems of the alternative. This does seem to suggest that whatever exchange-rate system is adopted by a nation, it will have its difficulties.

THE THEORY OF OPTIMUM CURRENCY AREAS

Whilst the general arguments for and against fixed and flexible exchange rates are well known and can be found in the majority of economics textbooks, the theory of optimum currency areas is less familiar and less commonly found in standard textbooks. However, it is clearly of importance when considering whether a certain area of Europe should adopt a single currency.

The theory of optimum currency areas attempts to lay down criteria which can be applied to regions of the world to help to judge whether such regions would perform best, maximise their economic welfare, by having just one currency or by having different currencies in different parts of the area under consideration. The theory does not necessarily have anything to do with national boundaries. It could equally be applied to regions within one particular country. An obvious example would be to consider whether the states of the USA form one optimum currency area or whether their economies would function more effectively with separate currencies.

The work of Mundell (1961) is often seen as the starting point for describing the criteria associated with an optimum currency area. In his article on the topic, Mundell suggests that an optimum currency area is characterised by internal factor mobility and external factor immobility. Taking the example of labour, workers can move relatively freely, both occupationally and geographically, within the area, but cannot move very freely between the area under consideration and other areas. If this is the case, then a separate currency for the area is likely to be justified. The reason for this is that necessary economic adjustments can take place when factors of production are mobile in a way that cannot occur when they are immobile. Thus, with immobile resources, it may be necessary to have separate currencies which allow for necessary adjustments to occur via changes in the exchange rate of the currencies. If considering just two areas, X and Y, then suppose that there was a fall in demand for the products of X and a corresponding increase in the demand for the products of Y. If labour and other factors of production are mobile, then this will allow production to expand in Y and contract in X without any great economic cost as the factors transfer from X to Y. However, if factors of production are immobile, then there will be problems. Output will not be able easily to expand in Y in response to the higher demand and thus there will be inflation in this region. On the other hand, output will contract in X, but factors of production will remain unemployed as they cannot easily move to employment in Y. Thus an undesirable mixture of inflation in Y and unemployment in X is created. If the two regions had separate currencies, then this would allow Y's currency to appreciate against X's, causing a relative rise in the price of Y's products compared with X's and thus helping to raise demand in X and lower it in Y. This should help to moderate inflation in Y and unemployment in X.

Mundell then goes on to point out, however, that if this is the only factor that is taken into account when deciding what may constitute an optimum currency area, then it is possible to envisage the whole world divided into vast numbers of small currency areas insofar as there is a degree of immobility of factors of production between any areas, no matter how small. Given this, it is also, therefore, important to remember the basic point that the fundamental function of money as a means of exchange becomes increasingly ineffective the larger the number of currencies that exist. Trading is less easily facilitated by money if many of the trades that take place require the exchange of currencies as well as goods and services. From this standpoint, the optimum position would be to have just one world currency, thus allowing money to perform its function as a medium of exchange as effectively as possible. In practice, then, the decision about what constitutes an optimum currency area is dictated by a balancing act between the benefit of separate currencies allowing economic adjustments to occur, but the cost of money being a less effective means of exchange. This cost will be greater the greater the number of transactions that take place between the regions with separate currencies.

Subsequent consideration of optimum currency areas has suggested that there may be other factors to be borne in mind when attempting to decide whether different regions are best suited to a single currency or to separate currencies. First, there may be no need for separate currencies in different areas even if there is factor immobility between the areas as long as prices are flexible in the regions concerned. Considering the example above, if prices were quickly to fall in X in response to the fall in demand, then this could see a healthy demand for X's products continuing and thus no significant rise in unemployment even with immobile resources. No adjustment through a changing exchange rate would be required. Another important point is that the need for separate currencies also depends upon the similarity, or symmetry, between the regions under consideration. If the ares concerned produce largely similar products, then any change in economic conditions is likely to affect both of them in a similar fashion. Thus, even with immobile resources and inflexible prices, there is not an argument for separate currencies as both regions are likely to be suffering in a similar fashion from unemployment or inflation due to any particular economic shock that may have occurred. A final point that is made is that the importance of having separate currencies will depend upon the level of specialisation that exists in the regions concerned. If the regions are highly specialised in their production, as might be suggested by the law of comparative advantage, then any economic shock could have a severe impact on a region. In that case, the need for a separate currency to permit adjustment through the exchange rate could be considerable. However, if the areas in question have diverse economies, then the impact of any economic shock will be far less and thus the need for a separate currency not as great.

ECONOMIC AND MONETARY UNION

Armed with the relevant economic theory, it should now be possible to consider the economic arguments concerning Economic and Monetary Union within the European Union. Before doing that, however, it is helpful to be aware of the historical background leading to EMU:

1962:   The Commission of European Communities drew up a draft of the first plan for monetary union within Europe. This was to be completed by 1971.

1970:   The Werner Report called for monetary union within ten years. This led in March 1972 to the creation of 'The Snake', a system through which all countries in the EEC were limited to exchange-rate movements of no more than $2 \frac{1}{4}$ per cent against each other's currencies. After the shocks to the European economy created by the oil price rises of 1973, this system effectively disintegrated.

1978:   The Bremen Summit led to the creation of the European Monetary System in 1979. The central element of this was the Exchange Rate Mechanism which aimed to stabilise members' exchange rates.

1986:   The Single European Act agreed to the establishment of the Single Market in Europe by the end of 1992.

1989:   The Delors Report (The Committee for the Study of Economic and Monetary Union) recommended a three-stage move to EMU to supplement the Single Market to be completed in less than ten years.

1991:   The Maastricht Treaty confirmed that monetary union was to be achieved in three stages:

Stage I The removal of all remaining controls on money capital, the convergence of inflation and interest rates amongst member states and exchange-rate stability.

Stage II Further convergence of national economic policies within the European Union.

Stage III The establishment of a single independent European Central Bank to be responsible for European monetary policy, the exchange rates of member states to be irrevocably fixed, and the Council of Ministers then to decide when to replace national currencies with a single European currency.

The idea of a single European currency is thus not entirely new. Nor indeed is the attempt to apply some concept of the theory of optimum currency areas to Europe. Meade (1957) and Scitovsky (1958) held differing views from each other in articles written in the 1950s. An advantage of attempting to use the theory of optimum currency areas to consider the issue of a single European currency is that if the theory is accepted then it might be possible to reduce some of the arguments to issues that can be resolved by discovering the appropriate empirical evidence.

The lack of resource mobility between European countries is a factor that could suggest the need to maintain separate currencies. If labour is often seen as immobile within countries, then it is considerably more immobile between different countries. Whilst movements to more standard educational qualifications across Europe and further improvements in the teaching of languages may help to increase mobility, it is hard to foresee the free and easy movement of labour amongst all European states in the near future. With regard to the flexibility of prices, it is perhaps now the accepted conventional wisdom that prices do not often adjust rapidly in the short run in advanced economies that are often characterised by oligopolistic industries (see Chapter 3 on microeconomics and macroeconomics). Thus, the need to preserve separate currencies from this point of view is also clear. Given these two points, it can be seen why much of the empirical work on this issue has tended to concentrate on the third factor which could suggest the lack of need for separate currencies, namely the similarity of the economies involved in any area. It is important to know how similarly all European countries are affected by external economic shocks. The greater the similarity, the stronger the case for a single currency as there will be no adjustments necessary between European countries. It is partly in this context that the so-called 'core' nations, based around France and Germany, and the 'periphery' nations of Europe have been identified, the suggestion being that some European economies share greater similarities than others. It is felt that the case for a single European currency is stronger amongst the 'core' nations than throughout the whole of the European Union. Studies such as those by Caparole (1993) have suggested that there are significant asymmetries in the way in which European economies are affected by shocks. Given this, perhaps a single currency in Europe would need to be accompanied by appropriate fiscal transfers from winning nations to losing nations when a significant shock affects European economies in differing ways. This could help to stop levels of unemployment becoming significantly different in different areas of the Union, as might happen otherwise. Caparole's study also pointed to the lack of any clear core and periphery areas in terms of this asymmetry. However, an important point to note here is that studies have equally suggested that there is no more asymmetry between European economies than there is between the different states of the USA. In this sense, the case for a single currency within Europe may be no greater and no less than the economic case for a single currency within the USA.

The final important point to consider with regard to the theory of optimum currency areas is the extent to which separate European currencies are hampering money within Europe from performing its full function as a means of exchange. To some extent, this can be measured by the level of the transactions costs that arise from swapping European currencies for trading purposes. Certainly, with the single market and ever-increasing trade amongst the member states of the European Union, the number of cross-border transactions is likely to continue to increase and with it the cost associated with maintaining separate currencies. The European Community's study, 'One Market, One Money' (Commission of the European Communities, 1990) suggested that the value of removing the transactions costs of exchanging European currencies with each other would be just under one-half of one per cent of the Gross Domestic Product of the European Community. This could be seen as a tangible economic benefit of creating a single currency, although to some extent there would be a redistribution effect as those previously involved in facilitating currency transactions would lose their source of income. Smaller nations would tend to gain more than larger nations since they rely on European trade for a greater percentage of their national income. A related point is that there could be further economic benefits accruing from the fact that price comparisons would be far easier with a single currency, thus permitting the market to function as efficiently as possible. It has been suggested that this could make the practice of price discrimination in certain European markets, such as the car market, more difficult to sustain given the improved information provided to consumers. This would provide a welfare gain to consumers, but at the expense of producers.

Further points both in favour and against a single European currency can be gleaned by recalling some of the important theoretical arguments for and against fixed exchange rates. There would be complete certainty regarding prices in different countries with the introduction of a single currency. The government of a country is not even able to realign the value of its currency in the face of economic difficulties as it could under virtually all fixed exchange rate systems. Thus, if increased business certainty is thought to raise economic welfare by encouraging investment and trade, then this would be an important benefit of adopting a single currency. Similarly, the value of the exchange rate cannot be undesirably affected by the activities of currency speculators as there are no currencies against which to speculate! This is perhaps the only sure way to end speculation in the currency market.

Another benefit claimed for fixed exchange rates was the discipline that they imposed upon countries with regard to their economic behaviour. In particular, it was felt that this would stop certain economies from following reckless inflationary tendencies. This argument applies in full force to a single currency. If one nation inflated faster than another with the same currency, then the costs would be high, as that country's products could no longer compete. Thus, a country would be very keen to avoid an inflation rate higher than its European competitors. The extent to which the overall inflationary tendencies that may exist within the European Union were moderated through Economic and Monetary Union would also depend upon the monetary policy adopted by the new European Central Bank. Insofar as this independent central bank was permitted to have a strong anti-inflationary mandate, then inflation throughout the European Union would be likely to be kept at a low level. To cover this point fully, it would be necessary to consider the various merits and demerits of having an independent central bank (see Chapter 13 on political business cycles and independent central banks). If a lower inflation rate is secured through the adoption of a single currency, then this will be associated with lower nominal rates of interest. It may be that real interest rates could, on average, be lower if it is the case that with separate currencies and monetary polices, some European countries have to have a premium included in their interest rates to cover the possibility of a future depreciation or devaluation of their currency. Clearly, there would be no need for such a premium with a single currency, except if it was required for the European Currency Unit against other world currencies.

The importance of the loss of adjustment available through a flexible exchange rate has largely been considered through the application of the theory of optimum currency areas. However, it should perhaps be emphasised that the efficacy of devaluation in restoring a country's international competitiveness is now generally doubted for the reasons discussed earlier. If imports are an important part of the production inputs of a country, and if there is significant real wage resistance on the part of workers, then the competitive gains through devaluation are lost with rising prices that are caused by the devaluation. If this view is held, then the loss of this policy weapon is of no great consequence.

A more serious concern about a single currency (as with any fixed exchange rate system), and one that is frequently voiced strongly in political debate, is that it would imply the loss of economic sovereignty. National governments would not be able to set their own economic policies. This is absolutely true with the case of monetary policy, given that this will be decided by the independent European Central Bank. Thus, a member of the European Union would not be able to set interest rates in its country at a level different from those in other member states. One possibility might be, therefore, that countries could make greater use of their fiscal policies in an effort to pursue particular domestic targets. However, there are various ways in which countries' fiscal policies will also be constrained. With the increasing integration of the European market, ever-increasing tax harmonisation is likely to be required. Raising indirect taxes above the Union average would lead to a loss of price competitiveness. If labour mobility does increase, then raising income tax above the average rate could lead to labour migration. This might still leave some flexibility in setting levels of public spending. However, a harmonisation of benefits levels may also be needed if there is not to be some migration of those eligible to receive state benefits (if mobility increases). Equally, the possibilities of any government running a budget deficit are severely constrained. The fiscal rules that are to be part of Economic and Monetary Union only permit for a country's Public Sector

Borrowing Requirement to be a maximum of 3 per cent of its GDP, and gross public debts to be 60 per cent of its GDP. Further, the financing of any budget deficit will not be easy. It would not be possible to raise interest rates as bond prices were lowered in an effort to sell government debt. Equally, financing a budget deficit by 'printing money' (borrowing from the central bank, also referred to as 'seignorage') is severely limited, given its monetary implications and the fact that it is thus part of the European Central Bank's monetary policy.

There are two points to bear in mind when considering the importance of this apparent loss of economic sovereignty. The first is to what extent members of the European Union have economic sovereignty while they possess their own currencies. No nation could lower or raise its interest rates very far from the Union average, given the likely size of the effect on the exchange rate. Equally, attempting to pursue any sort of expansionary economic policy in isolation would be likely to be doomed to failure given the large amount of any increased spending that would immediately leak out to other European nations due to the high level of integration of the economies. This leads on to the second point, namely that there may be important benefits to be derived from a more closely coordinated economic policy throughout Europe. It has been suggested that Europe has sometimes found itself in a prisoners' dilemma (see Chapter 4 on game theory) insofar as it would be in everyone's interest for economic policy to move in a particular direction, but not rational for any one nation to risk making that move in isolation. Thus, the forced coordination of economic policies could be deemed a benefit.

A further concern about fixed exchange rates was that they were felt to be susceptible to speculative 'runs' on the currency in the event of a potential devaluation. A clear advantage of a single currency over other fixed exchange rate systems is that this is logically no longer a problem. Given that any possibility of a change in the currency's value has been irrevocably removed, then there will be no speculative activity. A similar point is that the problem of requiring large foreign currency reserves will also no longer exist with a single currency as there is no longer an exchange rate for any individual country to have to support.

CONCLUSION

There are two main points which can be made in conclusion to this survey. The first is that a review of the relevant theory suggests that if the European Union does wish to adopt a fixed exchange rate system, then there appear to be greater advantages (or less disadvantages) associated with having a single currency than with attempting to fix the value of separate currencies. The second point is that the review cannot give a confident answer as to whether there are clear gains or losses in total to be associated with the adoption of a single currency. To some extent, this leaves a nagging feeling that it may not make a great deal of difference with regard to the net impact upon European economic welfare (although there must be a possibility that some nations may end up as net winners while others become net losers). In the words of Bean (1992) when considering the pros and cons of EMU, 'from a purely economic perspective, it seems to me something of a storm in a teacup'. Thus it is hard not to conclude that the real source of disagreement over the issue is not economic but rather political and nationalistic.

References

Bean, C. (1992) 'Economic and Monetary Union in Europe', *Journal of Economic Perspectives*, Fall.

Caparole, G. (1993) 'Is Europe an Optimum Currency Area? Symmetric Versus Asymmetric Shocks in the EC', *National Institute Economic Review*, May.

Commission of the European Communities (1990) 'One Market, One Money: An Evaluation of the Potential Benefits and Costs of Forming an Economic and Monetary Union', *European Economy*, no. 44 (October).

McKinnon, R. (1993) 'The Rules of the Game: International Money in Historical Perspective', *Journal of Economic Literature*, March.

Meade, J. (1957) 'The Balance of Payments Problem of a Free Trade Area', *Economic Journal*, no. 67.

Mundell, R. (1961) 'A Theory of Optimum Currency Areas', *American Economic Review*, no. 51.

Scitovsky, T. (1958) *Economic Theory and Western European Integration* (Stanford University Press).

13 Economics and Politics: Political Business Cycles and Independent Central Banks

The relationship between the subject disciplines of economics and politics has always been uncertain. Are the two clearly separate, or are they fundamentally intertwined? This conundrum is mirrored in different university degree courses, such as the Cambridge Economics course as opposed to the Oxford Politics, Philosophy and Economics course in the UK. A view of economics that attempted to be purely positive in its approach would shy away from any involvement with politics. Politics would be seen as the discipline where value judgements could be made that were not permitted through a positive approach (see Chapter 1 on economic methodology). Alternative approaches to economics which assert the intrinsic value judgements inherent in any study of the subject (such as a Marxist approach) would suggest that to study economics is to study politics, and vice versa.

One relatively recent theoretical development to emanate from the discipline of economics appears to suggest some common ground: an economic theory of politics. Using some of the fundamental postulates of mainstream/neoclassical economics, theories about political behaviour can be derived which may be capable of some sort of testing. This is the area of collective choice theory, often subdivided into social choice theory and public choice theory. The purpose of this chapter is to explain this area of economic theory and then to consider its major implications. The chapter contains three major parts:

1. An explanation of collective choice theory. An analysis of how collective decisions are made in a democracy and what are the important motivations behind those decisions. This suggests how the political process is likely to function.
2. The political business cycle. Perhaps the best-known implication of collective choice theory is the possible existence of the political business cycle. The arguments and evidence about this are considered.
3. Independent central banks. One recent further development of collective choice theory and the perceived political business cycle is the suggestion that a country's monetary policy would best be run by a fully independent central bank. This discussion has become particularly important in Europe

with the possibility of a European central bank running Europe's monetary policy. The arguments are examined within the framework of collective choice theory.

COLLECTIVE CHOICE THEORY

Collective choice theory examines the relationship between the preferences of individual members of society and the collective choices made (on behalf of individuals) by governments. The usual domain of economics is that of individual choice made by individual consumers in a market: how much less of a product will individuals buy if its price rises? However, not all decisions are of this individual nature. A classic example concerns the provision of public goods. Given the free-rider problem (see Chapter 7 on the public provision of goods and services), there is a need for a central authority (the government) to oversee the provision of such goods. However, this creates a difficulty because the decision rules are not as obvious as when individual consumers make individual decisions in the market-place. There must be a system which allows the decision-making to take place. The assumed system is that of a liberal democracy, as opposed to the major alternative, a dictatorship.

The fundamental problem of collective choice theory, then, is to consider how it is possible for diverse individual preferences to lead to a group decision. What are to be the objectives of the group, given that individuals will not all hold exactly the same utility structures? Economists often refer to this in another way, namely what is the social welfare function? The political constitution of a country effectively answers this question. It is through the political constitution that individual preferences are turned into collective government decisions. An interesting question for economists to address is whether some political constitutions may be better at maximising social welfare than others. As mentioned before, there tend to be two types of approaches to this study: social choice theory which examines the question in a highly theoretical (perhaps abstract) fashion; and public choice theory which concentrates upon the political institutions of a country and considers the implications of these structures for political decisions and behaviour. Both approaches can be of value in an economic understanding and explanation of politics.

The important starting point for collective choice theory is to set the framework for analysing political decisions. The key issue is the perceived motivations of the people (or players) involved in the political process. The approach of political science has traditionally been to suggest the notion of a 'public interest'. The essence of this is the idea that groups of people have interests and preferences. The focus is upon whole groups. This contrasts with what might be seen as the economic approach. This suggests that it is individuals, not groups, that have preferences. As in all neoclassical economic theory, rational individuals are seen as maximising their own utility subject to resource constraints. In this approach, the 'public interest' is seen as simply the adding of all the relevant individuals' interests. There is no sense of a group interest that is separate from individuals' interests.

The aggregation of individual interests into a group interest is not entirely straightforward. An obvious example of this is the existence of externalities. By definition, external costs and benefits are not relevant to individual decision-making. However, when adding lots of individual decisions into a group situation, the externalities are relevant as they will affect other members of the group. Hirsch (1976) in his *Social Limits to Growth* gives an interesting example of this. He suggests that an individual may decide that they do not feel it worthwhile to say 'Hello' to people they meet in their village. However, they enjoy the benefit derived when someone else says 'Hello' to them. If everyone feels the same way, then it might maximise utility for a convention to exist where everyone agrees to say 'Hello' to everyone else, even though from a purely individual decision-making standpoint it is a cost to say 'Hello' with no guarantee of an immediately associated benefit. Hirsch refers to this as the group benefit of 'As if' altruism. However, despite these complications, the point about this suggested approach to collective choices is that the correct focus is on individual motivation and behaviour.

Given the focus on individuals, the key question becomes: how can individual preferences lead to group decisions? As mentioned at the outset, there are essentially two possible answers: either there is a dictatorship where one person makes a decision for everyone else, or a democracy where a decision is made on the basis of majority voting. Collective choice theory focuses on majority voting in the form of a representative democracy, a system in which certain individuals are elected to make decisions on behalf of all individuals in a group.

One important theoretical point to emerge from the 'social choice' branch of this approach is that there are problems inherent in majority voting systems. The most famous of these problems is given by Arrow's (1951) 'impossibility theorem'. Arrow suggested that certain conditions were required for a political constitution to be deemed ethically acceptable:

1. The assumptions of rationality. In particular, it must be true that if *a* is preferred to *b* and *b* is preferred to *c*, then *a* must be preferred to *c*.
2. The independence of irrelevant alternatives. The only thing that can change a set of group preferences is a change in individual preferences.
3. The Pareto principle. *a* must be preferred to *b* if at least one person feels that way and no one prefers *b* to *a*.
4. An unrestricted area. All logically possible choices are available to individuals.
5. Non-dictatorship. One individual is not permitted to overrule the decision of others.

Arrow proceeds to demonstrate that these conditions are not met under a system of majority voting. Thus there is no ethically acceptable political constitution. One possible example of this is shown in Table 13.1. Three individuals have to

Table 13.1   *Preferences of three individuals given three alternative choices*

	1st choice	*2nd choice*	*3rd choice*
Individual 1	X	Y	Z
Individual 2	Y	Z	X
Individual 3	Z	X	Y

decide between three alternatives. Their preferences are indicated in the table. Which of the three alternatives will be chosen, given the use of majority voting?

X will win over Y, because both individuals 1 and 3 prefer X to Y. Z will win over X as both individuals 2 and 3 prefer prefer Z to X. Therefore, the winning choice, so it appears, must be Z. However, when comparing Z and Y, it appears that Y is more popular as both individuals 1 and 2 prefer Y to Z.

This example therefore contravenes the first of the conditions laid down by Arrow for a voting system to be ethically acceptable: it does not fulfil all the assumptions of rationality. Thus Arrow made it clear that it is, in fact, not possible to devise an ethically acceptable system of majority voting, if all of his suggested conditions are accepted. Obviously this could have implications regarding the process of economic decision-making. If different trade-offs are believed to exist in economics (such as between inflation, unemployment and the rate of economic growth) then how can the government decide which economic variable should be given the greatest weighting in its economic policy decisions? The above example suggests that a system of majority voting will not necessarily provide an acceptable means of making the decision.

Other difficulties with a system of majority voting have also been identified. It appears true that a majority voting system will not necessarily guarantee a position of Pareto efficiency (the situation where no one individual can be made better off without making someone else worse off). It is clear that unless the outcome of a voting procedure is unanimous, there will be winners and losers in every decision that is reached. This suggests that one group (the majority) is being made better off at the expense of another group (the minority). Thus the outcome does not fit within the definition of Pareto efficiency. It might be possible to achieve a unanimous decision by allowing individuals to veto any proposal that was put forward, thus forcing a situation where the only possible decisions that took place meant that no one was made worse off. However, achieving any decisions with this rule would require the use of many resources (the number of elections required would be great), and this is likely to be judged as inefficient. In some ways, the problem can be seen here as the fact that majority voting systems do not take account of the intensity of people's preferences. It makes a great deal of difference whether individuals slightly prefer or very greatly prefer one alternative to another. However, this will not be registered under a simple majority voting system. A system which allowed the intensity of people's feelings to be expressed could arrive at a different outcome from one that did not differentiate in this fashion.

A further difficulty with majority voting systems is the incentive that exists to try to manipulate voting by giving false information regarding an individual's preferences. It is possible for an individual to give false information regarding his or her most favoured alternative in order to avoid the least desired alternative from happening. This is really the case of tactical voting: an individual may vote for his or her second favourite political party in order simply to prevent his or her least favoured party from gaining victory. This suggests that if one individual owns more information than others about the voting procedure and the preferences of others, then he or she can manipulate the process in order to gain at the expense of others (something that would not be deemed to be Pareto efficient).

Thus this whole area of theory makes it clear that any decision that is made by majority voting faces difficulties. This is important within economics, because as soon as the decision is made that the economy could run more efficiently if a government intervenes in an effort to correct market failures (see Chapter 7 on the state provision of health care and education), then decisions have to be made about such things as how much of a public good should be provided (with accompanying implications about the appropriate tax level required in order to finance the decision). Allowing individuals to make this decision through some form of majority voting system will then suffer from all of the problems mentioned.

The problems identified by social choice theory concerning majority voting are obviously important. However, it is perhaps the implications that have been derived from Downs's analysis (1957) that have the greatest significance for the overlap between politics and economics. In particular, they can be seen as the basis of the theory behind the political business cycle and, more recently, the calls for central banks to be given full independence from governments. These two issues provide the major focus of the rest of this chapter.

Downs' model clearly fits within the neoclassical economic approach to politics mentioned earlier based upon the assumption of rational, utility-maximising individuals. Perhaps the most important part of Downs's analysis is to identify politicians as being rational vote-maximisers. Whether the individual politician's aim is to promote the social good or simply to gain benefit from political office, the rational politician must aim to maximise his or her votes. In a system of democracy, the perceived social good can only effectively be promoted from a position of political power. In keeping with the neoclassical approach, voters are assumed to be individual, rational utility-maximisers.

An important implication of Downs's identification of politicians as vote-maximisers is the key role of the median voter. If a democracy is characterised by a two-party system, as is the case in several western democracies, then capturing the vote of the median voter becomes the key to electoral success. This observation is merely an extension of Hotelling's observation concerning competition between two sellers. Hotelling (1929) pointed out that if two sellers, for example selling flowers, were in competition along the same stretch of road, then their aim would be to position themselves at the mid-point of the road in order to maximise the potential number of sales of flowers. Thus the two sellers could be anticipated to be next to each other on the road. The same would thus be true in a two-party political democracy. In order to gain a majority of votes, political parties can be expected to manoeuvre in the central ground of politics in an effort to capture the median voter. The implication is that vote-maximising politicians will produce consensus politics in any two-party system.

There are various reasons why the political system may not operate in precisely the fashion indicated above, even given the assumptions of neoclassical economics. One obvious point is that some western democracies are characterised by more than two major political parties. In such a situation, it is not so clear that capturing the vote of the median voter is the key to electoral success. Hotelling's model of competition suggests that an equilibrium between three sellers along a stretch of road may be reached when the sellers are positioned at equal distances from each other along the road. The same may be true of a three-party political system. Political parties may see their best chance of maximising votes as targeting certain key groups. This could imply the need for one political party deliberately to distance itself from others.

The most significant difficulty with Downs's model as outlined above is the lack of perfect information, both on the part of politicians and of voters. One obvious uncertainty regards the identification of the median voter. It is not always clear exactly where the middle ground lies. Given that, it seems likely that political pressure groups could succeed in exercising a disproportionate influence. As politicians are unaware of who is the median voter, they may be very willing to listen to the views of pressure groups who can claim to represent a large proportion of the electorate. It is sometimes suggested that this has led to the over-expansion of certain parts of government expenditure. For example, if the military establishment strongly emphasises to the government the importance of spending money on certain military projects, the government may be prepared to go along with the suggestion in an effort to capture this known section of votes as opposed to the unknown median voter.

A further difficulty with identifying the median voter arises due to the lack of voter participation in many elections. In economic terms, this may be explained by the fact that the perceived benefits of voting do not outweigh the perceived costs. The costs of voting could involve the time taken and the discomfort of bad weather. It may not appear worth enduring these costs if it is possible to 'free ride' on the votes of others who are prepared to vote. This may be particularly true in an electoral system where it is possible to believe that an individual vote could be of no importance. This may be the case in 'first past the post' systems. Equally, if the consensus politics postulated from the Downsian model emerges, there may be very little to choose between the two parties and thus little to gain or lose from voting.

Uncertainty on the part of the voter could lead to another type of decision rule being employed by voters. Given a further assumption about individual behaviour emanating from neoclassical economics, namely that individuals aim to minimise risks, then voters could operate a minimax regret voting rule. Voter uncertainty concerning the exact future policies of political parties means that voters may simply vote in a way that endeavours to avoid the worst outcome. This observation correlates well with the perceived rise in negative election campaigning in western democracies. If voters are concerned to avoid the most damaging outcomes for themselves, then any political party will see the importance of persuading the electorate of the possibility of other political parties inflicting unwanted policies upon the nation, if elected. The most common theme here appears to be to try to persuade voters that other political parties will raise tax rates, if elected.

The key point about Downs's analysis is to illustrate how the assumptions commonly employed within the framework of neoclassical economics can be applied to political behaviour to explain and predict the functioning of political democracies. The political business cycle is seen as one of the most important possible implications.

THE POLITICAL BUSINESS CYCLE

> All political history shows that the standing of the Government and its ability to hold the confidence of the electorate at a General Election depend upon the success of its economic policy.

These words of Harold Wilson, the former British Prime Minister, sum up the essence of the political business cycle. If Wilson is correct, and if Downs's assumption about politicians' vote-maximising behaviour is accurate, then the key task that any government will give itself is to manipulate the economy so that it is at its 'best' in the run-up to a General Election. This should maximise the chances of any incumbent government being re-elected. In the words of Downs: 'Parties formulate policies in order to win elections, rather than win elections in order to formulate policies.'

The usual assumption is that individual voters tend to hold utility functions that mean that they feel happier with the performance of the government during times of rising incomes and lower unemployment (the so-called 'feel good' factor) and less happy with the government during periods of stagnant or falling incomes and higher unemployment. Given the known tendency of market economies to progress in booms and slumps, rather than in a straight line, the suggestion is that governments may try to manipulate the economic cycle (perhaps even accentuating it) so that the 'best' performance of the economy arrives at the same time as a General Election. In this way a government stands the greatest chance of re-election, since voters are more likely to vote for the government when the economy is 'doing well'. Thus the development of a democratic market economy will tend to be as shown in Figure 13.1.

This argument is then sometimes taken a stage further to suggest that such a pattern is not in the long-term interests of the economy as it implies damaging

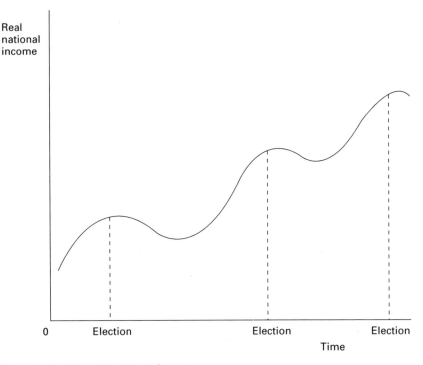

Figure 13.1   *The political business cycle*

fluctuations and economic policies being used to ensure short-term re-election rather than the effective long-run performance of the economy. Such views lie behind calls for independent central banks.

However, before this simple analysis is accepted, it needs to be subjected to closer scrutiny. It can be questioned in various ways. One important point to note is that although the logic that led to the suggestion of the existence of the political business cycle was seen as emanating from the assumptions of neoclassical economics, the possibility of such a cycle is contrary to some of the assumptions held within certain branches of the neoclassical approach. Certainly, it assumes that governments have the power to manipulate the economy in order to affect output and employment. Such a theory is contrary to 'new classical' macroeconomic views which argue that if individuals have rational expectations, then a government cannot engineer a fall in the rate of unemployment, even in the short run. However, the point about rational expectations goes further than this. Even if it is believed that the government does have the ability to manipulate short-run changes in employment and output, the political business cycle appears to suggest that voters do not learn from their experience. In other words, they do not have rational expectations. The fact that at some previous General Election the government had managed to manipulate the economy into a position of boom only to be followed by a recession after the Election does not lead voters to behave differently when at a present Election the government also manages to manipulate a rise in employment and output. Whether such a view of voters can be deemed to be in keeping with the assumption of rationality at the heart of neoclassical economics may be open to question.

A further uncertainty regarding the political business cycle concerns the accuracy and stability of the parameters of correlation between the government's popularity and certain important economic variables. The theory of the political business cycle is only applicable if there is some degree of stability and predicability about the economy's performance and the electoral chances of the incumbent government. A casual observation suggests that this may not be the case, given the re-election of many western governments in the 1980s, despite high levels of unemployment. Such an outcome would probably have seemed impossible in preceding decades. However, more specific measures are required than this. Research has suggested that three macroeconomic variables can have an impact upon government popularity:

1. The rate of unemployment (negative effect),
2. The rate of inflation (negative effect), and
3. The rate of growth in real disposable income (positive effect).

If the exact effect of each of these variables on government popularity is known, then any government can aim for the optimum position possible in the economy, given the constraints of such things as the trade-off between inflation and unemployment. However, the coefficients are seen as varying between countries and across time. The results of some of the surveys are given in Table 13.2.

The figures in the table suggest the correlations changed over a period of time in the United States. Perhaps even more notable is how much the correlations appear to have differed between countries. While there could have been clear political advantage in reducing unemployment at the expense of rising inflation in both the United States and the United Kingdom in the time periods indicated, the same is by no means true of Germany. Research has suggested that in

Table 13.2   *Estimates of the impact of economic conditions on government popularity*

Country and period	Estimated coefficient	
	Unemployment	*Inflation*
United States (1981–88)	–8.6	–0.1
United States (1953–75)	–4.2	–1.0
United Kingdom (1959–74)	–6.0	–0.7
West Germany (1951–75)	–0.9	–0.7

Source: W.D. Nordhaus (1989) 'Alternative Approaches to the political Business Cycle', *Brookings Papers on Economic Activity*, 2.

Switzerland in the 1970s there was more political gain available through restricting inflation than through reducing unemployment. Thus the political business cycle could have been the opposite of that usually suggested.

It is also important to note that all models of the political business cycle that have been developed recognise the importance of non-economic factors. These could override any economic variables. The most important of them are suggested to be:

1. The initial popularity level of the government.
2. An autonomous election cycle which sees government popularity decrease until the middle of the legislative period and then increase before elections. This is particularly notable in the United Kingdom.
3. Internal events of great importance, such as the Watergate issue in the United States.
4. External events of importance. These events often appear to have only a very short-term effect.

Perhaps the most important question to ask of the political business cycle, indeed of the whole Downsian model, is whether politicians will always seek re-election at any cost. In other words, is there any role for ideology in politics? Without this, it is not easy to see the reason for the continuing existence of different political parties which purport to have different political priorities. However, once the possibility of ideology is accepted, then the political business cycle cannot be taken as given. The political priorities of one party might lead it to pursue a different mixture of inflation and unemployment from another party. The mixture would not solely be due to what was deemed to be the most likely to gain re-election. If this is the case, then predictions concerning the political business cycle must be amended accordingly. It is, however, worth noting that even in a model that allows politicians to hold ideological differences, it could be rational for those politicians to compromise their ideology up to a certain point in order to gain re-election if this was seen as the only possible means of ensuring that the even worse alternative of the policies of an opposition political party never happened.

There appear, then, to be ways in which the simple political business cycle is unlikely to operate in precisely the fashion illustrated in Figure 13.1. However, if it is believed that all voters do not hold fully rational expectations and that an important motivation of politicians is indeed to ensure re-election, then the chances of any government attempting to manipulate some version of the political business cycle appear strong. If this is not in the best interests of the long-term strength of the economy (the fluctuations, for example, not being desirable from the point of view of long-term business investment plans) then there could be an argument for the economy creating structures that make it less easy for the economy to be manipulated for short-term political gain. This is the essence of the argument that suggests that western democracies are likely to have a better economic performance if they have an independent central bank.

INDEPENDENT CENTRAL BANKS

The argument for independent central banks is that if monetary policy is removed from the government and given to a country's central bank, then the policy can be used solely in the economic interest of the country, rather than being a political tool to help to ensure re-election. This argument has come into sharper focus within Europe given the imminence of decisions regarding Economic and Monetary Union and the nature of the European Central Bank that should control European monetary policy. The usual suggestion is that if the central bank is given independence and is given as its primary goal the control of inflation to within prescribed limits, then the overall performance of the economy will be better than if all economic policy is handled by the government.

A starting point for this suggestion is often a graph plotting the average rate of inflation on one axis and an index of the level of political independence of the central bank of a country on the other axis. A best fit line is then usually drawn in the fashion indicated in Figure 13.2.

The conclusion to be drawn is that the higher the level of central bank independence, the lower the average rate of inflation. Germany is usually held up as a clear example of this, possessing both a strongly independent central bank and a low post-war average rate of inflation. In addition to the problems of identifying the level of independence of a central bank, there are still other problems with this argument. Association need not imply cause and effect in a particular direction. Indeed, the example of Germany fits equally well within the framework of the political business cycle given that German governments appear to be able to gain as much popularity by reducing inflation as by reducing unemployment, unlike the governments of the United States and the United Kingdom. Thus, this could be the real cause of lower inflation in Germany when compared with the United States and the United Kingdom.

Indeed, when the behaviour of central banks is included within political business cycle models, the suggestion is that the central bank will pursue its preferred policy of a restrictive monetary policy to combat inflation, as long as that does not conflict with overall government economic policy. However, if there is a possible conflict with the government, it is assumed that the central bank will follow the government (who are stronger) and set an expansionary monetary policy to match the expansionary fiscal policy of the government. Certainly, it is important to consider the underlying motivations of central bankers. If this is to be in keeping with the vote-maximising behaviour of politicians, then job preservation may be deemed a high priority. As such, upsetting the government of the day too much may not be considered a likely course of action.

The argument for an independent central bank can be formalised within the framework of an expectations-augmented Phillips curve (see Chapter 11 on inflation and unemployment). This is shown in Figure 13.3.

Given the assumption of vote-maximising politicians, then in certain western democracies (but not all) there will be a tendency for governments to try to

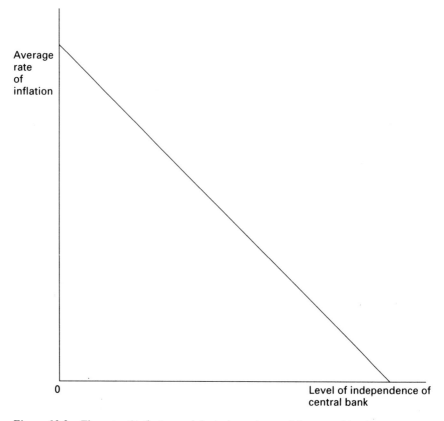

Figure 13.2   *The rate of inflation and the independence of the central bank*

reduce unemployment in the run-up to any General Election. This the basic suggestion of the political business cycle. Thus, governments may attempt to move
the economy from point A to point B on short-run Phillips curve 1. This may or
may not succeed in securing the re-election of the incumbent government. After
the election, the economy returns to position C at the natural rate of unemployment when workers realise that their real wages have not in fact risen (the standard behaviour assumed in the expectations-augmented Phillips curve). The
problem, of course, is that that point is associated with a higher level of
inflation than the starting point of A. The problem for the economy now is that
the government will not be able to reduce inflation below this level if it is
assumed that people learn from their experience of previous government behaviour as a General Election approaches. Now that people have learnt how a government is likely to behave as a General Election approaches, inflating the
economy in an effort to secure re-election, then any suggestion by the government that it wishes to reduce inflation and maintain inflation at a lower rate

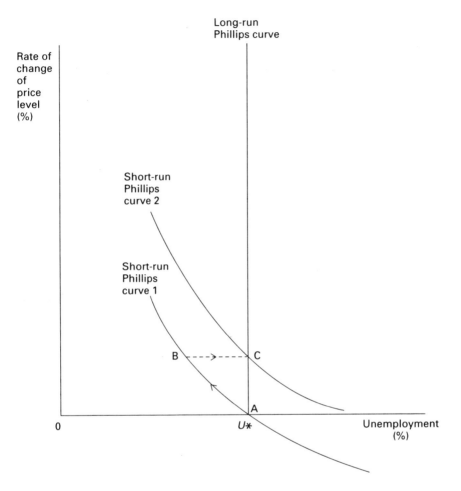

Figure 13.3 *The expectations-augmented Phillips curve*

cannot hold credibility. People will always expect inflation to return to its higher level as the General Election gets nearer. This means that all economic behaviour adjusts to take account of this expectation, including the level of wage demands. The government is then left in a position where it will be forced to allow the money supply to rise and inflation to stay at the higher anticipated rate if it wishes to avoid a rising level of unemployment. The price the country has had to pay for the government inflating the economy in an effort to be re-elected is a permanently higher rate of inflation.

The way out of this situation is to hand over control of monetary policy to an independent central bank. The bank then has the sole duty of maintaining a low or zero rate of inflation. When such a target was announced by the independent central bank, it would be seen as credible because there would be no incentive for the central bank to inflate the economy at a future date. Thus people would be prepared to adjust their behaviour, including wage demands, in line with a lower anticipated level of inflation. The country can have a lower rate of inflation with an independent central bank than it could without one.

The above appears to give a clear theoretical framework for suggesting that lower inflation (without any sacrifice in terms of output and employment) will be the reward for any country which is prepared to give its central bank independence. However, there are a number of questions that must be asked about this analysis. Clearly, it relies upon the expectations-augmented Phillips curve being an appropriate way in which to model the economy. Not all economists would agree with this. If there is the possibility of any longer-term trade-off between inflation and unemployment, then the analysis would not hold.

The assumption regarding voters that is used in the above model is not the same as that required for any persistence in the political business cycle. For the political business cycle to exist over any length of time, it is not possible for voters to have fully rational expectations. However, that is the assumption in the model described above. Once voters have learnt how governments behave, they never make the same mistake again. Thus the political business cycle does not exist. This seems ironic, given that the background to the argument about independent central banks is the existence of the political business cycle.

The above analysis also assumes that any inflation target announced by the central bank will be fully credible. However, if the assumption concerning central bank behaviour that is made in the theory of political business cycles is accurate, namely that central banks will fall in line with the government when there is the possibility of any conflict, then it is not clear that such an announcement will be credible. If a central bank is to be independent, it must be fiercely independent of any political control.

This last point raises an issue that returns to Arrow's impossibility theorem. A fully independent central bank with complete power to set monetary policy as it sees fit appears to contradict one of Arrow's requirements for an ethically acceptable voting system, namely non-dictatorship. The background to all of the analysis in this chapter has been that government economic policy decisions should have the backing of a democratic vote. It is interesting that the assumptions held about voter and politician behaviour appear to have led to the conclusion that an institution that is not democratically accountable may be needed in order to improve the performance of an economy.

CONCLUSION

Collective choice theory indicates how the assumptions of neoclassical economics can be applied to politics. The implication appears to be that there is the possibility that economic policy could become a tool for incumbent governments to try to ensure their own re-election. In order to try to reduce the damage that this may do to an economy, it has been suggested that certain tools of economic policy, notably monetary policy, should be taken out of the hands of governments and run by an independent institution. The validity of these arguments appears to depend heavily upon the level of voter rationality that is assumed. Thus, the suggestion appears to be that reducing the amount of economic policy that is dictated by democratic voting could be desirable. This probably requires ethical debates that are more clearly in the domain of politics than of economics, if one takes a positive methodological approach to the subject.

References

Arrow, K. (1951) *Social Choice and Individual Values* (New York: John Wiley and Sons, Inc.).
Downs, A. (1957) *An Economic Theory of Democracy* (New York: Harper & Row).
Hirsch, F. (1976) *Social Limits to Growth* (Cambridge, Mass: Harvard University Press).
Hotelling, H. (1929) 'Stability in Competition' in *Economic Journal*, vol. no. 39
Nordhaus, W. D. (1989) 'Alternative Approaches to the Political Business Cycle', *Brookings Papers on Economic Activity,* 2.
Wilson, H. (1981) Quoted in Hibbs and Fassbender (eds), *Contemporary Political Economy* (Amsterdam: North-Holland).

14 Economic Growth: Old Theories, New Theories and Government Policy

A consideration of what causes economies to grow is not a new one in the area of economic study. Adam Smith (1776) referred to it as *An Enquiry into the Nature and Causes of the Wealth of Nations*. From the time of the Industrial Revolution, industrialised countries have become accustomed to the fact that, on average, the value of their real national income and output will become greater every year. In other words, we expect economic growth to occur. We expect material living standards, as measured by per capita real income, to increase. In some ways, economic growth might be seen as fundamental to any 'solving' of the basic economic problem, implying that a greater number of infinite wants can be met. Despite increasing environmental concerns over the impact of economic growth upon all aspects of the world's environment (see Chapter 6 on the economics of the environment), there remains a belief that sustainable and 'appropriate' economic growth is desirable. Our expectation of improving education, health services and private consumption could never be met without it.

Given this centrality of economic growth to the subject-matter of economics, it is perhaps extraordinary that growth theory is so tentatively and sparsely handled in many economics textbooks; that, until recently, there have been little by way of theoretical developments in growth theory since the 1950s; and that growth theory has not been seen as anything of great relevance and help by the designers of government economic policy. The purpose of this chapter is to look at the older growth theories and consider some of the problems they appear to face when confronted with the pattern of world growth rates. In light of these concerns, there have been new theories developed in recent years. These are investigated. It then seems pertinent to consider where the theories of economic growth that exist today leave possible recommendations for economic policy to encourage economic growth. This chapter thus comprises of three main sections:

1. Old theories of economic growth. The two major models to be considered are those of Harrod (1939) and the neoclassical model of Solow (1956). The perceived empirical inadequacies of these models will be discussed.
2. New theories of economic growth. In recent years, new theories of economic growth have emerged which help to resolve some of the perceived empirical weaknesses of the older theories. These theories stress the importance of positive externalities in the growth process.

250

3. Government policies to encourage economic growth. Using the theories of economic growth, it is possible to make suggestions for different government economic policies which could enable the long-term growth rate of a nation to rise.

Before embarking on a consideration of theories of economic growth, it is important to be sure of what it is that is under consideration. Economic growth is any increase in a nation's real national income. However, we are not really interested here in a short-run increase in national income associated with a boom in the trade cycle and a fall in the level of national income associated with a downturn in the trade cycle. Rather we wish to consider the long-run trend growth of national income, around which the trade cycle may function. The difference between these two concepts is illustrated in Figure 14.1.

Thus, what is under consideration is not a movement of an economy from within its production possibility frontier, but rather what dictates the yearly average outward movement of that frontier (representing the productive

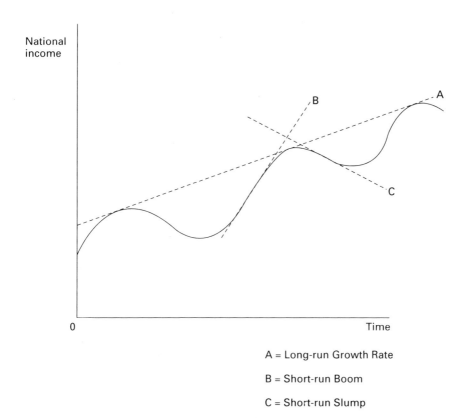

A = Long-run Growth Rate

B = Short-run Boom

C = Short-run Slump

Figure 14.1 *Identifying the rate of economic growth*

potential of a nation). Again, this is best understood with a diagram: see
Figure 14.2.

The production possibility frontier is also helpful in beginning to focus upon
the possible causes of economic growth. There are just two reasons why there
may be an outward movement of the country's production possibility frontier:
either there is an increase in the quantity of factors of production available, or
there is an improvement in the quality of the factors of production that already
exist. Any recorded long-run economic growth must be associated with either or
both these phenomena. The problem is that this offers no explanation as to why
the quantity or quality of factors of production may vary, and which factors may
make the more important contributions. Thus it is necessary to examine theories
of economic growth.

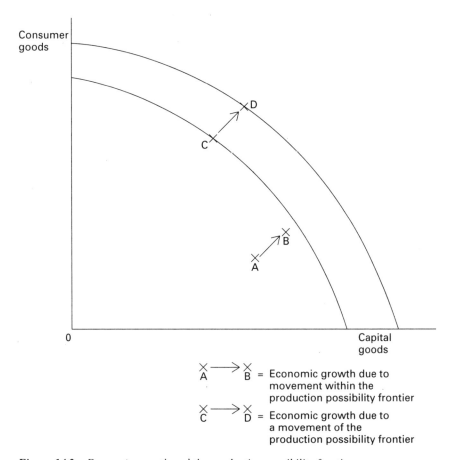

Figure 14.2 *Economic growth and the production possibility frontier*

OLD THEORIES OF ECONOMIC GROWTH:

An important assumption that lies behind the older theories of economic growth is the law of variable proportions or diminishing marginal returns. This simply states that for successive increases of a variable factor of production (perhaps labour) to a fixed factor of production (perhaps capital), there will be progressively smaller increases in total production. Thus, the increase in production gained through increasing labour while leaving the level of capital fixed could be illustrated as in Figure 14.3.

The other important assumption made is that if all factors of production are increased by the same amount, then there are constant returns to scale. Thus if the only two factors of production considered are labour and capital, then a doubling of the input of both labour and capital inputs will lead to a doubling of output. This assumption is necessary if there is to be the possibility of a competitive market, not usually to be seen as possible where there are increasing returns to scale which induce firms to become large thus tending to reduce competition. As the models tend to rely on the existence of competition (preferably perfect competition), this is a necessary assumption.

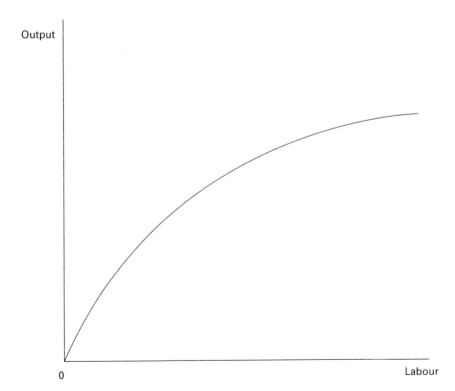

Figure 14.3 *The law of variable proportions*

Harrod's (1939) work attempted to use a Keynesian style of economic analysis to suggest a theory of long-run economic growth. Together with the work of Domar (1947), this led to the so-called Harrod–Domar model of economic growth. An important assumption lying behind this model was the assumed inflexibility of prices, particularly the long-run interest rate. Harrod assumed that the rate of interest was determined outside of the model, in the money market rather than the goods market. Using a simple Keynesian analysis, it is assumed that planned savings will be equal to planned investment, that the savings ratio (s) represents a certain percentage of national income, and that investment is dictated by the expected rate of change of income and expenditure multiplied by the required incremental capital–output ratio (Cr) (the amount by which capital, or investment, has to be increased in order to secure a certain increase in output. If it is assumed that that there is a fixed capital–labour ratio, then Cr will be fixed). This is the so-called accelerator mechanism. These simple relationships can be summarised as follows:

1. Planned savings (S) = Planned investment (I) (for equilibrium)
2. Planned savings (S) = Savings ratio (s) multiplied by national
   income (Y) = (sY)

3. Planned investment (I) = required incremental capital–output ratio
   (Cr) multiplied by anticipated change in
   national income ($*Y$)
   ($Cr*Y$)
   ($* = $ 'change in')

These simple summaries need to be slightly rearranged to give the fundamental relationship in the Harrod–Domar model. By combining:

1. $S = I$ with
2. $S = (sY)$ we get:
4. $I = (sY)$

By combining:

4. $I = (sY)$ with
3. $I = (Cr*Y)$ we get:
5. $(sY) = (Cr*Y)$

The final stage is to divide both sides of this relationship by both Cr and Y to arrive at the final relationship:

6. $s/Cr = *Y/Y$

This is what is termed the 'warranted' rate of growth, the rate of growth of national income that is consistent with equilibrium in the market for goods and services in the country (planned desired savings = planned desired investment).

An important part of the Harrod–Domar model is the suggestion that if the expected rate of growth of national income is not the same as the warranted growth rate then there will be instability. For example, if the expected rate of growth is below the warranted rate, then actual income will fall below expected income for the time period under consideration. This is because the level of investment that will occur for the expected rate of growth is below that for the warranted rate, given that income is expected to grow at a lower level and thus less investment is justified. This means that desired investment will be lower than desired saving, and therefore actual income will fall. This will create spare capacity in firms and lead to an expectation of even lower rates of growth, thus causing a fall in investment rates and a further fall in actual income. This is a cumulative movement which threatens to continue to move the economy in a downward direction. The process would work in the opposite direction if the expected growth rate were above the warranted rate. Thus, there is the suggestion that growth rates are poised on a 'knife edge'. There will be stable growth if the warranted rate is equal to the expected rate, but any divergence between the two will lead to the economy heading off in an upward or downward direction.

The possible growth of the supply side of the economy is characterised by what is called the 'natural' rate of growth. This is the maximum rate of growth that can be facilitated by the supply side of the economy. There are two things that, by definition, dictate the natural rate of growth: the rate of growth of the labour force and the rate of technical progress. These are the factors that increase the productive potential of the economy, shifting the production possibility frontier to the right. If the warranted rate of growth is equal to the natural rate of growth, then a steady state of economic growth will occur in the economy. However, if these two rates do not equal each other, then the economy faces difficulties. If the warranted rate of growth is lower than the natural rate, then there will be a steady state of economic growth but it will be characterised by a continually rising rate of unemployment. The level of investment is insufficient to provide enough capital to employ all the workers, and as long as the warranted rate remains below the natural rate, then this situation will continue to worsen. If the warranted rate is greater than the natural rate, then growth will become constrained by labour shortages. Planned saving will exceed planned investment and this will cause excess capacity and unemployment of the Keynesian variety. The excess capacity will cause a cut in investment by firms which will then produce a cumulative downward movement of the economy as previously described in the 'knife-edge' property of growth rates. Both of these problems could be tackled by appropriate government policy, as will be discussed later.

The principal difference between Solow's neoclassical model of economic growth (1956) and Harrod's (1939) model is that factor prices, including the long-run real rate of interest, are seen as being flexible. This significantly affects the predictions of the theory. There will not be the same problems for the economy that were seen as possibilities in Harrod's model. The existence of flexible prices implies that if there is a discrepancy between the warranted and the natural rate of growth, then the appropriate factor prices will change. This will permit the capital–output ratio (*Cr*) to vary, something that was not possible in Harrod's model, and thus mean that the warranted rate of growth will change until the warranted rate adjusts to a point where it is equal to the natural rate. For example, if the warranted rate were above the natural rate, then the shortage of labour that was created would force up the real wage, and the excess of capital would force down the real interest rate (as investment demand fell). This would cause firms to substitute capital for labour in order to minimise production costs, and thus the capital–output ratio would be raised. Given that the warranted rate of growth is equal to *s/Cr*, then an increase in the capital–output ratio (*Cr*) will lower the warranted growth rate. This process will continue until the warranted rate is once more equal to the natural rate. The implication of this is that the warranted and natural rates of growth will tend to equal each other, and thus that economies will generally be characterised by steady states of economic growth. Equally, the two determinants of long-run economic growth are the two things perceived as determining the natural rate of growth: the rate of growth of the labour force and the rate of technical change.

One point worthy of note in passing is that what has been described above suggests that a fundamental difference in the predictions of macroeconomic models can be traced to an assumption regarding the perceived flexibility of all, or particular, prices. This was a point noted in Chapter 3 (on microeconomics and macroeconomics) and is a vital theme in macroeconomics models.

Solow's neoclassical model of growth became accepted in most economic circles as a standard model of economic growth. A technique known as 'growth accounting' which attempted to identify the particular causes of economic growth for any particular nation or group of nations developed based on the assumptions of the theory (for example, Denison, 1967). Perhaps the most notable feature about these growth accounting surveys was that the largest contributor to economic growth was usually derived from a residual in the calculations. This residual was put down to technical progress. Technical progress was thus suggested as the major contributor to economic growth. However, this has been one of the areas of dissatisfaction with the traditional theory: no explanation is offered for the causes of technical change, and hence there is no explanation of the main cause of economic growth. Rather, technical progress is seen as something that just happens, raining down rather like manna from heaven, perhaps in the form of scientific breakthroughs. To put it another way, technical progress is exogenous to the model.

Some important implications can be derived from the neoclassical theory of economic growth:

1. As a nation's capital–output ratio rises, then so its growth rate will fall. This is the case due to the assumption of the law of diminishing marginal returns. If the use of capital is increased in the production process without a commensurate increase in the use of labour, as must be the case with developed nations if they wish their economies to grow at a rate that is not entirely

constrained by the size of their workforce, then the diminishing returns to capital will cause a fall in the rate of growth. The implication is thus that investment does not matter for long-term growth as the possible beneficial output effects of higher investment will be offset by a higher capital–output ratio.

2. Less-developed nations should be able to grow at a faster rate than more-developed nations (at least for the same investment ratio). In other words, there will be a tendency for countries with lower per capita incomes to 'catch up' with those with higher per capita incomes. Again, this relates to the law of variable proportions. Given that less-developed nations are working from a smaller capital base than more-developed nations, then an increase in investment, causing a rise in the capital–output ratio, will not suffer from diminishing returns to the same degree as any investment in a more-developed country.

3. Economies should grow at a steady state. It can be suggested that as the capital–output ratio can vary and that the warranted rate of growth will tend to equal the natural rate, then growth rates might be expected to be steady over a long period of time. There are unlikely to be periods of acceleration and deceleration in a nation's growth rate. However, it may not necessarily be true that steady state growth is the same thing as growth at the same rate. The trade cycle may still cause fluctuations in the short run.

The problem with all three of these predictions derived from Solow's model is that they appear to be inaccurate. Over a long period of time, there does not seem to have been a continual fall in the growth rate of developed economies. Nor does there appear to have been a tendency for the economies of Latin America and much of Asia and Africa to catch up with the western developed economies. An explanation is offered for this, namely that continuing technical progress succeeds in staving off the onset of diminishing returns. Economies keep moving on to new production functions. However, this point suffers from the same difficulty encountered with growth accounting: there is no explanation as to what might cause technical progress. The third observation of steady rates of economic growth equally does not appear to be accurate. Most of the developed world found their growth rates increasing in the 'Golden Age' of the 1950s and 1960s only to decelerate after 1973.

These perceived empirical inaccuracies of fundamental conclusions derived from the traditional theory of economic growth have proved to be an important factor in the deriving of new growth theories from the middle of the 1980s.

NEW THEORIES OF ECONOMIC GROWTH

While there have been several suggestions concerning growth theory which have elements in common with the more recent developments, such as Arrow's 'learning-by-doing' (1962) and Kaldor's emphasis on Verdorn's law and the importance of economies of scale (1966 among others elsewhere), the current theories are generally seen as starting with Romer's PhD thesis (1983). It is possible to identify certain important elements in the various versions of these new theories, referred to as 'endogenous growth theory', which distinguish them from Solow's model:

1. There is a broader view of what may constitute capital. In particular, there is an emphasis on the role and importance of knowledge as a part of capital, or perhaps even as a separate factor of production.
2. There are seen to be important positive externalities which are associated with the growth process.
3. The new theories are consistent with imperfect, rather than perfect, competition.

It is perhaps best to try to separate these new theories into two types. The first, associated with Romer (1986), assumes that there are constant returns to scale (as in the traditional model) but that there is a positive externality intrinsically involved within the growth process. The key point is that the act of capital accumulation causes positive learning externalities to take place. It is possible to think of many examples of this. The use of the silicon chip when first applied to production techniques was used in certain specific ways. However, it gradually became clear that there might be many further applications which could raise the productivity of labour. These further applications have spawned yet more alternatives. There is a cumulative process with positive externalities deriving from the initial application. This is very similar to Arrow's 'learning-by-doing'. Through applying the silicon chip, unintended lessons have been learnt which allow for further benefits. These unintended knowledge gains can be characterised as positive externalities. An alternative version of 'learning-by-doing' is 'learning-by-watching' (King and Robson, 1989). It is not necessary for a producer to be actively involved in the particular area of capital accumulation for it to benefit from the learning externalities. The further possible applications of the silicon chip may benefit many other producers not initially involved in its application.

The second type of these new growth theories stresses the role of a specific growth factor in raising the productivity of all of the factors of production, rather than an externality specifically associated with capital accumulation. This factor is itself subject to external increasing returns to scale. It is possible to think of several examples of such growth factors which raise the productivity of all factors and possess positive externalities. One example is human capital. The education of individuals raises productivity by increasing skills and generating new ideas. It is also associated with positive externalities as these skills and ideas are likely to benefit producers beyond the individual and his or her firm. Another example would be the knowledge gained through the process of research and development conducted by firms. This could raise productivity and is also associated with a positive externality insofar as other producers can use and benefit from the knowledge that is gained. A further suggested example is that of public investment, perhaps in the transport system. This helps to raise the productivity of all the factors of production and leads to positive benefits to a wide range of possible producers.

These new theories have several important implications. The first is that they are capable of explaining the empirical observations that were seen as contradicting the standard neoclassical theory. The positive externalities associated with the growth process explain why there is no slowdown in the growth rates of developed countries. The positive externalities prevent the capital–output ratio from rising, so that more investment in rich countries does not lead to slower growth. Thus the suggestion is that investment does matter to economic growth rates, unlike in Solow's model.

Once a certain level of investment is established, then it is clear that different nations could become established on different growth paths with different growth rates as they benefit from different levels of positive externalities. Thus, if certain nations, for example Germany and Japan, embark on a level of investment that is higher than others as they catch up other nations, then the catch-up could become overtake, as appears to have been the case. Equally, it has been suggested that the world has witnessed the formation of 'growth clubs' whereby certain regions of the world have benefited from high growth rates and managed to exclude others. In particular, these regions – perhaps the so-called East Asian Tigers might be an example – have excluded other areas from benefiting from the positive externalities involved in the growth process that are seen as so important in the new theories. This could certainly help to explain why less developed regions of the world have failed to catch up the more developed regions of the world. Advanced and high growth economies have enjoyed the positive externalities of economic growth without them spilling over to other regions.

The new theories may also help to explain the observed accelerations and decelerations of growth rates that have been observed in post-war history. If an external shock were to alter investment levels, then economies could be set on a different cumulative growth rate, as the changed level of investment generates changed levels of externalities. Thus the oil price shock of the early 1970s may have caused a generalised fall in investment because it raised world interest rates, lowered world expenditure and caused the governments of many advanced economies to adopt restrictive economic policies. Once investment was cut in many countries, then so the growth externalities were reduced, and economies became set on a lower growth path.

One important feature of these new growth theories is that they are incompatible with perfect competition. It is always the case that there will be market failure in the presence of externalities (see Chapter 7 on the state provision of goods and services). The standard situation with positive externalities is that production will be below its optimum level. Of all the examples mentioned which have characteristics of positive externalities, the best known is that of research and development. The problem is that research and development by firms shares some of the characteristics of public goods. Once a discovery has been made, it is very hard to stop others from benefiting, even with the existence of patents. The problem then is that firms are left in a prisoners' dilemma with regard to their research and development (see Chapter 4 on game theory). It is rational to wait for someone else to make a particular breakthrough (a new application of a silicon chip) and then to copy that, not having incurred the cost. This might be seen as 'learning-by-watching'. The problem is that if all firms behave in this fashion, then insufficient research and development will occur compared with what would be the optimum level. There would be a less extreme problem with education, but an under-provision would still be likely. As the individual undertaking education will only gain a part of the whole benefit to society, then the amount of education that the individual decides to receive, based solely on private benefit, will be less than the optimum level for society. Given these market failures, there will be a case for government intervention, the topic of the next section of the chapter.

GOVERNMENT POLICY AND ECONOMIC GROWTH

The growth theory that has the clearest implication for government policies to promote economic growth is Solow's model. The key point is that government policy will have no real effect on long-run growth rates. The growth rate is dictated by the natural rate of growth, and this in turn is dependent upon the growth of the labour supply (principally a function of the growth of the population) and technical change (which has no suggested cause other than fortunate discoveries and innovations). Government policy is ineffectual. Insofar as a role might be seen for government policy, it could be in ensuring that the market works as well as possible with prices adjusting rapidly. This would mean that any deviation of the warranted rate of growth from the natural rate would quickly be corrected through the necessary change in the capital–output ratio. Such a policy tends to be associated with the minimum level of government intervention so that the government is not responsible for creating any price rigidities in the economy.

Harrod's model of growth suggests a more active role for government policy. The economy could suffer economic difficulties if the warranted rate of growth is not equal to the natural rate, a situation that could persist due to the fixed capital–output ratio. It was suggested in the previous section that if the warranted rate were below the natural rate of growth then there would be unemployment on account of there being insufficient investment to create a capacity in the economy that is capable of employing all available labour. This is more likely to be a characteristic of developing countries than developed countries, because of their likely smaller savings ratio and higher natural rate of growth. The government could try to raise the warranted rate of growth in this situation. Given that the capital–output ratio is fixed, the government could alter the warranted rate by affecting the savings ratio. In order to raise the warranted rate, the savings ratio would have to be raised (as the warranted rate of growth was derived from the relationship *s/Cr*). The easiest way for the government to achieve this is deliberately to run a budget surplus since this will be the equivalent of net saving by the government. Resources will be taken from current consumption and will be available for investment. Thus, perhaps a policy of raising taxes would be a clear possibility.

The opposite situation in the Harrod–Domar growth model would be where the warranted rate of growth exceeded the natural rate. Here, the actual rate of growth is likely to be below the warranted rate due to the shortage of labour to fill the capacity of the economy created by the level of investment. This excess capacity will cause firms to lower their levels of investment, which in turn will lower the level of aggregate demand in the economy and create further excess capacity and thus induce further cuts in the level of investment in the economy. In this situation, the government needs to lower the warranted rate of growth in the economy. It can do this by reducing the savings ratio in the economy, the easiest way of achieving this being to run a budget deficit. Thus, this time the appropriate policy response could be to cut the level of taxation. Of course, this is the standard Keynesian macroeconomic policy response to a situation of excess capacity in the economy.

The most obvious point regarding the policy implications of the new theories of economic growth appears to stem from the importance of positive externalities in the growth process. Positive externalities lead to a sub-optimal level of production if the market is left alone. The standard government response to this situation is to subsidise products that display characteristics of positive externalities (see Chapter 7 on the state provision of goods and services). If this principle is to be applied to the new growth theories, then there is a case for subsidising such things as research and development, human capital (education) and perhaps even the whole area of investment. This could be further supplemented by public investment programmes subsidised from general taxation. The ideal subsidy would be to set a subsidy equal to the value of the positive externality so that firms are induced to produce the goods and services at a level where the social marginal cost of production is equal to the social marginal benefit. The problem with this is the unpredictable and uncertain nature of the growth externalities. This implies that setting a subsidy at the ideal level will be extremely difficult. Research and development is probably a good example, as by its very nature the results of any research and development must be unpredictable. However, it is interesting to note that the apparent theoretical implications of these theories are in fact what many governments already tend to do. There are many examples of free or subsidised education, public investment investment projects, research and development and indeed general investment throughout the world. This could be an example of theory catching up with practice in this area of economics.

A further possibility that might be suggested by the new theories is that the tax system should be designed in such a way as to be mindful of the positive externalities that are associated with investment. This could mean that taxes on savings and profits could be set at a lower level than other income taxes, as savings and profits are associated with the promotion of investment. The most obvious way to do this would be to have a tax system which only taxed expenditure, thus giving savings a tax benefit.

It is worthy of note that those responsible for the new growth theories have not generally suggested that they imply the need for considerable government intervention in the growth process. The reason for this is to do with perceived government failures (see Chapter 7 on the state provision of goods and services). One example of government failure has already been mentioned, namely the difficulty of measuring the size of the positive externalities involved in the growth process. However, any subsidy would involve the use of distortionary taxes which could be undesirable for the economy (see Chapter 8 on taxation). Further problems could arise due to the utility-maximising behaviour of politicians which might mean that subsidies were offered to particular interest groups rather than simply being based on economic calculation (see Chapter 13 on political business cycles).

Another suggested implication of the new growth theories for government policies concerns the value of attempting to foster the growth of knowledge between countries. In this sense, the promotion of free trade is likely to be an advantage, especially insofar as it could facilitate 'learning-by-watching'. Thus some countries could benefit from this through the completion of the single market in Europe. However, it might be even more pertinent for less-developed countries who would be able to benefit from significant learning economies through free trade with developed nations. This might be considered an important part of development policy.

It would not be right to finish this section without reference to the fact that the new theories have little or nothing to say about several factors that continue to be viewed as important in the growth process of many nations. Surveys point to the institutional and legal framework of nations as one such factor (for example, Crafts, 1992). Thus the collective bargaining framework in operation in a country could be seen as significant in dictating investment levels. Equally, financial frameworks that encourage long-term or short-term outlooks by the nations' producers could be important. Such factors, then, are likely to have different policy implications from those suggested thus far. Altering institutions could be a prerequisite of raising growth rates.

CONCLUSION

The new growth theories have made an important contribution to this area of economics: thinking has moved on from a period of relative stagnation. In particular, the new theories appear to explain some of the empirical observations that seemed inconsistent with traditional growth theory. They seem to imply a role for the government in subsidisation, given their emphasis on the role of positive externalities within the growth process. However, because of the uncertain nature of these externalities and the other concerns surrounding government failure, the new theories do not provide a clearcut case for government intervention. There remain other possible determinants of growth rates not covered by the new theories which could be significant for government policy. Thus, though the new theories have made an important contribution to growth theories, their practical importance is still unclear.

References

Arrow, K. J. (1962) 'The Economic Implications of Learning by Doing', *Review of Economic Studies*, vol. 29.

Crafts, N. (1992) 'Productivity Growth Reconsidered', *Economic Policy*, October.

Denison, R. F. (1967) *Why Growth Rates Differ: Postwar Experience in Nine Western Countries* (Washington DC: Brookings Institution).

Domar, E. (1947) 'Expansion and Employment', *American Economic Review*, vol. 37.

Harrod, R. F. (1939) 'An Essay in Dynamic Theory', *Economic Journal*, vol. 49.

Kaldor, N. (1966) *Causes of the Slow Rate of Economic Growth of the United Kingdom* (Cambridge University Press).

King, N. and M. Robson (1989) 'Endogenous Growth and the Role of History', *LSE Financial Markets Discussion Paper*, no. 63.

Romer, P. M. (1983) 'Dynamic Competitive Equilibria with Externalities, Increasing Returns and Unbounded Growth', unpublished doctoral dissertation, University of Chicago.

Romer, P. M. (1986) 'Increasing Returns and Long-run Growth', *Journal of Political Economy*, vol. 94.

Solow, R. M. (1956) 'A Contribution to the Theory of Economic Growth', *Quarterly Journal of Economics*, vol. 70.

Smith, A. (1776) *An Inquiry into the Nature and Causes of the Wealth of Nations* (Oxford: Clarendon Press, 1976).

Conclusion

It is hard to conclude a book that has tackled a wide range of different issues. However, through the different topics investigated, certain generalisations can perhaps be made. The approach of having a clear appreciation of certain fundamental economic principles and theories and then applying these to various areas can be fruitful. Even with a relatively limited range of principles and theories, a great deal of valid application is possible.

There is one theme that comes through most of the chapters more strongly than any other, and that is how well the free market works. How effectively does the market, left to its own devices, allocate scarce resources between competing uses? In light of this, the general review of the arguments for and against market provision in Chapter 7 must be seen as particularly important. To some extent, it enters into all of the issues investigated. It is also fundamental to considering what, if any, is the appropriate government policy in any particular situation. In macroeconomics, this manifests itself most notably when asking whether a market economy, if left to its own devices, tends towards a position that can reasonably be described as 'full employment'. This, in turn, appears to depend, at least in part, on whether prices can and do adjust properly. That is a microeconomic question that is all to do with how well markets do the job required of them by economies. One particular reason why markets may not always perform as desired is to do with the concept of externality. A proper and thorough understanding of that seems vital. The picture is further complicated by government failure. The fact that the market may not lead to the optimum allocation of scarce resources does not automatically imply the desirability of government intervention. It is possible that such intervention could create an even less desirable allocation of resources. Ultimately, the practical question may involve an investigation of where the level of failure is likely to be least: with free market provision or government intervention. This will vary from circumstance to circumstance. There is no such thing as an easy answer in economics.

Index